Eschatology

Joseph Ratzinger

Eschatology

Death and Eternal Life

Translated by Michael Waldstein
Translation edited by Aidan Nichols, O.P.

Second Edition

With a new foreword by
Joseph Ratzinger, Benedict XVI
And a preface by Peter Casarella

The Catholic University of America Press
Washington, D.C.

Originally published in German under the title *Eschatologie—
Tod und ewiges Leben*. Copyright © 1977 Friedrich Pustet Verlag,
Regensburg

Printed in the United States of America

The Library of Congress catalogued the original edition as follows:

LIBRARY OF CONGRESS CATALOGING-IN-PUBLICATION-DATA

Ratzinger, Joseph.
  [Eschatologie, Tod und ewiges Leben. English]
  Eschatology, death and eternal life / Joseph Ratzinger ;
translated by Michael Waldstein ; translation edited by Aidan
Nichols.
      p.   cm.—(Dogmatic theology ; 9)
  Translation of: Eschatologie, Tod und ewiges Leben.
  ISBN 0-8132-0632-4. ISBN 0-8132-0633-2 (pbk.)
    1. Eschatology.   2. Death—Religious aspects—
Catholic Church.   3. Future life—Christianity.
4. Catholic Church—Doctrines.   I. Title.   II. Series:
Auer, Johann, 1910– Dogmatic theology ; 9.
BT821.2R3713   1988
236—dc19   87-35107
ISBN 13: 978-0-8132-1516-7

For my students in Regensburg

Contents

Preface to the Second English Edition   xi

Preface to the First English Edition   xv

Foreword to This Edition   xvii

Foreword   xxiii

Abbreviations   xxvii

I. Introduction: The State of the Question   1

    1. On the Current State of the Eschatology Question   1

    2. The Historical Presuppositions of the Present Situation   4

Part One. The Eschatological Problem as a Question About the Very Essence of Christianity

II. The Exegetical Data   19

    1. A Word on Method   19

    2. The Meaning of Jesus' Proclamation of the Kingdom of God   24

    3. The Expectation of an Imminent End   35

III. Word and Reality in Contemporary Appreciation   46

    1. The Panorama of Solutions   47

    (a) Karl Barth   47

    (b) Rudolf Bultmann   48

    (c) Oscar Cullmann   51

viii   Contents

(d) C. H. Dodd   55
(e) The Theology of Hope and Political
    Theology   57
2. Preliminary Conclusions   60

Part Two. Death and Immortality. The Individual Dimension of Eschatology

IV. The Theology of Death   69

1. Posing the Question   69
2. The Historical Roots of the Question   72
    (a) The Prevailing View   72
    (b) An Attempt at Revisionism   75

3. The Development of the Question in
   Biblical Thought   80
    (a) The Old Testament   80
    (b) The Interpretation of Death and Life in the
        New Testament   92

4. Some Conclusions on the Ethos of Death
   in Christianity   101
    (a) Assent to Life as a Whole   101
    (b) The Meaning of Suffering   101

V. The Immortality of the Soul and the
   Resurrection of the Dead   104

1. The State of the Question   104
2. The Biblical Data   112
    (a) The Resurrection from the Dead   112
    (b) The "Intermediate State" Between Death
        and Resurrection   119
        i. Early Judaism, 120   ii. The New
        Testament, 123
    (c) Conclusions and Implications   129

3. The Documents of the Church's
   Magisterium   132

4. Theological Unfolding   140
   (a) The Heritage of Antiquity   140
   (b) The New Concept of Soul   146
   (c) The Dialogical Character of Immortality   150
   (d) Immortality and Creation   153
   (e) Summary: The Principal Features of the
       Christian Faith in Eternal Life   157

Part Three. The Future Life

VI. The Resurrection of the Dead and the
    Return of Christ   165

   1. What Does "The Resurrection of the
      Dead" Mean?   165
      (a) The State of the Question   165
      (b) The Tradition   168
          i. The New Testament, 168   ii. The
          Clarification of the Formula "The
          Resurrection of the Flesh" in the First
          Three Centuries, 172   iii. The Debate
          About the Risen Body in the History of
          Theology, 176
      (c) What Is "Resurrection on the Last Day"?   181
      (d) The Risen Body   191

   2. The Return of Christ and the Final
      Judgment   194
      (a) The Biblical Data   194
          i. The Signs of Christ's Return, 194   ii. The
          Return of Christ, 201   iii. The Judgment,
          204
      (b) Theological Evaluation   209

VII. Hell, Purgatory, Heaven   215
   1. Hell   215
   2. Purgatory   218
      (a) The Problem of the Historical Data   218

*(b) The Permanent Content of the Doctrine of
Purgatory* 228

3. Heaven 233

Appendix I. Between Death and Resurrection:
Some Supplementary Reflections 241

1. A Clarification from the Congregation for the
Doctrine of the Faith on the Question of
Eschatology 241
2. The Background of the Modern Controversy 246
3. Content and Problematic of the New Attempts
at a Solution 251
4. Basic Outline of a New Consensus 255

Appendix II. Afterword to the English Edition 261

1. Short Report on the Further Progress of the
Controversy About Resurrection and
Immortality 262
2. Further Fundamental Matters from My Book 270

Notes 275
Select Bibliography 291
Index of Names 299
Index of Subjects 302
Index of References 305

Preface to the Second English Edition

The fine English translation of Joseph Ratzinger's *Eschatologie—Tod und ewiges Leben* first appeared in 1988 through the collaborative efforts of Fr. Aidan Nichols, O.P., and Dr. Michael Waldstein. For the reasons given in the Holy Father's new foreword, it seemed superfluous for the second edition to retain any references to the book series that was left incomplete long ago.

Since 1988 Pope Benedict has written a considerable amount about the themes treated in this book, especially as they relate to the question of the kingdom of God and politics.[1] A least one German work of Cardinal Ratzinger cited as such in the original translation has now appeared in English translation.[2] The papal encyclical of December 25, 2005, *Deus Caritas Est*, can even be seen as a further specification in the light of new concerns about the problem of hope mentioned in the new foreword. At the very least, the treatment of the proper meeting of faith and politics in that encyclical develops a conversation that the young theologian Ratzinger had already seriously engaged at least as early as his completion of the original manuscript on eschatology in the autumn of 1976.[3]

1. See, for example, Joseph Ratzinger, *Truth and Tolerance: Christian Belief and World Religions* (San Francisco: Ignatius Press, 2004).
2. Joseph Ratzinger, *The Church, Ecumenism, and Politics: New Essays in Ecclesiology* (New York: Crossroad, 1988).
3. The German original included a dedication "to his students at the University of Regensburg, 1969–1977." In his preface to that edi-

The Pope's new foreword includes references to some recent secondary literature in German on Ratzinger's *Eschatology*. The Holy Father does not follow the practice of the
earlier appendices of engaging these debates on questions
of substance, but he acknowledges the continuation to the
present day of a discussion that he has been addressing for
several decades. It seems quite odd that in the English-
speaking world the reaction to Ratzinger's text has never
been equivalent to that in Germany (of either a positive or
a negative sort!).[4] Although new stirrings in the field of eschatology are now plentiful in the Anglo-Saxon world, the
engagement with Ratzinger's thought still seems largely
ignored.[5] With the issuing of a new foreword, it is my renewed hope that theologians outside of Germany will ben-
efit from the important conversations kept alive by, for example, Josef Wohlmuth and Tobias Kläden.

This is not to say that Pope Benedict's thoughts on
death and eternal life are a purely academic affair. Many
spiritual nuggets may be culled from this work: the idea,
for example, that we live because we are inscribed into
God's memory or the definition of the human soul as
"nothing other than man's capacity for relatedness with
truth, with love eternal." Each of these thoughts merits

tion, Ratzinger mentions lecturing on eschatology as early as 1957.
Thus, the ideas contained in the volume were the subject matter of
his intellectual work at a much earlier date than the completion of
the manuscript.

4. There are astonishingly few exceptions to this generalization.
See, for example, Terence McGuckin, "The Eschatology of the Cross,"
New Blackfriars 7 (July-August 1994): 364–77, and Aidan Nichols,
*The Thought of Benedict XVI: An Introduction to the Theology of Jo-
seph Ratzinger* (New York: Burns and Oates, 2005).

5. Among the many examples that could be given of the renewed
interest among English-speaking theologians, I cite two exemplary
works: John Polkinghorne, *The God of Hope and the End of Time*
(New Haven: Yale University Press, 2002), and Nicholas J. Healey,
The Eschatology of Hans Urs von Balthasar: Being as Communion
(Oxford: Oxford University Press, 2005).

the sort of meditative time and reflection for which the incomplete book series was also intended. Sometimes it is hard in the English-speaking world to see how intimate the connection is between the Bavarian academic theologian Joseph Ratzinger and the pastor of a global Church, Pope Benedict XVI. The clear focus in this volume on the Biblical unfolding of Jesus' preaching of the kingdom, as well as the accents placed on the personal dimensions of what the Church has taught about the embodied, immortal soul fully open for communion with God and neighbor, makes it easier to grasp the unity of the man and the clarity and consistency of his message.

PETER CASARELLA

DEPAUL UNIVERSITY

FEAST OF ST. DOMINIC, 2007

Preface to the First English Edition

Dogmatic Theology of Johann Auer and Joseph Ratzinger is now being offered to an English-speaking public in the belief that the three characteristic emphases of the series mentioned in the German preface—informedness by Scripture, attention to the history of doctrine, concern with the systematic coherence of theological teaching—are as desirable in the Anglophone world, far-flung and diverse as that now is, as in the Bavaria which is the authors' home. Both men belong to the milieu of South German Catholic theology which has produced, over the last hundred and fifty years, several great schools or centers. In each of these, a rigorously academic theology, concerned to rise to the challenges of documentary accuracy and conceptual orderliness set by universities, was placed at the service of the Church—bishops, clergy and people—and hence obliged to meet the differing but no less exigent requirements of doctrinal orthodoxy and pastoral good sense. It is typical of German Catholic theological work in this inheritance that it is simultaneously open to biblical scholarship, to Church tradition in all its phases and monuments, and to the philosophical culture of its day which, however, it sifts critically, bearing in mind the Johannine dictum, "Test the spirits, to see if they come from God" (I John 4, 1).

Students of dogmatic theology are frequently to be heard making three complaints about the state of the subject. First, they find it difficult to employ contemporary biblical criticism in a constructive fashion in the sphere of doctrine. This Dogmatic Theology, while showing no hostility to historical-critical tools as such, which occupy a limited but legitimate place in its enquiry, seeks to penetrate beyond the historical-critical problems to the revelatory witness that shines forth from the Scriptures. Secondly, students lament the sheer quantity of detailed monographs now available on the history of doctrine. Sinking as one may well do beneath this weight of erudition, the main contours of doctrinal development are easily lost to view. In the Dogmatic Theology, by a judicious selection of *topoi*, an attempt is made to point out the lie of the land to those who cannot see the wood for the trees. Or, to change the metaphor once again, theologically acute historical highlighting illuminates what is of lasting significance for the Church's sensibility, teaching and practice. Thirdly, students do not always find it easy to see how the different facets of doctrinal believing belong together as a unitary whole. Dogmatic Theology addresses itself to this problem in a conscious effort to lead back all the ways of doctrinal reflection to their living center, the Gospel of grace.

Although the series is aimed in the first place at the theological student, whether in university or seminary, the needs it tries to meet are felt much more widely by clergy and laity alike. May that "quest for understanding," to which all Christians are summoned by the gift of faith itself, be stimulated, assisted and brought closer to its goal in the vision of God by the contemplative study of these pages.

AIDAN NICHOLS, O.P.
Blackfriars, Cambridge
Memorial day of St. Isidore,
bishop and doctor of the Church,
1987

Foreword to This Edition

When I accepted the appointment to teach (*der Ruf*) at the newly founded University of Regensburg in the fall of 1969, I met up once again with Professor Johann Auer. We had spent several wonderful years of collaboration at the University of Bonn. Auer had already developed the idea of a "Short Catholic Dogmatics" when he was in Bonn, the volumes of which were to be published in pocket-book format. According to their common foreword, they were intended to be used as "as a thought-provoking student's companion."[1] Auer had begun the undertaking in 1947, and its just completed fruit was the fifth volume, *The Gospel of Grace*, which was already submitted to the publishing house Pustet. He had prepared extensive drafts for the other short volumes as well. So when I arrived at Regensburg, he urged me to contact the publisher, Dr. Friedrich Pustet. This got me involved in the project and made it into a jointly authored work. At first I hesitated since I had already agreed to publish a work in dogmatics with the publishing house Wewel. Later I was convinced by my friend to accept the offer. When I had finally finished one of the two volumes assigned to me, namely, the one on eschatology, I was named archbishop of Munich and Freising. That is why this book remained with my episcopal consecration my sole contribution to the common undertaking.

---

1. The original German phrase "Begleiter des Studierenden auch auf besinnlichen Wegen" conveys the idea of combining a textbook for beginning students of theology with a volume that also lends itself to spiritual meditation.

The other volume assigned to me, i.e., the *Introduction to Dogmatic Theology*, remained unwritten because Professor Auer departed from this life in 1989, before he could lend a hand with the project.

Thirty years have passed since the first edition [of *Eschatology*]. In these years theological advances have not ceased. When the book was written, two profound upheavals were under way in the general realm of a theology of hope. Hope was reconceived as an active virtue, a deed that could change the world, from which a new humanity, the so-called better world would emerge. Hope became political, and man himself appeared to be charged with its execution. The kingdom of God, upon which all depends in Christendom, became man's kingdom, the "better world" of tomorrow. God is no longer considered to be "above" but rather "right in front of us." When theology joined forces with a current of philosophical and political reflection that kept getting stronger and stronger, a second development was then joined to the heart of the theological enterprise. In its own way the general intellectual context in this matter had an equivalent effect. The crisis of tradition, which became virulent in the Catholic Church in conjunction with the Second Vatican Council, led many to believe that faith came strictly speaking from the Bible and that [therefore] tradition could be set aside. In this manner, it was thought that there was no notion of the immortality of the soul in the Bible but only the hope for resurrection. These people dismissed "immortality of the soul" as Platonism and thought it had obscured belief in the resurrection. So by employing a noteworthy philosophy of timelessness that held sway beyond death, it was now explained that resurrection takes place in death. This theory was also hastily assimilated into the discourse of preaching so that in many places the act of worship in which one offered petitions for the dead now became known as "a celebration of resurrection."

In my *Eschatology* I tried to deal with both of these developments without leaving aside issues of the whole tradition regarding belief, hope, and prayer as they had developed in the history of the Church, at least those that were important for a manual of this kind. With respect to the first theme, it seemed important to me not to allow eschatology always to be transformed into political theology of whatever kind. I hope to have restricted myself basically to having indicated a problem. I attempted to set forth the perduring significance of hope in God's own action in history because this activity lends an inner context to what man accomplishes and transforms from within the transitory into something that endures.

By contrast, a closer scrutiny of the question of resurrection in death was unavoidable; this topic fills up chapter 5 of the book. It is first and foremost the case that the Bible does not offer a definitive anthropological conceptuality but rather utilizes diverse conceptual models. But it is just as clear that the Bible does not recognize the thought of resurrection in death. It even denies it explicitly (cf. 2 Tm 2:18). On the other hand, the Bible does acknowledge "being with the Lord" between death and resurrection (e.g., Phil. 1:23).

I attempted to show that the anthropological conceptuality that used the language of body and soul (as it had occurred in the tradition and was formulated at the Council of Vienne) was another development thoroughly in line with the precepts of Biblical anthropology. In the wake of my book, a lively dispute ensued, in which my position was treated as little more than a defense of Platonism. In the two appendices to the sixth [German] edition, I sought to comment in detail on the dispute and thereby also ac-

knowledged with gratitude the approximations and medi-
ations that resulted and thus added vigor to my thinking
about the "last things."[2] The most recent presentation of
eschatology brought to my attention has worked through
all sides of the dispute.[3] The author claims to have ascer-
tained further narrowing of the standpoints (especially on
pages 169–76). I would not like to enter into the whole debate again but only to underscore once again what was and
is my main concern. Above all else, I am not concerned
with an empty abstraction or with "Platonism" but with
a strictly theological interpretation (in the sense of what
Jesus taught) of our life beyond death. Accordingly, we
live because we are inscribed into God's memory. In God's
memory we are not a shadow, a mere "recollection." Remaining in God's memory means we are alive, in a full
sense of life. We are fully a "we." The Sadduccees, relying
upon an esoteric tradition, tried to convince people that
belief in the resurrection was absurd. Jesus responded un-
waveringly to them not with abstract lectures on anthropology but by pointing to God's memory: "As for the dead
being raised, have you not read in the book of Moses, in
the passage about the bush, how God told him, 'I am the
God of Abraham, (the) God of Isaac, and (the) God of Jacob'? He is not God of the dead but of the living. You are
greatly misled."[4] This theo-logical interpretation is just
as much a dia-logical interpretation of the human being
and of human immortality.[5] I was thus able to summarize
my idea of the soul in the second appendix of the sixth

2. These two appendices were consolidated into Appendix I of the
English translation. Tr.

3. J. Wohlmuth, *Mysterium der Verwandlungen: Eine Eschatologie
aus katholischer Perspektive im Gespräch mit jüdischen Denken der
Gegenwart* (Paderborn: Ferdinand Schöningh, 2005).

4. Mark 12:26. See also in this book pp. 113–14.

5. "Theo-logy" discloses a discourse about *theos*, God. A "dia-logical" interpretation is a sharing of the *logos* in the form of a conversation *(diálogos)*. Tr.

German edition with this phrase: "Soul is nothing other than man's capacity for relatedness with truth, with love eternal."[6] The relationship to that which is eternal, viz., remaining in communion with Him, is partaking in His eternity. This theo-logical interpretation of eternal life incorporates the christological concretization of our faith in God. In other words, God's dialogue with us takes on flesh in Christ. Since we belong to the body of Christ, we are united to the flesh of the resurrected one, to his resurrection: "God . . . raised us up with him, and seated us with him in the heavens in Christ Jesus."[7] Beginning with our baptism, we belong to the body of the resurrected one and are in this sense already attached to our future.[8] Never again are we totally disembodied (a mere *anima separata*) even if our pilgrim state cannot reach its end while history is still in motion. Thus arises a fourth point—the bodiliness of Christ, who retains a body in eternity, signifies the taking seriously of history and of matter. I have tried to show this on pages 184–89. Finally, it is important to me that what we say about the human person must be entirely theological and christological. Precisely for this reason, the capacity for dialogue with reason stays open—a capacity for dialogue with modern anthropology that is mediated by philosophy. I emphasized this point in the two appendices to the sixth German edition. Meanwhile the discussion has taken another step forward. The contribution of Tobias Kläden offers valuable hints for the contemporary state of this question.[9]

In the preface to the whole of the "Short Catholic Dog-

6. See p. 259 of the present translation. Tr.
7. Ephesians 2:4, 6.
8. This theme in Ratzinger's theology is treated admirably in Paolo Sottopietra's *Wissen aus der Taufe: die Aporien der neuzeitlichen Vernunft und der christliche Weg im Werk Joseph Ratzinger* (Regensburg: Pustet, 2003).
9. The Pope refers here to Kläden's journal article: "Die aktuelle

matics," mentioned at the outset, Johann Auer had said that a hastily composed textbook could not offer in every treatise the comprehensive knowledge of a manual prepared by many contributors. I am very conscious of the limitation of what I attempted in 1977. In spite of its insufficiencies, I nonetheless hope that what I tried to do can still help others to understand better the hope that faith in Christ grants to us and to see that hope anew as a living promise made to us.

I would like to thank Friedrich Pustet of the Pustet publishing house for making the decision to send the little work once again on its way to the readers.

JOSEPH RATZINGER, BENEDICT XVI

ROME

FEAST OF ALL SAINTS, 2006

Debatte um das Leib-Seele-Problem," *Theologische Revue* 102 (2006): 183–202, as well as to a review in the same volume by F. A. Peters of E. Richter, *Wohin führt uns die moderne Hirnforschung? Ein Beitrag aus phänomenologisch und erkenntniskritischer Sicht* (Berlin, 2005). The reader may also consult Tobias Kläden, *Mit Leib und Seele . . . Die mind-brain-Debatte in der Philosophie des Geistes und die anima-forma-corporis-Lehre des Thomas von Aquin* (Regensburg: Pustet, 2005). Tr.

Foreword

Dogmatic Theology is intended to be a textbook for theology students—in brief compass. It has come out in a pocket book format because it is meant to accompany the student, not just in the classroom but on his or her meditative walks as well. Anyone who has had the task of preparing a three-year dogmatics course will know how impossible it is to achieve for each and every area of dogma that scientific presentation which can be expected from a multi-authored, collaborative work such as *Mysterium Salutis*. By way of compensation, a concise textbook, through its selectivity and inner coherence, may make certain points more clearly than is the case in such team products.

We have decided to publish this little textbook because we believe it fills a gap. It is intended to provide a foundation which appropriate lectures can extend and build upon. In this way it will offer a basis for theological discussion, something which is only meaningful in dogmatics if it can presuppose a certain knowledge of the subject matter.

We have tried to pay special attention to the three dimensions which are important for dogmatics today:

1. The biblical foundation of doctrine. This is why we cite biblical texts so frequently. The quotations are there in order to communicate not simply the doctrinal truths themselves but also their spirit.

2. The history of individual doctrines. The historian of doctrine is well placed to show the many facets of the underlying problem as well as the multiplicity of possible human answers.

3. The systematic inner coherence of doctrine. Doctrinal formulations always tell us about some part of the
whole, but the whole is more than the sum of its parts. In
the exposition of the individual parts, it is vital to preserve
the whole and keep it in view at all times. The main problem in teaching dogmatics is really this: by means of a
large number of statements scattered through three or
more years of the student's academic life, dogmatics must
unfold before the learner's eyes a single reality and a single
truth. This fundamentally single whole can stand before
the student in its greatness and profundity only to the extent that he or she is able to absorb it in its unity at a
single glance.

It is our hope that this book will be used not just as a
textbook but also as a collection of materials capable of
enriching theological thinking, reflection and meditation.
We hope, moreover, that it may thus stimulate that attitude
which all true theologizing requires. That attitude may be
summed up under five heads: respect for the uniqueness of
the object of theology; sensitivity to the various methods that object demands, and preparedness for practicing
them; the realization that faith must accompany knowledge, and that both life and action flow from this knowledge of faith; receptivity to the way that an individual's
theological endeavor needs for its completion the achievement of others, both past and present, and will thus take
its place in the noble history of theology in our Church,
there to find itself in the act of losing itself—and finally, the
awareness that all theology, as reflection on the Church's
teaching, shares in the "historicity" both of the Church
herself and of the individual theologian within her.

JOHANN AUER
JOSEPH RATZINGER

Exactly twenty years ago I lectured on eschatology for the first time in the cycle of courses that fell to me to teach. Since then I have come up against its questions at regular intervals, and have had to face them anew each time. Next to ecclesiology, eschatology is the dogmatic treatise I have taught most often. This emboldens me to make it the first I shall offer in unified form to the public. My experience with this subject has been somewhat curious. I began rather boldly with a set of theses which were then still uncommon but are now almost universally accepted in Catholic circles: that is, I tried to construct a "de-Platonized" eschatology. However, the more I dealt with the questions and immersed myself in the sources, the more the antitheses I had set up fell to pieces in my hands and in their place I saw the inner logic of the Church's tradition stand forth. Thus the result of two decades' work, which I am presenting here, runs contrary to the currently prevailing opinion—but in an opposite sense from the way that was so with my first attempts in this area. This is not because I enjoy being contradictory, but because of what I have found to be the exigencies of the subject matter. This is not to say that my vision of the whole has not been affected—deepened, purified and clarified—by the specifically modern-day questions.

The compass of my treatment has been determined by the form of Dogmatic Theology, so that I have had to forgo much detailed discussion that would have been desirable. However, I hope that the essential questions have been sufficiently addressed in a way befitting a textbook. The manuscript was finished in the autumn of 1976. I have not been able to take account of the literature which appeared after this date, and this includes, unfortunately, the extensive treatment of eschatology offered in J. Feiner and M. Löhrer (eds.) *Mysterium Salutis* V (Einsiedeln, Zürich, Co-

logne 1976), pp. 553–890, by Schütz, Gross, Schelkle and
Breuning. As I see things at present, their comments
would not have caused me to change my mind. And perhaps it is instructive and helpful to have two presentations
of the theme made in genuine independence of each other
and without reciprocal influence.

I do not want this book to appear without offering suitable thanks. First of all, I must thank my secretary, Frau
Elisabeth Anthofer, for the patience and care she devoted
to the manuscript. My gratitude is also due to Herr Josef
Zöhrer, who was of great service to me in producing the
bibliography and in helping to read the proofs. Herr Zöhrer
also made the indices, together with my two assistants,
Dr. Stephan Horn and Dr. Siegfried Wiedenhofer. Finally, I
must thank the publishing house Pustet, and especially
Frau Monica Bock, for the work involved in publication.

As it happens, the book is going into print at the moment when my teaching activity comes to an end and I
embark upon the episcopal office. I take this opportunity,
therefore, to dedicate it to the students of my years in Regensburg—in grateful memory.

JOSEPH RATZINGER,
Pentling,
Feast of the Ascension, 1977

Abbreviations

CSEL   *Corpus Scriptorum Ecclesiasticorum Latino-*
        rum (Vienna 1886 ff.)
DS   H. Denzinger and A. Schönmetzer, *Enchiridion*
        Symbolorum, Definitionum et Declarationum
        de rebus fidei et morum, 34th ed. (Freiburg im
        Breisgau 1967).
LThK   *Lexikon für Theologie und Kirche,* 2nd Ed. eds.
        J. Höfer and K. Rahner (Freiburg im Breisgau
        1957–1967).
NCE   *New Catholic Encyclopedia* (New York 1967).
PG   *Patrologia Graeca,* ed. J. P. Migne (Paris 1857–
        1866).
PL   *Patrologia Latina,* ed. J. P. Migne (Paris 1844–
        1855).
TDNT   *Theological Dictionary of the New Testament*
        (ET of TWNT, *vide infra*), ed. G. Bromiley
        (Grand Rapids 1965–1974).
TWNT   *Theologisches Wörterbuch zum Neuen Testa-*
        ment, eds. G. Kittel and G. Friedrich (Stuttgart
        1933–1974).

I

Introduction: The State of the Question

I. ON THE CURRENT STATE OF THE ESCHATOLOGY QUESTION

For centuries eschatology was content to lead a quiet life as the final chapter of theology where it was dubbed "the doctrine of the last things." But in our own time, with the historical process in crisis, eschatology has moved into the very center of the theological stage. Some twenty years ago, Hans Urs von Balthasar called it the "storm-zone" of contemporary theology.[1] Today it appears to dominate the entire theological landscape. A recent synod of the German bishops published a confession of faith under the title "Our Hope"—thus placing faith itself in hope's perspective.

How did this shift come about? And how should we evaluate it? So far as chronology is concerned, it can be dated to the writings of Johannes Weiss as well as to Albert Schweitzer's early exegetical studies.[2] With the assistance of modern scholarship, people reestablished an insight which, in the age of the rationalist Enlightenment, had been virtually dismissed as the brainchild of eccentrics. This insight consisted in the awareness that Jesus' preaching was soaked through with eschatology. The inner impetus of that preaching came from the fact that Jesus, in an authoritative fashion, proclaimed the imminent end of the world, the breaking-in of the Kingdom of God. The novelty and greatness of Jesus, his bursting of old wineskins, cannot be separated from the momentum which this expectation created. Without exception his sayings must be understood in the light of this central concern. Being a Christian in the sense Jesus intended is summed up in the central petition of the *Our Father:* "Thy Kingdom come." In this petition, early Christians prayed for the end of the world, and the breaking-in of a new reality which only God can create. From such a perspective, all subsequent Church history might seem like a saga of "de-eschatologizing." And in point of fact, the historian of doctrine Martin Werner *did* attempt to offer a comprehensive description of the making of the Church in precisely these terms.[3]

In the course of this book, we shall have to deal in some detail with the theses thus baldly stated. They touch not only the central point of eschatology, but the heart of Christianity itself. Its very identity is called into question. But to begin with, we can content ourselves with noting the wider human context of this "eschatology question." The revolutionary invasion of a new eschatological awareness into biblical studies, which has gone so far as to subsume the entire confession of faith under the single theme of hope, cannot simply be explained by reference to the refinement of scholarly methods. Whenever people adopt an absolutely fresh starting point for their investigation of historical sources, this is always a telltale sign of some change in consciousness by which they are looking at reality with new eyes, and so getting new answers from it. In our case, it is surely obvious that the sudden intensification of our capacity to pick up the eschatological undertones and overtones of the New Testament must have something to do with the emerging crisis of European civilization. Since the turn of the century, human minds have been increasingly aware of a decline and fall, like the premonition of some imminent earthquake in world history. The First World War gave this sense its earliest tragic confirmation, undermining as it did so the then dominant theological Liberalism with its optimistic assessment of a purely cultural Christianity. Theology then moved into the new key of Existentialism, a philosophy of preparedness and decision which at the same time offered itself as a reasonable interpretation of the real meaning of Jesus' message about the End.

In the meantime, a second and more powerful current has flowed into theology. This is Marxism, a movement marked by much greater realism. Here we encounter something of the primordial potency of Old Testament messianism, now gone anti-theistic and demanding an unconditional commitment through its claim that here at last all reality has become scientifically knowable, the past, present and future of humankind receiving their exact interpretation. All resistance to this claim must mean for Marxism relegation to the lower rungs of the ladder of history. And yet this movement draws its passion, and its fascination, from the root of prophetism, which promised a world the signs of whose coming had no rational index. The very attack on God and the historical religions fosters a religious pathos which attracts the often deracinated religious energies of numerous contemporary men and women to itself, as a magnet draws ore. This pathos also affects theology, which detects in it the opportunity to fill the eschatological message with a tangible, realistic content. It is curious, and yet, in the light of Barth's violent separation of faith and religion, also understandable that when theology is thus placed before the alternatives of faith in God and a religious pathos directed to futurity, it is willing to choose religion over against God.

It is thus possible in our day to write an eschatology which would be nothing but a dialogue (whether in agreement or disagreement) with the theology of futurity, the theology of hope and the theology of liberation. This has in fact been done in a study where the classical themes of the doctrine of the last things—heaven and hell, purgatory and judgment, death and the immortality of the soul—are conspicuous by their absence.[4] It is perfectly true that the question of the future and its relation to the present, and with that the whole theme of hope and its attendant "praxis," rightly belongs to the subject matter of eschatology. But a textbook in Catholic dogmatics cannot surrender to the transformation of perspective implied in the reduction of eschatology to these things. This is so not merely on the extrinsic grounds that a textbook should contain the information classically offered by a work of its genre. It is also the case that these omitted topics belong intrinsically to what is specific in the Christian view of the age-to-come and its presence here and now. And that is why we have a duty to attend to these questions, as necessary components of Christianity, no matter how out of tune with the spirit of the age they may for various reasons appear.

2. THE HISTORICAL PRESUPPOSITIONS OF THE PRESENT SITUATION

But just why is it that this message often seems so alien to people today? If this question is susceptible of an answer, it must needs be an answer of a highly differentiated kind. Yet what we find around us is the wide diffusion of a remarkably simple answer, whose criticism must occupy

the second part of this preamble on the "state of the question." What is being said is that in official Christianity the
currency of eschatological discourse has been thoroughly
debased, so much so that the history of eschatology is
nothing less than the history of an apostasy. The shift
from a praxis of hope to a doctrine of the last things involves, people maintain, a systematic reversal of the original intention. If this be true, then it is only logical that
evil cannot be cured save through a return to the source.
Such a return to, and reactualizing of, the origins is what
liberation theologies frequently intend to be.

The evidence for this thesis of a past apostasy seems to
lie all around us. Scholars have long drawn attention to
the contrast between the early Christian invocation *maranatha* and the mediaeval *Dies Irae*. In the former, there is
a joyful hope for the Christ who will come soon, a hope
which takes on particular intensity in the early second
century *Didache* with its cry: "May grace come, and this
world pass away."[5] In the *Dies Irae*, on the other hand,
we hear only of the fear of judgment, which contemplates
the End under the appearances of horror and of threat to
the soul's salvation. Or again, there is that characteristic
motto of mass mission in the nineteenth and twentieth
centuries: "Save your soul." Like a lightning-flash, this
motto seems to expose the true facts as to how Christianity has been reduced to the level of individual persons, to
the detriment of what was once the core of both eschatology and the Christian message itself: the confident, corporate hope for the imminent salvation of all the world.

Yet historical reflection hooked on to the pegs of a
few formulae must always be problematic, even if on occasion such formulae can be illuminating. For instance, the
meaning of the invocation *maranatha* is by no means self-
evident. It can be read as a petition: "Come, Lord Jesus"; it

can also be read as a statement: "The Lord has come." Some scholars even take it to be a strong attestation intended to safeguard the sanctity of the Eucharist: "As surely as our Lord has come. . . ."[6] At the very least, it is certain that the expression belongs in the context of early Christian eucharistic celebration. As such, it must be understood in terms of the mode of prayer proper to that celebration which always carries a reference to both present and future. The Eucharist is at once the joyful proclamation of the Lord's presence and a supplication to the already present Lord that he may come, since, paradoxically, even as the One who is present he remains the One who is to come.

To clarify this point, it may be helpful to bear in mind the conclusions of F. J. Dölger and E. Peterson about the typical modality of early Christian prayer, based on their researches into the tangible monuments which that prayer has left behind.[7] They found that in the early Church body and soul still prayed in unison. Through the body, prayer became part of the cosmos and its history. When the ancient Israelite prayed, he turned towards the Jerusalem temple. In this way, he linked his prayer to the salvation history which united God with Israel and was focussed and made present in the temple. He prayed to the God who willed to be glorified in that temple, and, in so doing, integrated his prayer with Israel's law of faith, the order established by God himself. By contrast, early Christians as they prayed turned towards the East, the rising sun, which is the symbol of the risen Christ who rose from death's night into the glory of the Father and now reigns over all. At the same time, the rising sun is also the sign of the returning Christ who makes his definitive epiphany out of hiddenness, thus establishing the Kingdom of God in this world. The fusing together of these two kinds of sym-

bolism in the image of the rising sun suggests how intimately related faith in the resurrection and hope for the
parousia really are. The two are one in the figure of the
Lord who has already returned as the risen One, continues
to return in the Eucharist, and so remains he who is to
come, the hope of the world. Peterson has shown that,
from early times, this orientation of prayer towards the
East, by which the cosmos becomes a sign of Christ and
thus a space for prayer, was underlined visually by the
tracing of a cross on the east wall of the buildings where
the Christian assembly met. This cross was understood as
a sign of the returning Son of Man, and also as a threat of
eschatological punishment:

. . . Every eye will see him, every one who pierced him, and all
tribes of the earth shall wail on account of him.[8]

As Peterson himself put it:

Such apsidal representations of the Cross derive from the liturgical custom of eastward oriented prayer by means of a Cross which
symbolises eschatological faith.[9]

In this cross, the triumphal procession of the returning
Christ reaches in some sense the believing community itself. By turning to the east, the community declares the
temple to be superseded by Christ who is the true temple,
the world's future in the world's present.

    What conclusions may we draw from this discussion? If
turning to God through Christ in prayer was then as now
the heart of all Christian existence, it follows that analyzing the structure of prayer should help us to grasp the
inner makeup of early Christianity. Though it would be
unrealistic to expect such a brief report to yield some
definitive formula, we can nevertheless say that in the
prayer of the early Church, where East displaced Jerusa-

lem, a powerful eschatological expectation made itself felt. But we should also add that this eschatological hope is bound up with the spiritual expectation of prayer and the corporate authority of faith within the unity of the Church. It is inseparable from the experience of the presence of the final reality in the eucharistic feast. What this means is that the Christian hope is not some news item about tomorrow or the day after tomorrow. We might put it this way: hope is now personalized. Its focus is not space and time, the question of "Where?" and "When?," but relationship with Christ's person and longing for him to come close.

Has Christianity preserved this expectation faithfully? However did we arrive at that tedious and tedium-laden Christianity which we moderns observe and, indeed, know from our own experience? So far as the expectation of the end of time is concerned, history shows a certain fluctuation. Around the year 1000, a downright eschatological hysteria breaks out, the result of invoking ancient typological methods of dating world history—but perhaps the term *eschatological* is something of a misnomer in this context. In the later Middle Ages an intensified expectation of the imminent end of the world resurfaced. But these are emphatically not the places in which to seek the authentic eschatological approach of Christianity. Once again, we may be well advised to look for its most central manifestation in major prayer texts. The *Dies Irae*, a religious lyric with a marked subjective character, is, admittedly, not the best place to start. The immediate stuff of the prayer life of the Christian people in its corporate anxiety and hope is perhaps best grasped in the Litany of the Saints. By a development not all of whose phases are as yet clearly seen, this litany grew up by degrees from the Late Antique period onwards. It absorbed into itself all those concerns with which time harries us, while counterposing to them the pledge of hope through whose agency we may endure them. The first thing to strike us here is that the person who is thus set about by dangers in time and eternity finds a shelter in the communion of the saints. He gathers the redeemed of all ages around him and finds safety under their mantle. This signifies that the walls separating heaven and earth, and past, present and future, are now as glass. The Christian lives in the presence of the saints as his own proper ambience, and so lives "eschatologically." It is true that here the decisively determining element is the Church of those who have already been saved, the already achieved history of faith. And to this extent it would not be unfair to say that the stress lies more on the past than on the future, or even that, whereas consolation and certitude flow from the past, all the future holds is fear. But the real significance of this entry of the saints onto the Christian stage would not be captured in such an allotting of meaning to time. Much more important is the fact that in them the Christian promise has already proved its worth. They count for something not as the past but as the present of the Lord's power to save.

A second observation is pertinent in this connection. Surely the last petition of the Our Father has so overtaken the first and second as to eat up the whole force of the Lord's Prayer? What speaks to hearts is no longer "Thy kingdom come" but "Deliver us from evil." "Evil" here is not simply wickedness. As the unfolding of the petition into no less than ten invocations of the Litany suggests, "evil" is a portmanteau word spacious enough to include everything human beings find fearful and so, by contrast, all those prayers which spring from their necessities. The supreme evil here is death itself, the final foe and gaunt presence behind all other enemies, from whom one must flee for protection to the Lord surrounded by his saints.

As the Litany moves on, a further group of invocations

summons the great events of salvation history as powers of deliverance to our aid. Through prayer, they are to become a protective shield against the dangers that threaten us. Surprisingly, the actual events of the history of salvation seem to have moved completely into the past. Of sole pertinence to the future is the single petition: "On the day of judgment, Lord, deliver us" (or, "redeem us"). The term *adventus,* the translation of the ancient Greek *parousia,* has lost its eschatological meaning. We find it used twice: once for the "coming" of the Holy Spirit, that is, for Pentecost, itself an event which continues to unfold in the Christian community, and once for the coming of the Lord Christ himself. But in this latter case, the petition actually occupies a midway position between references to the Incarnation and the birth of Jesus, and so very likely alludes to his conception in the flesh. But is it not obvious, then, that what we are dealing with is a Christianity for which grace and salvation are past, and the future holds only threat and judgment? Isn't this shifting of the axis the real cause of the crisis in Christianity? Hasn't Christianity elected to make the past its preferred moment in time and so deprived itself of the future?

It is quite implausible to deny that there *is* a danger of this kind implicit in the pattern of the Litany prayer. I have to confess that my impression is of a sensibility welling up from the late mediaeval period by which Christendom became so attached to its past that it lost hold of both present and future. In part, it must be admitted, Gospel preaching was itself responsible for this deadly development through a one-sided emphasis on the threat of doomsday. But what I cannot let pass is the claim that all this satisfactorily sums up the state of Christianity in the Middle Ages. To begin with, the pervasive power of the thought of judgment is in any case perfectly characteristic

of the ancient Church as well. As we have seen, it was inseparably bound up with both the *maranatha* and the
eastward facing cross. Then there is the consideration that
the formal qualities of these prayers as appeals for liberation necessarily highlight the theme of judgment. But
above all, we have to remember that the Lord of judgment
is himself addressed as the liberator who has the power to
transform the act of judgment into an act of redemption. If
one may put it so, the judge who is to come is confronted
with the Savior who has already come. His coming, his actions, his sufferings and his gifts become so many promises of mercy with which the suppliant steps before him.
The believer holds up the mirror of the Savior to the face
of the Judge. Since he cannot place his hope in himself, he
finds shelter with the One who was his Savior and cannot
fail to be so everlastingly.

Also helpful in this connection is a glance at the structure of the Creed. The article on judgment was quite self-
consciously moved into the christological section as the
conclusion of the part of the Creed on God the Son, thus
leaving the section on God the Holy Spirit in exclusive
charge of the statements on salvation where the positive
perspective of Christian hope would be found.[10]

What can we learn from all this? In the first place, the
decisive consideration is still *looking to our Lord*. Eschatology's meaning and driving force depend upon the
power of this waiting on Christ, not on temporal expectations of the world's end or transformation, no matter of
what kind. Furthermore, though past Christian history receives very considerable emphasis, that history is invoked
in the Litany as a generator of hope, and so contains a
dynamism directed to the future. Lastly, the threat of
personal death and the powers that can encompass it
moves unmistakably into the center of the picture. The es-

chatological question becomes the question of my own dying. Accordingly, the really urgent question becomes that of personal salvation, which thus overlays that of the meaning of history as a whole. But note that this is possible precisely because the individual has found shelter in a history filled with salvific energy and so not in and of itself a dubious quantity. It follows from this that it is a mistake to speak of an absence of eschatology in the Middle Ages or a total transformation of eschatology's content. The truly constant factor is Christology. It is upon the integrity of Christology that the integrity of all the rest depends, and not the other way around. Though the shift of stress in eschatology, as in Christology, is undeniable, it has not only negative but also positive aspects. The question of the meaning of one's own dying cannot be suppressed. To attempt to obliterate or to shelve the progressive deepening of that question in Christian reflection would be not a return to the source but a barbarianization that would quickly recoil on its perpetrators. We have only to look at the complete impotence of Marxist thought when it comes to the topic of death to see how little chance there is of sidestepping that particular question. Thus it is by an inner logic that the doctrine of the "last things" grew up within the framework of eschatology. That doctrine remains indispensable for eschatology today. But the negative aspect of what happened is the real danger of reducing Christianity to individualism and otherworldliness. Both of these rob the Christian faith of its vital power. Here, in fact, lies the task of contemporary eschatology: to marry perspectives, so that person and community, present and future, are seen in their unity.

By way of conclusion, let us try to trace, very schematically, the path that leads from the Middle Ages to the early modern period and so, finally, to ourselves. Of great importance was the work of the south Italian abbot Joachim of Fiore (c. 1130–1202), who deduced a threefold periodization of history from faith in the triune God. The age of the Father, the Old Testament, and the age of the Son, the Church as found hitherto, would be followed by an age of the Holy Spirit, characterized by a Church living in spontaneous fulfilment of the Sermon on the Mount, through the universally efficacious activity of the Holy Spirit. There were anticipations of this view of things in Chiliasm, the expectation, founded on the Johannine Apocalypse, of a thousand-year reign of Christ on earth before the end of the world and the final judgment.[11] Although the chiliastic viewpoint had practically disappeared by the fifth century, Joachim revived it as a systematic doctrine of God. It was even made into something of a program of practical action, in that one could work toward the awaited third age by founding suitable religious Orders. The hope aroused by Joachim's teaching was first taken up by a segment of the Franciscan Order, but subsequently underwent increasing secularization until eventually it was turned into political utopia. The goad of the utopian vision remained embedded in Western consciousness, stimulating a quest for its own realization and preparing the way for that interest in concrete utopias which has become such a determinative element in political thought since the nineteenth century. This secularization of Christian eschatological thought has clearly sucked the sap out of faith awareness. People still have hopes for the historical process, but these impulses, now strangers to faith, have been transformed into a secular faith in progress. The specifically Christian element seems, therefore, ever more confined to the soul, and its reality ever more emaciated.

The "well-being" (*Heil*) which faith promises is thus diluted to the condition of the "salvation of the soul" (*Seelen-heil*), from which the "happiness" (*Glück*) sought by human beings in this life is now disconnected.[12] "Well-being" had once meant a totality: the well-being of the world through which I too am happy. But now the soul's salvation is but a fragment, and happiness another, and soon these two parts will be seen as natural enemies. The future salvation of my soul is the adversary of my present happiness, the Christian promise an impairment and menace to the earthly present. This opposition is the source of the resentment one can sense among many theologians against the doctrine of the last things. The traditional eschatology is felt to be suspicious of human happiness, which it would fain whittle down by appeal to the spectre of an uncertain tomorrow.

But meanwhile, by a remarkable development, this phase of theological sensibility represents what is by and large a thing of the past in the consciousness of most people. The more "happiness" was liberated and left to its own devices, making good its claims against the "salvation of the soul," the more impoverished and vacuous it became. Since it no longer admits any possibility of correction outside itself, it has to require the utmost of every passing moment and measure its pretentions by the highest possibilities human existence affords. The "little bit of luck" of the individual turns stale when left to itself. The greater happiness of other people, and the insatiable nature of one's own passions, become its new enemies just at the point when it has emancipated itself from the threat posed by the idea of the soul's salvation.

In order for happiness to become possible, the world must be transformed. So just at the point when its goal seems at hand, the quest for happiness must go into temporary suspension for the sake of the future of the world.

"Happiness" takes on the features of a petty-minded little *bourgeois,* whereas the human person in his full dimensions responds rather to the claims of hope, whose expectations of the future now drive him on as their willing captive.

At the end of our introductory reflections we find ourselves back at the point where we started. But we may have gained in understanding of one matter *en route:* humanity is waking up to the significance of eschatology because the question of the future of the whole has once again become urgent. The creation of a new world: this is the task which now absorbs all energies. As a result, the older eschatology has been pushed back into a corner where it stands bearing the dismissive label "salvation for the soul." No contribution here, or so it seems, to the "praxis" of a new age. This is the situation in which we are to do eschatology, but while we must not lose sight of the particular preoccupations of the present we ought not to make it the measuring-stick of everything we say. Instead, we need to integrate the opposing elements in the light of the Christian center, to strike a fair balance and come to understand the real promise of faith more deeply.

Part One

The Eschatological Problem as a Question About the Very Essence of Christianity

II

The Exegetical Data

I. A WORD ON METHOD

a. We noted at the outset that, ever since the work of Johannes Weiss, the question of Jesus' relation to eschatology has been formulated with ever-increasing clarity. To what extent did the historical Jesus include in his preaching the expectation of an imminent end to the world and an imminent epiphany of the Kingdom of God? How central was such an expectation to his proclamation as a whole? To what degree can a faith that does not wish to be such expectation of an imminent *eschaton* claim authentic continuity with the historical Jesus? The issue is no longer the relatively superficial question as to any errors that may have been contained within Jesus' world view and his perspective on future time. Rather is it the much more fundamental question of the essential character of his message as such. Is the expectation of an imminent end its true center? Does his message retain any significant content once the expectation of an imminent end is eliminated?

On closer inspection, we can distinguish here two levels whose confusion continually distorts the whole debate. On the one hand, we face a historical problem, an issue of textual interpretation. What does the historian make of the New Testament on this point? What, according to the sources, was the proclamation at that time?

What are the most ancient strata that can be traced and how did subsequent development proceed? The historian —in this particular case, the exegete—deals with questions that have to do with the past. He wants to find out exactly "what happened," and so he should. On the other hand, the question as to the meaning of these data from the past for the person who believes, or is searching for faith today, belongs to a quite different plane. The issue of appropriation, of the transposition of the past into the present should be carefully distinguished from that of research into historical data. In no way can it be answered by historical methods. It requires quite different methodological tools, corresponding to a different modality of the enquiring spirit. The very supposition that an ancient text has something of value to say to the present and should be interpretatively transposed for contemporary digestion already far exceeds the departure point of the historical method. But both sides are guilty of boundary violation. Dogmatics is always tempted to correct the data for the sake of the results. Exegesis wants to perform the task of transposition into the present, claiming the competence of an interpreter for work that simply cannot be carried out in that fashion. Not infrequently, historical analysis suffers from too much touching-up with a view to subsequent reinterpretation.

Naturally, the historical method in its distinterested quest for the truth of the past can hardly attain its ideal form in the case of texts whose affirmations touch the most basic human questions. The concepts employed in such investigation necessarily bring into play the preunderstanding of the interpreter. Without a sympathetic understanding, in which one's own view of reality is risked as in a wager, the interpreter can hardly expect to grasp anything at all. Take, for instance, the question as to what

Jesus actually meant by "the nearness of the Kingdom." This calls for an understanding of both "nearness" and "Kingdom" which can scarcely be disentangled entirely from one's own views. In any case, it is downright impossible for the historian to decide whether Jesus' assertion was true or false. The historian seeks the correct interpretation of texts but the leap to truth itself lies quite beyond his method. For the sake of our present concern, it might be helpful to look more closely at the fundamental problem which the issue of the truth of Jesus' expectation of the Kingdom engages. It should give us a rather more concrete grasp of the methodological limitations of pure scholarship.

Whether or not we think there is truth in the assertion that the Kingdom has come close depends upon what we understand by reality at large: what we consider real and what vantage point within reality we take as our own. Two hundred years ago, the assertion that the Christian hope was illusory would have been completely meaningless for most people in Europe. Though that assertion was in fact made, it remained for most people insubstantial and inconsequential, because the presence of Christianity governed their sense of reality. The Christian message was continually engaged in demonstrating its own reality as something on whose basis one could live and die. The joy which such certitude brought forth, even amid a host of afflictions, found expression in the radiant beauty of Baroque church-building and music. Today, we are faced with a phenomenon of an absolutely contrary kind. To maintain today that Christianity is the reality which bears up the world is to make an empty claim so far as the average person is concerned. For many, Christianity is nothing more than a gush of pious words which only the naive could accept as a substitute for reality. And these two attitudes dispose one to hear the same text in completely different ways. What we hear reflects the persons we who listen are, and not simply what it is we are listening to.

b. A second methodological comment is important for evaluating the kind of knowledge which is at stake here. During the last one hundred and fifty years, the epistemological ideal has been that of the natural sciences, where knowledge commends itself as certain and useful by techniques of verification and technological application. The historical-critical method tries where possible to transfer this characteristic form which knowledge takes in the natural sciences to the realm of history and to establish a certitude in this sphere that resembles that of the natural sciences themselves. To a remarkable extent this attempt has succeeded in such matters as ascertaining archaeological data, deciphering writings, dating documents, recognizing pseudepigraphy, and determining the succession of events. But this method soon discovers its own limitations when called upon to interpret texts with some more weighty significance where such a mode of comprehension is out of the question. The elimination of the observer, never fully possible even in natural science, now becomes a mere chimera. And yet people continue to approach the opinions of historical exegetes with a natural scientific model in mind, when the model they should be using is that proper to human history itself.

What does this last statement mean? It is beyond a shadow of doubt that natural scientific discovery depends upon certain preconditions in intellectual history. That Euclidean geometry was discovered by the Greeks, while non-Euclidean geometry took shape only in the nineteenth century, can be ascribed to the fundamental intellectual attitudes dominant in those two periods. Those attitudes were eye-opening for the one system, but obfuscating for the other. Yet once such results are achieved, they are in principle independent from the then prevailing world view and the historical preconditions of their discovery. For instance, one need not become a full-fledged Pythagorean to understand and employ the Pythagorean theorem. The achieved results slough off the skin of their historical preconditioning. Together they constitute the enduring materials of a gradually maturing body of knowledge. The sum total of reliable data is continually on the increase, from Pythagoras to Einstein, and scientific research draws upon it as on a self-contained intellectual treasury. The history within which a given idea is formed does not belong to its internal structure. For that idea it is not so much its own living history as a prehistory which is over and done with. The natural scientist has no need of it.

It is according to this nonhistorical model of the natural sciences that exegetical results are very largely assessed today. They are thought of as a sum of fixed results, a body of knowledge with immaculate credentials, acquired in such a fashion that it has left behind its own history as a mere prehistory, and is now at our disposal like a set of mathematical measurements. The measuring of the human spirit, however, differs from the quantification of the physical world. To follow the history of exegesis over the last hundred years is to become aware that it reflects the whole spiritual history of that period. Here the observer speaks of the observed only through speaking of himself: the object becomes eloquent only in this indirect refraction. Now this does not mean that at the end of the day all we know is ourselves. Rather are we faced at this point with a kind of knowledge familiar to us from philosophy. (Not that the two are identical: nevertheless, they have a family resemblance.) The "results" of the history of philosophy do not consist in a catalogue of formulae which

can be totted up into a final sum. Instead, they are a series
of raids on the deep places of being, carried out according
to the possibilities of their own time. The history in which
these explorations were made remains a living history,
not a dead prehistory. As philosophizing continues, Plato,
Aristotle, Thomas do not become prehistory: they remain
the originating figures of an enduring approach to the
Ground of what is. In their way of thought, and its access
to the Origin, a certain aspect of reality, a dimension of
being, is caught as in a mirror. None of them *is* philosophy
or *the* philosopher. It is in the multivalent message of the
entire history, and its overall critical evaluation, that truth
is disclosed and with it the possibility of fresh knowledge.
Something analogous to this is true of such a foundational
text as the Bible. Here, too, and especially where the heart
of the scriptural message is concerned, there is no such
thing as a definitive acquisition of scholarship: no interpretation from the past is ever completely old hat if in its
time it turned to the text in true openness. Unfortunately,
historical reason's criticism of itself is still in its infancy.
But one thing is certain: to employ in this domain the
paradigm of knowledge characteristic of the natural sciences is fallacious. Only by listening to the whole history
of interpretation can the present be purified by criticism
and so brought into a position of genuine encounter with
the text concerned.

2. THE MEANING OF JESUS' PROCLAMATION OF THE KINGDOM OF GOD

For the New Testament, the phrase "Kingdom of God,"
basileia tou theou, or "Kingdom of heaven," *basileia tōn
ouranōn*, is the true *Leitmotiv* of Jesus' preaching. Looking at the statistics makes this plain. There are in all 122

occurrences of the word in the New Testament, 99 being in the three Synoptic Gospels and 90 on the lips of Jesus himself. This in itself makes it clear that the phrase has a fundamental importance in the tradition stemming from Jesus. By contrast, in the post–Easter proclamation of the Church it speedily lost its place. In terms of frequency and importance it faded into the background. In point of fact, one can say that, whereas the fulcrum of the pre–Easter preaching of Jesus is the message of the Kingdom of God, the equivalent place in the post–Easter apostolic preaching is occupied by Christology. This historically verifiable sequence, in itself a sign of fidelity toward the words of Jesus, can also be seen as the symptom of a rupture between pre–Easter and post–Easter preaching, or even as the expression of an act of apostasy.

And yet one can legitimately ask whether this very change in the *Leitmotiv* of preaching may not be the way in which a self-identical theme was preserved under different conditions. Be that as it may, the making of Christology gave expression to the first Christian generation's faithfulness towards not only the person of Jesus, but also his teaching and work. Its preservation of his teaching in its original form in the Gospel tradition shows how that teaching remained a present reality for the first Christians: to listen to it in no way meant a self-distancing from the empirical life of the Church around one. It is already clear in this example just how difficult it is to visualize the historical *donné*. What strikes the modern reader, and inevitably so, as a most radical transformation, was evidently not so perceived by the living faith of that period. But if Christology is, in point of fact, the consistent continuation of the theme of the "Kingdom of God," this naturally tells us something about the original content of that phrase and the spiritual expectation which lay behind it. It helps us to grasp something of the relation to time, and to reality at large, which forged the language of the Kingdom as its self-expression.

And here a comment on a second linguistic fact is in order. Matthew speaks of the 'Kingdom of heaven' where Mark and Luke have 'Kingdom of God'. The meaning is the same in each case. Behind the Matthaean usage lies the Jewish linguistic rule of not using the Name of God, nor even the conceptual denomination "God," out of reverence for the greatness of this word. One spoke of him only by circumlocution. "Heaven," then, is simply a periphrasis for "God." This is an important point, because it shows that Matthew is not concerned, any more than are Mark and Luke, with something which is primarily in the world beyond. What is at stake is not the beyond, but *God*, in his personal activity. This observation gains in force if we add that in Jewish usage, the term *basileia*, normally translated "kingdom," does not signify a sphere of governance, but an active reality like our words "reign" or "command." Thus the phrase "the Kingdom of God" points to God's rule, his living power over the world. Following Joachim Jeremias, the affirmation that "the Kingdom of God is at hand" can be paraphrased "God is close."[1] First and foremost Jesus is speaking not of a heavenly reality but of something God is doing and will do in the future here on earth.

Sensitivity to the meaning of words is already leading us, without more ado, to the interpretation of the reality those words are about. But so as not to mistake that reality, we still have to consider the fact that Jesus' whole message was indebted to a prior tradition of language and thought, an earlier history of faith and prayer. The novel element in Jesus is manifested in the way he takes up, continues and transforms this tradition. So far back as we can follow it, the faith of Israel was marked from the outset by the element of promise, and therefore by hopeful expectation. The Old Testament books witness to a development of this hope as it crystallizes into various patterns which can be described only allusively here. From the Davidic "court theology," as we meet that in the figure of the prophet Nathan, there emerged the expectation that the Davidic monarchy would last forever. And from this expectation there sprang the hope for the Messiah, a king of David's lineage who would shape the kingdom of Israel into its perfected form. Little by little an image of the future came to be, the hopes of those who entertained it being strongly influenced by the political aspirations of the Davidic national idea.

But the acerbic controversies of the great prophets with the ruling dynasty favored a more transcendent kind of hope: an immediate intervention of God, his direct rule over the world. At the level of particular prophetic spokesmen, the mediation of such future divine rule was thought of in different ways: with Daniel, the figure of the Son of Man; with Deutero-Isaiah, the figure of the Servant of Yahweh; with Zechariah, the notion of the two Messiahs, sacerdotal and kingly. In so-called early Judaism, the panorama is even more diversified. It is customary to distinguish two main types of expectation: rabbinic and apocalyptic, though these two have many variants and are linked by many different cross-connections.[2] For the rabbinic tradition, God is always Lord and Ruler of this world, yet there is an expectation that he will step forth some day from his hiddenness and show his power openly. This provides the basis for a distinction between two ages or aeons. The time of the Messiah belongs to the present aeon, but his rule mediates the transition to the aeon to come. Herein lies the distinctive feature of the Zealot position.

Attempting to bring about the messianic kingdom by political means, it politicizes Israel's eschatology by interpreting the hope of Israel as a fundamentally political program. Another way of translating hope into practice is
exemplified by those rabbis who held that redemption, the
days of the Messiah, could be brought nearer through repentance, keeping the commandments and good works.[3]
Typical here is a saying of rabbi Joḥanan (d. 279 B.C.):

God spoke to the Israelites: 'Since I have fixed a definite time for
the end at which it will come, whether they do penance or not, it
will come at a determined time. But if they repent, even just for
one day, I will let it come outside (before) a determined time'. See
psalm 95,7: 'Today, if you will hear my voice'.[4]

By contrast, the apocalyptic brand of expectation stressed,
rather, the radical difference between the two aeons. It had
grown up in situations where Jews were acutely conscious
of their minority status: It was a hope-filled expression of
hopelessness. In the concrete, however, it became fused
with the other varieties of hope.

Jesus' preaching belongs within this situation. Its novelty lies not so much in new ideas as in the authority of
his mission, whereby he set asunder wheat and chaff. The
Davidic-dynastic component, which found its continuation in Zealot policy, evidently had no place in his message. Thus he never directly referred to himself as the
Messiah. Only in the inscription on the Cross does the
title Messiah, *Christos*, makes its appearance, from which
point it would enter the Christian confession of faith
though transformed in meaning through the catalyzing
power of the crucifixion.[5] Jesus himself belongs to the tradition of prophetic expectation. This is nowhere clearer
than in his promise of God's Kingdom to the poor, in the
many meanings of that term, and his linking of the gift of
the Kingdom, in indissoluble manner, with repentance.[6]

Mark put this very well in the summary of Jesus' message which he placed at the very beginning of Jesus' way and work: "The time is fulfilled and the Kingdom of God is at hand: repent, *metanoeite*, and believe in the Gospel."[7]

This linkage, and its supreme importance, is especially finely expressed in a very ancient group of texts describing Jesus' mission by reference to the figure of the prophet Jonah.[8] When some scribes and Pharisees demand a sign, Jesus replies that no sign shall be given to this generation save the sign of Jonah. The exact meaning of this saying was seemingly no longer clear even in the early tradition. In Matthew 12, 38–42, it referred to Jesus' death and resurrection, prefigured in the fate of Jonah, who spent three days and three nights in the belly of the whale before preaching repentance in Nineveh. In Luke, on the other hand, Jesus' generation is compared directly to the Ninevites who received no other sign than the person of the prophet and his message of repentance. There is a lot to be said for the view that the latter corresponds better to the original intention. But be that as it may, the two strands of tradition share a pair of common features. The sign Jesus offers is Jesus himself, and yet at the same time that sign must be sought in the form of his message. If one reflects on the implications of the "sign of Jonah" this correlation between grace and eschatology on the one side and repentance on the other becomes plain. Nineveh had forfeited its salvation and deserved to be destroyed. But amid all the sinful city's forgetfulness of God a prophet is sent to it by unexpected and undeserved grace. This prophet discloses the city's doom yet offers it the chance of repentance. The improbable happens, and the city repents. Moreover, something even more improbable—and unmerited—follows: the city is spared, to the great scandal of the prophet who protests loudly against such a *dénouement*. In this story repentance is itself grace: firstly, as offered, and secondly as accepted. The preaching of Jesus belongs within such a framework. With authority he proclaims repentance as a grace, thus opening himself to sinners and being understood by them.

Appropriately enough, given this foundation, Jesus' proclamation of the Kingdom of God is shot through with a sense of the urgency of the present moment. It does not take as its subject speculations about the where and when of space-time. At its heart stands the person of Jesus himself. Its fundamental categories are grace and repentance, grace and behavior—each bound to the other in an indissoluble unity. Though this connection is all-important, the historical background of contemporary exegesis makes it difficult to grasp. To get some idea of the range of interpretation, and so the measure of the problem itself, it may be helpful to compare two examples of such exegesis. Roughly of a date, they take up quite contrary positions on the meaning of the text. Here is the first:

> Jesus makes entry into God's kingdom something dependent on fulfilling God's will, on a certain attitude, a certain level of performance, on the part of the individual person. This lends his teaching an individualistic ... and decidedly ethical character. . . . Jesus mentions specifically religious and ethical preconditions for entering the Kingdom. . . . It is in accordance with a man's works of love, whether performed or left undone, that, on the day of judgment, he will enter the Kingdom or be shut out and swallowed up by eternal perdition.[9]

And here the second:

> The Kingdom of God belongs to a realm beyond ethics. The person whose lode-star is ethics naturally thinks in terms of the individual. But for Jesus and his apostles the promise is not directed to the individual as such, but to the community, with the individual attaining to salvation as a member of that community. . . . The negative assertion that the Kingdom of God is sheer miracle

must be preserved in its strict negativity. This negative assertion
. . . is the most positive affirmation there can be.[10]

Such a comparison is extremely instructive for the understanding of the text. It becomes clear at once how much
the results of interpretation depend upon the manner in
which questions are asked, and how tellingly they mirror
the questioners themselves. But it is also clear that both
interpretations bring out something genuinely present in
the text, though neither expresses its totality. In order to
perceive the whole meaning one would have to make a
kind of collage of the two interpretations. With the second
(but by no means over against the first), we must agree
that Jesus is opposed to any form of righteousness, whether
political or ethical, that tries to achieve the Kingdom of
God by its own volition. He contrasts such self-made
righteousness with a redemption which is pure gift, something sheerly received.[11] However, we must also maintain
that the Kingdom of God does find expression in ethical
categories.[12]

In a somewhat different and indeed deepened form, the
same connection between grace and ethics recurs in the
Beatitudes of the Sermon on the Mount. Here too ethical categories play a decisive part. The poor, the last and
least, are the bearers of the Kingdom and so first and foremost among its citizens. Yet they are also described as
meek, hungering for justice, merciful, pure in heart, peace-
makers, and persecuted for righteousness' sake. Here grace
appears as God's transformation of the lopsided order of
this world. God inverts this order, taking to himself those
who themselves have made a 'U-turn' and now stand in
opposition to the world. Ethos, right behavior, is found
now in the folly of embracing poverty, in opting out of secular achievement, in drawing close to God's own poverty
and so in the ever-increasing capacity to receive his riches.

The tension between these polarities is also expressed in another study in contrasts in Jesus' preaching of the Kingdom. The Kingdom is announced beneath the signs of joy, festivity and beauty, as in the parables of the Wedding Feast and the Great Banquet, as well as through images of powerlessness, as in the parables of the Mustard Seed, the Leaven, the Haul of Good and Bad Fish, the Field of Wheat and Tares. It is this paradox which, more than anything else, excludes the interpreting of Jesus' proclamation in terms of an imminent end. By virtue of this same paradox Jesus steps out of the framework of both apocalyptic and rabbinic thought. The victory of God under the species of insignificance, of the Passion: this is his new image of the Kingdom.

All of this leads us back with inner logic to our starting point, the type of Jonah. Jesus did not proclaim an explicit Christology. But the great lines of his preaching converge upon himself as the eschatological sign of God. They point to his destiny as the "now" of God. Jesus' own person is the "vanishing point," *Fluchtpunkt*, of everything he has to say about God's Kingdom. A difficult text, Luke 17, 20, when seen against the foil of Jesus' self-consciousness, irradiating, ubiquitous, indicates how we should evaluate the meaning of his message as a whole. To the Pharisees' question about when the Kingdom of God will come, Jesus replies:

The Kingdom of God is not coming with signs to be observed, *meta paratēreseōs*; nor will they say, 'Lo, here it is!' or 'There!' for behold, the kingdom of God is in the midst of you, *entos humōn estin.*

This statement is so hard to translate that every translation must be an interpretation. Precisely in this, it reflects the *chiaroscuro* of Jesus' whole message about the King-

dom. In its entirety that message shrinks from mere spec-
tating, "observation." Its "translations" are always interpretations. The term "observation," used in this text, was
commonly employed in the medical practice of the ancient world for the observation of symptoms. It also turns
up in the context of predicting the future through observations, something assiduously cultivated in astrology and
the pagan cultus. The mystery of the Kingdom does not
disclose itself to this kind of observation. Its coming calls
out for another kind of seeing.

What could this other kind of seeing be? In the history
of exegesis, three varieties of interpretation of our text are
identified. Comparing them will show yet again how in-
escapably every answer brings into play the factor of the
questioner. The first kind may be termed "idealistic":
with many different nuances of meaning it was dominant
from Origen until the start of this century. Here *entos
humōn* is translated "within you"—which, in purely linguistic terms, may not be incorrect. The meaning would
then be: the Kingdom of God is not outside you, but inside. Its proper space is personal interiority, and there one
must seek it, on the path which leads inwards and there
alone. But can we accept that Jesus would have voiced
such an exaltation of inwardness? After all, we have sayings like "You who are evil . . ."[13] that manifest his human
realism, together with his knowledge that "God alone is
good."[14]

And so a second type of interpretation has gained the
upper hand since the turn of the century: we might call it
the "eschatological" type. Here our text is read in the light
of the basic conviction that Jesus thought exclusively in
terms of imminent eschatology, expecting the Kingdom in
the form of a cataclysmic transformation of the very near
future. Exegetes of this mold conclude that, over against

the idea of a Kingdom which comes slowly, and thus observably, Jesus is setting forth his own idea of a Kingdom that comes suddenly. An appropriate translation would be, then: "The Kingdom will suddenly be in your midst."[15] Yet such a contrast is surely too superficial. "Observation" would simply be cut off in mid-course by the speed of arrival of what is observed, the Kingdom itself remaining in other respects something external. And in any case, there is no mention of "suddenly" in the text.

And so a third interpretation is becoming ever more popular at the present time. We could call it christological if we include the doctrine of the Holy Spirit within christology. Jesus is speaking in the present tense: the Kingdom of God cannot be observed, yet, unobserved, it is among those to whom he is speaking. It stands among them—in his own person.

Jesus in person is the 'mystery of the Kingdom, made over as gift' to the disciples by God.[16]

In him the future is present, God's Kingdom at hand, but in such a way that a mere observer, concerned with recording symptoms or plotting the movements of the stars, might well overlook the fact. In a splendid coinage of Origen's, Jesus is *hē autobasileia*, "the Kingdom in person."[17] This leads on to another text about the Kingdom whose reference to the present is (even) less debatable. In Luke and Matthew we read:

If it is by the finger of God that I cast out demons then the Kingdom of God has come upon you.[18]

This verse carries the above reflections to a deeper level and clarifies them in the light of the Gospel's own inner logic. Jesus is the Kingdom, not simply by virtue of his physical presence but through the Holy Spirit's radiant power flowing forth from him. In his Spirit-filled activity, smashing the demonic enslavement of man, the Kingdom of God becomes reality, God taking the government of this world into his own hands. Let us remember that God's Kingdom is an event, not a sphere. Jesus' actions, words, sufferings break the power of that alienation which lies so heavily on human life. In liberating people, they establish God's Kingdom. Jesus *is* that Kingdom since through him the Spirit of God acts in the world.

Here we glimpse the inner unity of the pre–Easter and post–Easter *kerygma*. The motif of the Kingdom is transformed into christology, because it is from Christ that the Spirit, the reign of God, comes.

3. THE EXPECTATION OF AN IMMINENT END

Beyond a shadow of a doubt, the New Testament does contain unmistakable traces of an expectation that the world will end soon. Where do these traces come from? Do they go back to Jesus? Do they point, indeed, to the true center of his message? This is how "thorough-going eschatology" has seen the matter since Weiss and Schweitzer. The style of New Testament interpretation which they founded adopted a maxim which was immediately plausible and offered a helpful kind of guiding thread for following the successive stages of development of the Christian message. According to this maxim, the greater the stress on expectation of an imminent end, the older a text must be. The more mitigated such eschatological expectation appears, the more recent the text. In certain parables, Matthew and Luke speak of the "delay of the arrival" of the Lord, or the bridegroom: *chronizei mou ho Kurios.*[19] In such texts the waiting Church retrojects its own experience of the "delay" of the Parousia into the earlier sayings of Jesus. Second Peter responds to the urgent question, "Where is the promise of his return?"[20] by citing Psalm 90 (89), 4, according to which a thousand years are but a day in the Lord's sight. In this epistle one sees even more clearly how a later period reached a compromise between imminence and remoteness, and explained the Parousia's delay in theological fashion.

In themselves the examples given are doubtless cogent evidence for the thesis. They disclose the Christian religion struggling to preserve the characteristic form of its own hope, and put into words an experience of disappointment which demanded an answer. Nevertheless, it is open to question whether one can infer from this anything like a general chronological principle whereby Christian origins are marked by an eschatology of radical imminence which would then be gradually toned down until finally one arrives at John where, for Bultmann at least, temporal eschatology has been wholly eliminated in favor of its existential counterpart. On Bultmann's view, John no longer has any expectations for the temporal process. It was up to an ecclesiastical redactor to put back into the Fourth Gospel a doctrine of the Last Things. Here eschatology has ceased to be a temporal category, and become instead a category dealing with authenticity in human existence. Bultmann believes that in this shift of key from time to existence a genuinely Christian vision has at last been achieved. Johannine Christianity is the single valid interpretation of Christianity at large. Naturally, he has to claim that John understood Jesus better than Jesus understood himself, demythologizing a Jewish prophecy of the imminent end so as to draw out its profound existential qualities. This raises important, indeed fundamental, questions of method. Can a later interpretation understand more of the origin than the accounts that come before it? May not an aboriginal understanding probe more deeply into the ground of some given reality than a purely historical reconstruction can do? In Bultmann such questions are masked by the schema of development, according to which deeper insights evolve at a leisurely pace from imminent eschatology.

It is this very maxim which has been rudely shaken by works produced within the Bultmann school itself. Hans Conzelmann has shown that a Synoptic evangelist, Luke, already had a conception of the Gospel in which imminent eschatology was lacking. For him, Christ is not the end but the mid-point of time. The path he traces does not lead to an immediate parousia, but to the Church of the Gentiles, the horizon of his gospel, the spacious room of the future it envisages. Conzelmann's findings have been summed up by saying that for Luke the present is no longer an intermediate state: it is an abiding state.[21] On the other hand, the same commentator has shown that the gospel of Matthew, composed contemporaneously with Luke's (or perhaps even later) contains an undiminished imminent eschatology which may even be described as heightened in comparison with Mark.[22]

Matthew keeps grim hold on an expectation of the imminent end. . . . How in his own mind he reconciled this with the actual course of history—granted that he is writing after the year 70—is the riddle Matthew has bequeathed us.[23]

From these discoveries one basic fact emerges. Where the expectation of an imminent end is concerned, there is no linear development. Depending on circumstances, each period either heightened or relaxed the tension of time. In some circumstances, an extreme form of temporal expectation might well be the product of a re-Judaizing process. The Judaism of Jesus' day had an overwhelming expectation of the imminent end. Such an expectation cannot be regarded, then, as something peculiarly characteristic of Jesus. The schema of linear development simply does not correspond to the facts. The real course of history offers no clear criteria of judgment of this kind. Imminent eschatology might just as well be later rather than earlier.

Let us try to deepen this insight by turning to the text which lies at the heart of our problem: Jesus' eschatological discourse in Mark 13 together with its parallels. We are not committing ourselves to offering an exegesis of the details of these texts: our center of interest will be the manner in which statements about the ultimate end receive temporal qualification.

First of all, let us take a trio of parallel texts: Matthew 24, 15–22; Mark 13, 14–20 and Luke 21, 20–23, all of which describe the fall of Jerusalem. One distinguishing characteristic of Luke's account is the way it supplements the apocalyptic symbolism by concrete reference to Roman siege techniques. Its most striking feature, however, is the way it substitutes for the book of Daniel's "abomination of desolation which stands in the holy place,"[24] the destruction, desolation and echoing emptiness of the city of Jerusalem. Furthermore, in the light of the Old Testament prophecies, the events are described as "days of vengeance" in which the words of Scripture find fulfilment.[25] By and large, the effect of all this is to soften the apocalyptic tone, to bring out the historical nature of the event and give it its due place within salvation history. Matthew 24, 22 and Mark 13, 20 include a reference, absent in Luke, to the frightfulness of the final tribulation. Furthermore, Matthew 24, 23–24 and Mark 13, 21–23 carry a warning against false proclamation of the Parousia, against pseudo-prophecy and spurious miracles. Matthew 24, 26–28 is the sole text to speak of the suddenness with which the

"Parousia of the Son of Man" will come. For that matter, it is the only gospel to use the actual term "parousia."

After the prediction of the destruction of Jerusalem, another trio of texts—Matthew 24, 29–31; Mark 13, 24–27 and Luke 21, 25–28—speak of the Son of Man's return. So far as our problem is concerned, it is extremely important to note how these two aspects—the imminent destruction of Jerusalem and the Parousia—are temporally related. In point of fact, the three evangelists, each with his own distinct perspective, connect the two events in quite characteristic ways. Luke makes the connection, in the context of predictions about Jerusalem, by means of a verse found only in his gospel:

> They will fall by the edge of the sword, and be led captive among all nations; and Jerusalem will be trodden down by the Gentiles, until the times of the Gentiles are fulfilled.[26]

In these few words, broad vistas open before us. The fall of Jerusalem is not the end of the world but the start of a new age in salvation history. Here begins the dispersion of Israel: the hour of the Gentiles has struck. Luke's "today" points not to the Parousia but to the time of the Gentiles when the Word wings its way to the nations after the scattering of Israel. No expectation here of an "imminent End."

By contrast, Mark appears to present a direct temporal link between the fall of the city and the consummation of the world. As he writes: "But in those days, after that tribulation. . . ." Yet, looked at in the light of Mark's redactional technique as a whole, the issue is more complex. The formula "in those days" is a typical Marcan redactional device, a formula he uses to link the units of text he inherited. *In illo tempore* is an editor's construction, not the reporting of a date in a diary. It tells us nothing, therefore, about the inner relation of events in time and space.

In comparing these two gospels, we realize that Luke is engaged in outlining a definite historical picture in which the coming of the time of the Gentiles marks the beginning of an open-ended future for the world. Mark, on the other hand, confines himself to a purely technical welding together of bits and pieces from the Gospel tradition—leaving open, then, the true nature of their interconnection.

The problem is treated in a different fashion again in Matthew. He begins with the words: "Immediately, after the tribulation of those days."[27] Here there really is a temporal connection. Mark's schematic *in illo tempore* is converted into Matthew's "immediately" which seems to move the events of the end of the world into direct proximity with the destruction of Jerusalem. Still, we must take into account the fact that 'immediately' picks up here the tone of the preceding verses with their contrast between the kind of calculation that weighs up signs and symptoms and the sudden, incalculable arrival of this unique event. It follows that the *euthys* of the text should be translated not as "immediately" but as "suddenly," and the entire assertion interpreted accordingly. Nevertheless, the impression persists that the trials and tribulations entailed in the destruction of Jerusalem *are* connected in time with the events of the end of the world.

What ought we to think of these internal divergences within the Synoptic tradition and the issue which they concern? Three points are worthy of note. In the first place, the single Gospel is heard only in the quartet of the four evangelists (for John belongs here too!). The word of Jesus persists only as something heard and received by the Church. After all, it can scarcely enter the historical arena save by being heard and, once heard, assimilated. But all hearing, and so all tradition, is also interpretation: in throwing light on one aspect, it allows another to fall into the shadow. The Church was right to reject Tatian's attempt to create a unified gospel: no such literal harmonization can be the Gospel itself. It is as a choir of four that the Gospel comes before the understanding of faith, as fresh today as ever.

Accordingly, the Gospel does not confront the Church as a self-enclosed *Ding-an-sich*. Herein lies the fundamental methodological error of trying to reconstruct the *ipsissima vox Jesu* as a yardstick for Church and New Testament alike. Realizing this should not turn us into sceptics, even though we are touching here on the limits of historical knowledge. Jesus' message becomes intelligible for us through the echo effect it has created in history. In this echo, the intrinsic potential of that message, with its various strata and configurations, still resounds. Through its resonance we learn more about the real than we shall ever do from free-floating critical reconstructions.

The decisive point is surely that the New Testament writings leave open the nature of the difference between literary schema and reality in this connection. Even when seen from the side of the author, the literary expression is schematic. After all, it can hardly tell the story of the future as it might with something past. Schema and reality are differently related by different authors, but none of them makes the bald claim to an identity between the two. They do not attempt that kind of reconstruction of the past which derives its coherence from a sense of historical genesis. Since what interests them is not the question of exact chronological succession or a possible causality of development but the inner unity of the whole, they are quite able to present their material in schematic *blocs*, united by schematic connections. This is all the more true of their perspective on future time, which, from the nature of things, can hardly be described by means of a strict and seamless chronology. It can only be laid out in some way that the governing affirmations of their message suggest. There are classical techniques in narrative construction which can help link these affirmations together. But even they cannot turn into straightforward descriptive history what is still to come and so has not yet been experienced.

What cannot be narrated in empirical terms is, nevertheless, still genuinely *told* by means of the inherited resources of narrative technique. The schematic character of the statements we are considering is not owing to some accidental absence of ability on the part of the evangelists which could in principle be overcome. The difference between schema and reality plays an essential role in this context. It cannot be erased by purely literary means. Only reality itself, in its own forward movement, can clarify what the schema leaves obscure. Only as the actual course of history unfolds does reality fill the schema with content and shed light on the meaning and interrelatedness of its various aspects. The fundamental and all-important hermeneutical insight here is that subsequent history belongs intrinsically to the inner momentum of the text itself. That is: it does not simply provide retrospective commentary on the text. Rather, through the appearing of the reality which was still to come, the full dimensions of the word carried by the text come to light. For this reason, the interpretation of these texts must be, by its very nature, incomplete. For this reason also, a generation later, John could penetrate in authoritative fashion the depth of the word, and understand what was meant by it with greater purity than could his predecessors. For this reason, once again, his own message is not simply a subsequent adaptation of the word to a changed situation, but reproduces the inner movement of the word itself. For this reason, finally, that kind of reconstruction which confines itself to the text in its earliest form and permits interpretation only on that basis is fundamentally out of order. The open nature of the relationship between schema and reality invites the reality of subsequent history to enter into the text. Only through the harvest of historical experience does the word gradually gain its full meaning, and the schema fill itself with reality. In contrast, by insisting on definitive conclusions drawn from the most primitive wording the exegete can reconstruct, one condemns oneself to idling with an empty schematism. And so the reader himself is taken up into the adventure of the word. He can understand it only as a participator, not as a spectator.

Naturally, the other side of the coin must also be stressed. The difference between schema and reality makes space for the forward movement of reality, but this does not mean that the word is in itself content-less and thus abandoned to the whims of all-and-sundry. Yet this is just what happens in those theologies which make "situation" the highest source and norm of Christianity. Authentic appropriation of the word must make its way on the narrow path which leads between archaism and modernism. Issuing as it does from the crucified and risen Christ, the word indicates a given direction which is wide enough to receive all reality into itself, yet clear enough to confront it with a definite measuring-rod of its own.

And so the history of the Church continues in a certain respect what happened by way of foundation in the time of Jesus. For the difference between schema and reality takes its basic form from the difference between the word of the Old Testament and the historical reality of Jesus. The words of the Old Testament, in which Israel's faith-experience of the word of God is reflected, anticipate the history of Jesus, the living Word of God in this world. It is only in the light of that earlier word that the figure of

Jesus becomes theologically intelligible. Jesus is interpreted on its basis, and only thus can his whole existence
be acknowledged as itself substantially "Word." And yet,
no matter to what degree the biblical word interpreted
him ahead of time, only the real figure of him-who-came
makes visible what remained hidden within the linguistic
word alone and resisted extraction by purely historical
means. This tension between old word and new reality remains the fundamental form of Christian faith. Only by
means of it can the hidden reality of God become known.
This is why it is senseless to try to trace a linear chronology of de-eschatologizing or re-eschatologizing. The
experiences of man with the word, and with time, run on
no straight course. It also becomes more intelligible, and
that on a deeper level, why there must be differences
within the Gospel tradition and how, nevertheless, that
tradition remains a unity. As should by now be conclu-
sively apparent, the unity of faith cannot rest upon a hypo-
thetical reconstruction of some primitive nucleus. Rather
does it find its support in the unity of the believing subject—the Church, which is responsible for our different experiences with the word and holds them together as one.[28]

On these presuppositions, then, what, in a nutshell, can
we take from our reflections so far? In many-faceted parables, Jesus proclaimed the good news of the Kingdom of
God as a reality which is both present and still to come.
The early Church knew itself to be faithful to this original
message by proclaiming Jesus as the Christ, as he who acts
in the Spirit, and so constitutes the present form of the
Kingdom. By gazing on the risen Christ, Christianity
knew that a most significant coming had already taken
place. It no longer proclaimed a pure theology of hope,
living from mere expectation of the future, but pointed to
a "now" in which the promise had already become pres-

ence. Such a present was, of course, itself hope, for it bears the future within itself.

Transposed into spiritual terms, this means that believers knew God's joy, but were still beset by violent tribulation. They knew the Lord's closeness, but also that he has his own time, for which the time of the Gentiles must first be fulfilled. They themselves lived in the time of the Gentiles, which is simultaneously an age when God is afflicted in this world and an age of world-wide fruitfulness for the grain of wheat which fell into the ground in Jesus. And all this means, finally, that the tension between schema and reality is what marks out the confines where Christian existence takes place—then just as much as now.

III

Word and Reality in Contemporary Appreciation

In the above section, we recognized the tension between reality on the one hand and the literary schemata used by the word on the other as the necessary form of eschatological discourse. This tension is tolerable so long as the Church takes responsibility for the word. By this is meant: the tension is bearable so long as the Church retains its integrity as the factor uniting word and reality despite the changing readings on the geiger counter of eschatological radioactivity that the turmoil of the centuries may bring in its train. The tension becomes problematic or unacceptable only when the Church's standing as the locus of the word comes under question, or is rejected altogether, especially in a period when the surface of time seems unsafe, being broken by telltale fissures. In such a situation, the now naked word, duly divested of the Church's tradition, seems either meaningless or in need of a radical transformation to be brought into significant relation with the new look of reality. It was in this way that the eschatological feverishness of the twentieth century developed, giving the previous century something of the idyllic quality of the legend of Sleeping Beauty in comparison. In the various interpretative models which emerged, we can see the refraction of different experiences of the present in the prism of the word, an open word, not yet fully determined by events. In the effort of appropriating the word such experiences must be heard even if, in the last analysis, they are somewhat lacking in weight when only the authority of an individual theologian stands behind them. If the communal life of the Church, which vouches for the permanence and thus the future of the word, is no longer recognized then all interpretations are simply predictions without validating authority. Nevertheless, the reciprocal criticism of the authors of these various projections can help to clear the way for a new interpretation of the word.

I. THE PANORAMA OF SOLUTIONS

(a) Karl Barth

When Johannes Weiss and Albert Schweitzer proclaimed the strictly eschatological character of the message of Jesus, they were speaking as historians. So far as systematic theology was concerned, they had not the faintest idea of what to do with their discovery, still moving as they were along the tramlines of theological liberalism. But the work of the early Barth marked a real turning point: his commentary on the Letter to the Romans was a bugle blast announcing a new epoch in theology:

A Christianity which is not wholly eschatology and nothing but eschatology has absolutely nothing to do with Christ.[29]

How can that be so? Barth presupposes the truth of Ernst Troeltsch's idea that the Last Things stand in no real relationship with time. Phrases like "the end of time" or "after time is finished" can only be conceptual makeshifts because human thought is imprisoned in the temporal. In reality, eternity is not commensurable with time, being of a wholly other order. Each wave of the ocean of time rushes up eternity's shore in much the same way.[30] And so, for the early Barth, "to await the Parousia" does not mean working out the date of a temporal event which will take place at some given point. What it means is, rather, something in the highest degree immediate for everybody: looking at the limits my existence comes up against. Or, as Barth puts it: "taking our empirical situation in life with the seriousness which actually belongs to it."[31] "Resurrection *is* eternity"[32]: the imagery of the Last Days symbolizes what is metaphysically ultimate—namely, the absolute transcendence of God.[33] Against the background of such philosophical convictions as these, to see Christianity as all eschatology with nothing left over is to see it as being not a doctrine or an institution—far from it!—but an act of decision whereby we expose ourselves to the wholly other God. The word "eschatological" no longer qualifies time. Instead, it qualifies existence. It interprets Christianity as an ever renewed act of encounter.

The exigent earnestness of this message proved able to arouse an entire generation. Yet it could not be a lasting answer, because of the shapeless actualism to which it necessarily leads us. So the argument had to continue. One line of development led from the early to the later Barth of the *Church Dogmatics* where theology is conceived in a radically Christocentric way.[34] This line of advance threw the inner logic of the New Testament's own development into particularly clear relief. But another line of development led to the systematization of the Existentialist-eschatological standpoint. And this was the way of Rudolf Bultmann.

(b) Rudolf Bultmann

For Bultmann, "existing eschatologically" is what being a Christian means. At a stroke, the concept of eschatology is stripped of any temporal component. It is defined in terms of contrast to a "subject-object" way of looking at reality, whereby we would stand back from a manipulable reality and dissect it. Such "objective" reality is deemed "inauthentic." If one falls prey to it, and treats it as the only reality there is, then authenticity passes one by. What is authentic for the human person is not found in the things that lie around us and over against us, but in an event of encounter. The essential bearing of man is only a potentiality: it becomes actual in decision. But this decision is not something we can simply posit from within our own resources. It becomes available to us in the moment when we encounter the claim of a "thou." Against this background, the significance of Christ can be expressed by saying of him that he is in himself the "eschatological event." So being a Christian means *breaking through* to authenticity in an encounter-event that is true eschatology because it is the means of *breaking out* from the circle of subject-object relations. In this way, it is escape from the thralldom of time, indeed the end of time, and radical liberation from the grip of the world. Eschatology is an act of self-abandonment. Naturally, such an act can only be performed on odd occasions. If it gained any continuity, it would itself become time and not the end of time.[35]

The undoubted ethical earnestness of this philosophical theology seems strangely empty to us today. Its extraordinary success can only be explained by historical factors at work in the time when it was written. Its appeal lay in its apparently solving the dilemma of the modern Christian who seems obliged either to excise substantial portions of his faith under the pressure of modern knowledge, thus losing his religious integrity, or to resist modern discoveries in the name of that integrity, thus entering what to any self-respecting human being could only be an intellectual no-man's-land. What was at work in Bultmann was the leaven of a deeply serious faith whereby Christianity was lived as a new birth, a wholly other condition of self-abandonment to eschatological existence. By a seeming paradox, it was precisely this rupture with the compromises of liberal theology, this rigorous faith, which then handed secular knowledge unlimited freedom. No longer were the secular disciplines required to demonstrate the historicity of at any rate a certain minimum Christian content, as had still been the case with Adolf von Harnack. For after all, everything that can be grasped by scholarship belongs to the world of subject-object relations and so has nothing to do with faith. A collision of the two spheres is definitionally impossible. It is impossible, because Christianity must be understood as eschatology. Eschatology, once a thicket of problems for faith, has now been transmogrified into the sword which cut the Gordian knot.

Blinking in astonishment at this transformation, one might overlook the fact that the solution is purchased at too dear a price. For it depends on displacing Christianity from its home in the midst of reality and resettling it on the pinhead of the present moment. A faith which cannot come into conflict with history, and with experienced reality in general, no longer has anything to say to the historical process. The void hollowed out by Bultmann's "eschatologically" conceived Christianity was one of the reasons for the fascination soon to be exerted in theology by the promises of Marxism. Where Christianity has denied the world, the world will make a powerful comeback. A merely formal and actualistic concept of faith cannot possibly win through in the struggle for the soul of humanity. Wherever a particular generation is made to feel the impact of the world's hopes and sufferings alike, such a concept of faith will dissolve into what, by a prophetic irony, it has itself hailed as the non-objective: the truly pointless.

(c) Oscar Cullmann

The Swiss exegete Oscar Cullmann worked out in his writings a position diametrically opposed to Bultmann's concept of Christianity. He stands in the succession of salvation-history theologians initiated by the Erlangen School in the nineteenth century. "Salvation history" is just as much the essence of Christianity for him as "eschatology" is for Bultmann. In other words, what Bultmann discards as the husk, the historical process in all its facticity and continuity, Cullmann hails as the heart of the matter.

Admittedly, Cullmann did not develop his ideas solely by way of excluding Bultmann's. He was no less opposed to that bequest of the Greek spirit which is metaphysics, something that plays a decisive role in Catholic theology in particular. For Cullmann, two opposed concepts of time confront each other here. The Greek way of seeing time is cyclic. Time is a closed circle and thus an eternal return of the selfsame. Hence it is experienced as enslavement and malediction. On this view, to seek salvation in time is a hopeless impossibility. Salvation can consist only in escaping the circle of time, in a flight towards a timeless eternity.[36] "Metaphysics," understood as the quest for a salvation which lies outside time, embodies the negation of time and so, according to Cullmann, is in flagrant contradiction to the fundamental insights of Christian faith.

The dissolution into metaphysics of the original Christian view of salvation history, tied as that was to an ascending time-curve, is the very root of heresy—if by heresy we mean apostasy from aboriginal Christianity.[37]

By contrast to the Greek cyclic view of time, Scripture's understanding of time is linear. What time is may be known by looking at the ladder whose steps are: yesterday, today, tomorrow. Because it is a line of ascent, it offers the space in which the fulfilment of a divine plan may take place. In other words, salvation occurs within time, and the two are reciprocally related. Cullmann, indeed, is reluctant to apply the concept of timelessness even to God himself. "His eternity can and must be seen 'naively' as an infinite temporality."[38] Cullmann regards a triadic division of time as the quite basic shared perception of Old and New Testament alike. He depicts it graphically in this way:[39]

Midpoint of time

←————————•——————— * ————————————→

1. Before creation

2. Between creation and Parousia

3. From the Parousia on

Against the foil of this background, the novel element in the message of Jesus stands out. It is his eschatology, which, by a remarkably painless piece of surgery, he attached to the very substance of salvation history itself. As Cullmann sees it, Jewish thought knew only one decisive demarcation of time after the creation. This was the moment of the Parousia with which the new aeon is to begin. The "midpoint of time" which thus separates the aeons lies in the future. But Jesus' message transformed this fundamental conception in a decisive way, producing the following scheme:

Midpoint of time

←————————•——————— * ——————•————————→

1. Before creation

2. Between creation and Parousia

3. From the Parousia on

Here the midpoint of time lies no longer in the future, but in the past, in the presence of Jesus and his apostles. "His coming meant to Jesus himself that the mid-point of time had been reached even in his own life-time."[40] Cullmann's book, which appeared at the close of the Second World War, uses for illustration's sake a comparison with the events of the War itself, wherein a considerable time had elapsed between "D-Day," the decisive military engagement, and "V-Day," the moment of victory. However long one might have to wait to see the final results, the decisive moment was the battle that turned the tide. It is just the same with Christ's coming. The turning point, the midpoint of time, is already here, though it does not coincide with the end of world history. That history may go on long afterwards in the public realm. As a result of his awareness of constituting the midpoint, Christ communicated a new vision of salvation history. In the separating of midpoint and end, and the resultant shift of time's midpoint to time past, the Gospel proclaimed a new epoch: the age of the "already" and "not yet," the already realized midpoint and the still future end. This vital distinction was part and parcel of Jesus' own message.

Compared to this central perception, by which Jesus shaped a new understanding of history and eschatology, the question of how long the intermediate age will last is very secondary. The problem of the expectation of an imminent end ceases, therefore, to be a pressing one. The all-important factor in the message of Jesus is not the question of how short the time will be until the Parousia, but the dramatic prominence he gives to the midpoint as something already achieved. The concept, and the reality, of an "intermediate age" were created by Jesus himself. This new phase of salvation history, not envisaged by Jewish thought, so far from contradicting his message is its very fruit—even if it is lasting longer than might have been expected.

In comparison with Bultmann's presentation, Cullmann's ideas were at a twofold disadvantage. In the first place, they provided much less elbowroom for critical adventurousness in New Testament interpretation. In the second place, and much more importantly, they had a good deal less to offer in terms of personal spirituality. The whole thing could easily look like a piece of apologetics. Above all, it gave the impression of falling under the heading of philosophical "objectivism" with eschatology a theory, rather than a challenge to human existence.

Cullmann made a lengthy response to these objections in his book *Salvation as History*. Here he refined his earlier scheme by making his original straight line into a wavy one, whose undulations represent the ups and downs of history, the discontinuous elements in its continuity. He was especially careful on this occasion to bring out the "existential" content of salvation history. Faith means entering into solidarity with salvation history, taking up its "already" and, on that basis, working towards the "not yet." The "existential" categories of faith, hope and love are brought into relation with salvation history's own constitutive dimensions. Faith is the appropriation of the past history, which finds itself transposed through love into the present and so becomes once more hope for the future.[41] Salvation history is, therefore, not merely the past. It is also the present and the future, as we continue on our pilgrimage till the Lord's return.

Although the present mood of theology is not favorable to this departure-point in salvation history, it must be said that it is both more concrete and closer to the actual content of Scripture than the other models we have encountered so far. To this degree, the advantages offered by this kind of translation and appropriation of the biblical word exceed those of its competitors. But its view of the relation between time and eternity, drawn as that claims to be from Scripture, is philosophically somewhat problematic, and not entirely convincing even at the exegetical level. The question as to how the biblical message is mediated— what we call the *hermeneutical* question—is treated much too cavalierly. Nor does Cullmann pay sufficient attention to the limitations of the message of Scripture which is certainly not concerned with settling the philosophical issues of time and eternity.

(d) C. H. Dodd

The English scholar C. H. Dodd proposed an eschatological perspective very different from the types of solution prevalent in Germany. In his book on the parables of the Kingdom, repeatedly republished since its first appearance in 1935, he sums up the most characteristic features of Jesus' message in the catchphrase "realised eschatology." In the activity of Jesus, God's own action has broken into history in the here-and-now.[42]

He declared that the eternal order was present in the actual situation, and that this situation was the 'harvest' of history that had gone before.[43]

The dramatic character of Jesus' proclamation does not stem from some particularly intense expectation of an imminent end, but from its claim to bring with it the presence of God. Dodd connects this interpretation of Jesus' message of the Kingdom with a christological and sacramental view of things fully in continuity with the inner development of historic Christianity. In his parables Jesus calls on people to keep watch for an unexpected event now on its way. Then the curtain falls on the stage set whose spotlights the parables had been. The blow is struck with the suddenness Jesus had predicted. When it comes, Jesus no longer *talks:* he acts, and he suffers. The disciples are thunderstruck, bewildered. Yet in the light of the resurrection, they understand that in Jesus' dying and rising again the mystery of the Kingdom is at last revealed.[44] The Church, for her part, looks back to this moment when the decisive happening took place. She recapitulates it in the efficacious sign of the Eucharist which is for Dodd "a sacrament of realised eschatology."[45] The presence of the past event in the Church's sacrament unites us to the exalted Lord, thus throwing open the door of eternal life, which is man's destiny.

Eye hath not seen, nor ear heard, neither hath it entered into the heart of man, what things the Lord hath prepared for those who love him.[46]

From his starting point in modern exegesis, Dodd thus recreated that synthesis whereby the faith of the Church throughout the centuries has interpreted the relation of past, present and future, in the eschatological message of the New Testament. In German-language exegetical studies, and the theology which took its cue from them, such a view could find neither house nor home. Admittedly, the methodological basis of this mediation of the Church's synthesis needs to be thought out afresh. Yet it should be clear that the native power of Christianity, something which will outlive all the ideas of the academics, draws its strength from just this synthesis. This is what binds together faith and human living in a real and effective manner, whereas neither the actualism of the early Barth, nor Bultmann's theological Existentialism, nor a theology with the formal structure of salvation history but deprived of this life-giving background will ever be more than somebody's compilation.

(e) The Theology of Hope and Political Theology

By glancing at the work of Cullmann and Dodd we have wandered off the main line of development in German-language theology and must now, by way of conclusion, return to our old road. Bultmann's formalistic eschatology of decision was able to exercise the fascination it did because it united deep spirituality and complete freedom from the world with a continuing acceptance of secular rationality. However, in the process it robbed faith of all content and cut off the question of the meaning of the world and its history in mid-sentence. This could be no lasting solution. Once the phase of reconstructing the question of the future had yielded to that of setting new practical agendas and construing new meanings, its hour was at an end. The roll on the kettledrums which announced its passing was Jürgen Moltmann's *Theology of Hope,* followed in quick succession by the "Political Theology" of Johann Baptist Metz. For Moltmann eschatology was just as much the central concern of theology as it had been to Bultmann, but in a far-reaching shift of perspective he saw it not as liberation from the world but as "the suffering and passion which arise for the Messiah."[47] Accordingly, the main point at issue in eschatology is not the status of the present, or the significance of some special "moment," nor a past "midpoint of time," nor eternity itself. The time of the eschaton, and thus the all-important time for Christianity, is the *future.* The contradiction between faith and the present world order is not resolved by reference to some privileged moment nor to the world of eternity. Instead, that contradiction is quite consciously preserved by opposing the facts of the present to the hope of the future. This is what, for Moltmann, being a Christian means.

Doctrinal statements have their truth in a controllable correspondence with the reality which is at hand and can be experienced as such. The propositions of hope found in the promise, by contrast, are necessarily in contradiction with the presently experienced reality. They are not the result of experience, but the condition of possibility for new experience. They are not meant to illumine the reality which is here, but that which is to come. . . . Their wish is to carry a torch before reality, not to carry reality's train after her.[48]

The new manifesto ran: put Christianity into practice by transforming the world, using the criterion of hope. The torch, which was thus to be set to the tinder of the facts, blazed up soon enough. It became Political Theology, the Theology of Revolution, Liberation Theology, Black Theology.[49] After Bultmann's abstractions theology had become realistic in a way long regarded as impossible. It had become a theology of action with consequences on a world scale. Moltmann's theological model is so rich and complex that it would be inappropriate to try and weigh it up in terms of those consequences—and even more so to dismiss it hook, line and sinker by the same token. Besides, in the theologies of liberation and revolution themselves there are here and there gleams of real gold.

Though this is true, and no definitive separation of wheat and chaff can be made in this area, two fundamental objections have to be made. If Christianity is to be interpreted as a strategy of hope, the question naturally arises: But *which* hope? The Kingdom of God, not being itself a political concept, cannot serve as a political criterion by which to construct in direct fashion a program of political action and to criticize the political efforts of other people. The realization of God's Kingdom is not itself a political process. To misconceive it as such is to falsify both politics and theology. The inevitable result is the rise of false messianic movements which of their very nature and from the inner logic of messianic claims finish up in totalitarianism.

So the first objection is that the transformation of eschatology into political utopianism involves the emascula-
tion of Christian hope. Though to all intents and purposes
that hope is simply being re-expressed in humanly realistic
terms, in fact its own essential content is draining away,
leaving behind nothing but a deceptive surrogate. The second objection maintains that in this process politics itself
is also falsified. The mystery of God is invoked in order to
justify political irrationalism, and so is reduced to being a
pseudo-mystery. The transformation of human nature, and
the world with it, is possible only as a miracle of grace.
Where it is regarded as being, rather, the building-site
where the house of politics is under construction, a rank
impossibility is taken as the foundation for all human reality. The upshot can only be the violent self-destruction
of nature and humanity alike.[50]

But this by no means signifies that the proclamation of
the Kingdom of God can be pushed aside as of no practical
importance, and so transformed into a surreptitious justification of the *status quo.* The Kingdom of God is not a *political* norm of political activity, but it is a *moral* norm of
that activity. Political activity stands under moral norms,
even if morality as such is not politics nor politics as such
morality. In other words, the message of the Kingdom of
God is significant for political life not by way of eschatology but by way of political ethics. The issue of a politics
that will be genuinely responsible in Christian terms belongs to moral theology, not eschatology. In this very distinction, the message of the Kingdom of God has something very important to say to politics. It is healthy for
politics to learn that its own content is not eschatological.
The setting asunder of eschatology and politics is one of
the fundamental tasks of Christian theology. In carrying it
out, the theologian can know himself to be following
Jesus' own path in opposing the eschatology of his Zealot

rivals. Only by taking this route can we preserve the hope which eschatology carries, and prevent its turning into the terror of a "Gulag Archipelago." And conversely, only along this way can we preserve the morality of politics and so its true humanity. Where eschatology and politics are made to coincide, morality decrees its own dissolution, becoming no more than the question of how to find the most efficient way of reaching the *unum necessarium* of the absolute goal.[51]

2. PRELIMINARY CONCLUSIONS

So what conclusions may we draw from all of this? In the first place, the importance of courage in evaluating the latest theories of one's age with greater equanimity, noting in a historically informed way their role in that criticism which historical reason carries out in its own regard, and understanding their place in the movement of history as a whole. The obverse of this courage should be the modesty of not claiming to have just discovered what Christianity is really all about by dint of one's own ingenuity. Out of such modesty something even more valuable could emerge: the kind of humility that submits to reality, not inventing Christian truth as a newly discovered "find," but truly finding it in the sacramental community of the faith of all periods.

Something about the content of that faith may also have become a little clearer. To extend and deepen what has been said, let us go back once more to Oscar Cullmann's central thesis. The interval between the "midpoint" and the "end" is a decisive factor in Jesus' message. Cosmic transformation and the coming of God's Kingdom do not coincide. In this *diastasis* lies our difficulty, the root of our impatience and embarrassment. It really is *scandal-*

ous. But wait! Did not Christ want to be a *skandalon*, something one trips over? That is how, providentially, one becomes alert to the essential thing, finding the Corner-stone in the stone which causes one to stumble.

What, then, is the nature of this interval, this remark-able postponement of "Victory day" which obliges us to agree that the real event has already happened and yet for-bids us to say where it has, in point of fact, arrived? It surely means more than a mere chronological postpone-ment. In itself, a more finely differentiated division of time might signify very little, whereas the separation of midpoint and End before which we now stand has the effect of radically transforming both the idea and the real-ity of what we call salvation. Or to put it perhaps more ac-curately: it forces us to realize the true extent of the disas-ter entailed in the *absence* of salvation. At the time of Jesus, the Jewish people were expecting salvation in the form of a change of circumstances affecting the whole cos-mos: a kind of religiously grounded *shangri-la*. The temp-tations of Jesus, as described in Matthew and Luke, express this expectation to perfection: bread from desert soil, sen-sational signs and wonders, assured political power over the entire world. The Messiah of the temptations in the wilderness—the Messiah of human expectation—is de-fined by his promises of consumer satisfaction and power over others. Anyone who thinks hard about this will real-ize that here "the Jews" represent humanity in general. Were we to plan salvation for ourselves and our world it would not be any different. All political propaganda lives off such attitudes of expectation. As we know, the story of the modern belief in progress and its transformation into Marxist messianism demonstrates that one cannot stop at this point. By an inner necessity, freedom and equality en-ter into mutual conflict. Yet neither of them can be satisfying without the other. Unrestrained consumption shows up the tragic alienation there is between the cosmos and the human species, and between human beings themselves. What seemed a gift becomes a destroying curse. And so the program takes on a more radical color. Eventually, it turns into a desire for emancipation so total that it is equivalent to asking that men become God. At this point, faith in progress changes over into a dialectic of the negative: emancipation in the sense just outlined presupposes the tearing down of present reality.

In the past hundred years, humankind has moved with inexorable logic from one link of this chain to another. But the structural flaw in the whole is that, while man is capable of destruction, he lacks the power to conjure emancipation from the ashes. There is only one objective that can suffice for him: liberation from the constraints of cosmos and history alike so as to achieve equality with God. But this goal is manifestly unattainable. So what is left? Nothing more than a portrait of man as the one animal which is intrinsically absurd?

It is here that we may be able to encounter the figure of Jesus Christ in a new way. The Kingdom of God which Christ promises does not consist in a modification of our earthly circumstances—which, in any case, to judge from general human experience, might not mean much anyway. That Kingdom is found in those persons whom the finger of God has touched and who have allowed themselves to be made God's sons and daughters.[52] Clearly, such a transformation can only take place through death. For this reason, the Kingdom of God, salvation in its fulness, cannot be deprived of its connection with dying. The resemblance between the basic pattern of the New Testament message and the experience of our century is at once exciting and alarming, because that resemblance coexists with move-

ment on the part of the human spirit in diametrically opposed directions.

Man seeks total emancipation, freedom without limitations of any kind. He seeks an equality in which all alienation is eliminated, and his own unity with himself, with
nature and with humanity-at-large is at last made real.
What this means is that man wants Godhead. The New
Testament tells him that he is right in this desire but
wrong in his manner of looking for it. The christological
hymn in the Letter to the Philippians addresses this entire
problematic in a visionary statement which sums up the
whole of biblical theology. It reads:

Have this mind among yourselves, which is yours in Christ Jesus,
who, though he was in the form of God did not count equality
with God a thing to be grasped, but emptied himself, taking the
form of a servant, being born in the likeness of men. And being
found in human form, he humbled himself and became obedient
unto death, even death on a cross. Therefore God has highly exalted him and bestowed on him the name which is above every
name, that at the name of Jesus every knee should bow, in heaven
and on earth and under the earth, and every tongue confess that
Jesus Christ is Lord, to the glory of God the Father.[53]

Embedded in these verses is a divine oath found in the
book of Isaiah:

To me every knee shall bow,
every tongue shall swear.
Only in the Lord, it shall be said of me,
are righteousness and strength.[54]

In these words from the end of the exilic period one senses
the exultant joy of the Israelites returning from their cap-
tivity. Israel is experiencing the triumph of its God who
uses mighty kings—Nebuchadnezzar, Cyrus—as his ser-
vants. Through the fact of the Exile as well as its ending,
through the victory and the downfall of Babylon, God

proves himself to be history's true Lord, the only Ruler of the kings of the earth. In the last resort, all stand and serve him. Yet, despite the experience of fulfilment, the Isaiah verse must be taken as referring to the future. The Gentiles do not yet know that they are serving Yahweh, rather than carrying out the plans of their own hearts. The hour when they will confess his Name is still to come. In Philippians, Isaiah's future is transposed into the present. Christian believers are experiencing the quite unheard-of happiness of a future now become present. The unthinkable has happened. The Gentiles are actually bending the knee before Yahweh in the figure of Jesus. They pray by confessing him as God of the whole earth. Christian faith and liturgy are borne along by this deep current of joyous fulfilment. The word of prophecy came true.

But the thrilling part is that this triumph of Yahweh, whom all the nations now adore, took place in the utter humiliation of the Cross. In order to explain how this could be so, the hymn opens up that perspective on humanity as a whole which has been our topic. Verse six, alluding to a version of the Adam myth in the book of Job reminds us that man wishes to be God.[55] Nor is this desire of his entirely misconceived. Yet man pursues it in the style of a Prometheus, hunting the prey which is equality with God, taking it by violence. But man is not God. By making himself like unto God he sets himself over against truth, and so the adventure ends in that nothingness where truth is not. The actual God-man does just the opposite. He is God's Son, his whole being a gesture of gratitude and self-offering. In reality, the Cross is but the definitive radicalization of that gesture which the Son is. Not the grasping audacity of Prometheus but the Son's obedience on the Cross is the place where man's divinization is accomplished. Man can become God, not by making himself

God, but by allowing himself to be made "Son." Here in this gesture of Jesus as the Son, and nowhere else, the Kingdom of God is realized. This is why the first are to be last, and the last first. This is the reason for the Beatitudes about those whose life-style is cruciform and therefore Son-like. This is why little ones are lauded, and all called to become as children. In her theology of childhood, Thérèse of Lisieux rediscovered this mystery of the Son. Here is where equality with God happens, for God himself is Son, and as Son he is man.

The answer to the question of the Kingdom is, therefore, no other than the Son in whom the unbridgeable gulf between already and not yet is spanned. In him death and life, annihilation and being, are held together. The Cross of the *Pontifex* joins shore to shore. But if the answer to the question of the Kingdom is indeed the Son, then manifestly, the message of Jesus cannot make its peace with any eschatology of (merely) changed living conditions. Our departure-point is a person, not a program. But by the same token it is equally apparent that redemption does not reach us through the satisfaction of our ego, as we may dreamily imagine in the tranquillity of our privy chamber. Redemption cannot come through the repletion of the ego but only by a total turnabout in which we march away from egotism in the opposite direction. This is why true eschatology must be universal and aim at the salvation of all. Thus the time of the Gentiles, as the prelude to the End, is not an arbitrary item in the Gospel tradition: it follows by inner necessity from the very nature of salvation. Salvation must be willed for all and offered to all. A further consequence is that salvation cannot simply be given people in some external way, as one might hand over a sum of money. Rather does it claim the entire personal subject who receives it. And once again, the interval between midpoint and end becomes intelligible when seen from this angle. Man with his ambiguous story of acceptance and rejection of grace is an acting subject in God's saving plan, and it is on this basis that he inhabits time. He is a true subject in his own right, but not as one who would produce the Kingdom of God from his own resources. The "right" in which he is a subject he receives from the 'Thou' of God. He possesses genuine subjecthood only because he has become a son. Divinization, "emancipation" as a sharer in the Kingdom of God, is not a product but a gift. Sheer love can only be so. It is because entry into the Kingdom comes about through love that the Kingdom is hope. In a laboratory—which is how Ernst Bloch defined the world—there is nothing to hope for. Hope exists only where there is love. Since, in the crucified Christ, love prevailed and death fled vanquished, human hope can truly "spring eternal."

Part Two

Death and Immortality.
The Individual Dimension
of Eschatology

IV

The Theology of Death

I. POSING THE QUESTION

At first glance, our society's attitude to death seems remarkably contradictory. On the one hand death is placed under a taboo. It is unseemly. So far as possible, it must be hidden away, the thought of it repressed in waking consciousness. On the other hand, one is also aware of a tendency to put death on show, which corresponds to the general pulling down of shame-barriers everywhere. How can this contradiction be accounted for? On closer inspection, we seem to find a two-fold development whose phases affect each other in various ways yet remain in themselves distinct.

Bourgeois society hides death away. Josef Pieper has made a collection of a number of significant variations on this theme. Thus, for instance, a distinguished American newspaper does not allow the word "death" to be printed.[1] In the United States, even funeral homes themselves devise special arrangements so as to avoid mentioning the fact of death. Something similar happens in our hospitals, where death is carefully concealed so far as may be possible. This tendency to hide death away receives effective support from the very structure of modern society in which the corporate life of the family is increasingly displaced by the logic of production and the specializations which it has developed. As a result, the family home frequently seems no more than a sleeping-bag. In the daytime it effectively dematerializes. No more can it be that sheltering space which brings human beings together in birth and living, in sickness and dying. Indeed, sickness and death are becoming purely technological problems to be handled by the appropriate institution. These basic human things are thus pushed to the margins, not just so far as our deliberate thoughts about them are concerned, but socially, structurally. They cease to be physical and metaphysical problems which must be suffered and borne in a communion of life, and become instead technical tasks technically handled by technical people.

And so the taboo of death is at first strengthened by the outer structure of society. Yet other processes are coming more and more into prominence where a rather different evolution seems to be taking place. I am not thinking here of that Nihilist defiance of death also mentioned by Pieper. Such an attitude is for the chosen few who, refusing to play the game of hide-the-slipper with death, attempt to bear the meaningless by looking straight into its eyes. The growing phenomenon I have in mind is in fact a third attitude which Pieper, once again, has aptly called the "materialistic trivialisation of death." On television, death is presented as a thrilling spectacle tailor-made for alleviating the general boredom of life. In the last analysis, of course, the covert aim of this reduction of death to the status of an object is just the same as with the bourgeois taboo on the subject. Death is to be deprived of its character as a place where the metaphysical breaks through. Death is rendered banal, so as to quell the unsettling question which arises from it. Schleiermacher once spoke of birth and death as "hewed out perspectives" through which man peers into the infinite. But the infinite calls

his ordinary life-style into question. And therefore, under-
standably, humankind puts it to the ban. The repression of
death is so much easier when death has been naturalized.
Death must become so object-like, so ordinary, so public
that no remnant of the metaphysical question is left
within it.

All of this has momentous consequences for man's relation to himself and to reality in general. The Litany of the
Saints expresses the attitude of Christian faith vis-à-vis
death in the petition: *A subitanea morte, libera nos,
Domine,* "from a death that is sudden and unprepared for,
deliver us, o Lord." To be taken away suddenly, without
being able to make oneself ready, without having had time
to prepare—this is the supreme danger from which man
wants to be saved. He wants to be alert as he sets out on
that final journey. He wants dying to be his own action. If
one were to formulate today a Litany of the Unbelievers
the petition would, no doubt, be just the opposite: a sudden and unprovided death grant to us, o Lord. Death really
ought to happen at a stroke, and leave no time for reflection or suffering.

Yet it is apparent that the total ban on metaphysical fear
did not succeed. It had to be followed up by actually turning
death into an object of production. By becoming a product,
death is supposed to vanish as a question mark about the
nature of being human, a more-than-technological enquiry. The issue of euthanasia is becoming increasingly
important because people wish to avoid death as something which happens *to me,* and replace it with a technical
cessation of function which I do not need to carry out myself. The purpose is to slam the door on metaphysics before it has a chance to come in.

But the price for this ban on fear is very high. The de-
humanizing of death necessarily brings with it the de-

humanizing of life as well. When human sickness and dying are reduced to the level of technological activity, so is man himself. Where it becomes too dangerous to accept death in a human way, being human has itself become too dangerous. Oddly enough, it is in this attempt to renege on being human that the most contrary present-day positions find their common ground. For on the one hand we find people moving towards a positivistic, technocratic world view, and on the other they are equally attracted by a nostalgic yearning for some unspoiled state of nature. In this latter tendency, rational self-consciousness is regarded as the culprit that breached the peace of paradise, and man as the one animal that took a wrong turning. Attitudes to dying determine attitudes to living. Death becomes the key to the question: What really *is* man? The mounting callousness towards human life which we are experiencing today is intimately bound up with the refusal to confront the question of death. Repression and trivilization can only "solve" the riddle by dissolving humanity itself.

2. THE HISTORICAL ROOTS OF THE QUESTION

(a) The Prevailing View

Since positivist and materialist answers leave us finally perplexed at this crucial juncture, it should be clear that the issues of life and death are not among those which progress in the exact sciences can clarify. There is a set of questions—the really human questions—where other approaches towards an answer must be brought in. In this respect, the experience comprised in the wisdom of the tradition remains of central importance. And yet, if one seeks counsel here from the theologians, who are the professional guardians of tradition in Christianity, one discovers, by and large, a somewhat depressing state of affairs.

In recent discussion, one can identify two phases which are distinct though they cannot be separated chronologically in any watertight fashion. The first tendency is particularly well represented by the works of P. Althaus and E. Jüngel.[2] It is based on that antithesis between biblical and Greek thought which since the sixteenth century has increasingly stamped itself on theological work. So far as our question is concerned, the application of this rather schematic contrast has it that the Greek understanding of death, decisively shaped by Plato, was idealistic and dualistic. Matter was looked upon as in itself a bad thing. Only spirit and idea count as genuinely positive, God-like, the really real. On this view, man is a strange creature in which the two contrary realities of matter and spirit have come to coincide. The being thus moulded is self-contradictory, fatal. The divine flame of the spirit is imprisoned in the dungeon of the body. The way of the wise man, accordingly, is to treat the body as the tomb of the soul and to prepare himself for immortality through such enmity to the prison house. Death, then, is the great moment when the gates of that prison house are flung wide open and the soul steps forth into that freedom and immortality which are its by right. Death is man's true friend, his liberator from the unnatural chains of matter. Socrates, as presented by Plato, is an exponent of this idealist interpretation of death. He celebrates his own dying as a festal journey from the sickness of bodily life to the health of true living. At the moment of death, he asks that a cock be sacrificed to Aesculapius, the customary sacrifice offered in gratitude for a recovery. Death here is interpreted as emergence from the diseased semblance of life which is this world into real and lasting health.

At this point we get our first glimpse of a conclusion which in recent years has become of great importance for Christian faith and preaching. Some people are saying that belief in immortality belongs to this dualistic, body-hating Platonist thinking, and has nothing whatever to do with the ideas of Scripture. In biblical thought, by contrast, man is seen in his undivided wholeness and unity as God's creature and cannot be sliced down the middle into body and soul. This is why the biblical authors do not submit death to an idealistic transfiguration in their descriptions of it, but present it, rather, in its full, unvarnished reality as the destroying enemy of life. Only Jesus' resurrection brings new hope. However, this hope in no way softens the stark reality of death in which not the body alone but the entire human being dies. Language itself indicates this truth, for we say "I will die," not "My body will die." You can't get away from the totality of death: it devours you, leaving nothing behind. True, the risen Christ gives us the hope that, by God's grace, the entire person will be raised again into newness of life. This biblical hope, expressed only in the term "resurrection," presupposes the finality of death. The immortality of the soul must be firmly rejected as an idea which goes against the grain of biblical thought. We shall return in some detail to the question of immortality in a moment. The prior question facing us now is how death itself is to be interpreted.

In certain segments of contemporary theological literature the thesis of "total death" has undergone such a radicalization that its biblical aspect is visibly stripped away.[3] In a thorough-going fashion writers take over that archaizing view of the Old Testament once found among the Sadducees, and claim that the Jewish Scriptures in themselves know nothing of either immortality or resurrection. These ideas, it is insinuated, are invoked only in a marginal way, on loan from Iranian thought. Congruently with this, some authors insist on isolating "Q," the reconstructed sayings-source lying behind Matthew and Luke, as the original form of a "Christianity before Christ." Here not only the theme of the Church, but also that of death and resurrection, sacrifice and atonement, are conspicuous by their absence. Only on such an approach, it is said, can the total death of each human being retain that irrevocable finality which is proper to it. Resurrection becomes a mere cipher whose content mutates according to the philosophical convictions of the writers concerned. Such views are not without a certain inner consistency. A resurrection juxtaposed with total death in an immediate and unconnected manner *does* become a fantastic sort of miracle, unsupported by any coherent anthropological vision. The suggestive power of this new view of things derives from the perfect correspondence between the most advanced demands of the spirit of the age on the one hand and, on the other, the biblical message as suitably doctored by source-critical manipulation. However, this also means that faith abdicates its responsibility of offering an authoritative response to man's ultimate questions. Faith here simply points to the general experience of absence of meaning as to its own final comment on the human situation. But for such an office faith is superfluous anyhow.

(b) An Attempt at Revisionism

If, for the sake of scientific objectivity, one tries to take a closer look at the historical data, the following picture emerges. First of all, the contrasting of cultures and thought forms as though these were fixed quantities—in this case Greek versus biblical—makes no historical sense. Great cultures, and the thinking which grows up on their soil, are not static formations with settled boundaries. The grandeur of a culture is manifested in its capacity for reception, for permitting itself to be enriched and transformed. A truly great culture does not enclose itself hermetically in its own sphere, like a capsule. Rather does it carry within itself a dynamic capacity to grow, for which the interplay of giving and receiving is an essential condition.

With respect to our theme, this means that in the face of the question of death all cultures and milieux of intellectual reflection have been subject to change. The individual phases of this process show certain marked similarities. Originally, all cultures found shelter in the very structure of the cycle of life and death, a shelter which myth built for their repose. They knew a contented this-worldliness, a desire for fulfilment in the richness of long life and continued existence in one's children and their posterity. This is not just how things were seen in the Old Testament world in early times. It is just as much true of the early Hellenes. Achilles, after all, preferred the life of a beggar in this world to being sovereign of the shades whose life is hardly a life at all. And this description also applies to the early period of that most spiritual of all cultures, India.[4] I should add that nowhere is death conceived as being absolutely the end. Everywhere some kind of subsequent existence is assumed. Complete nothingness was not even thinkable. This afterlife, which is not life but a curious mixture of being and nothingness, on the one hand was rendered possible by rites of passage with their provision of food for the dead, and on the other was in itself an object of great fear. The dead, and the nothingness they carry, might break through into the sphere of life. Thus rites on behalf of the dead are also apotropaic rites which protect life by sealing the departed into their own realm. Some form of ancestor cult and belief about the dead is coextensive with humanity as such. As the ancient historian Johann Jakob Bachofen put it, it is down streets of graves that we make our way into the past.

This shared view of all early cultures according to which

only this life is really life, whilst death is being-suspended-in-nothingness was everywhere superseded as man's final word on the matter in the course of his own spiritual evolution. When the unreflecting shelter of the tribal state collapsed and the individual stepped forth to claim his full personal identity, this view of things underwent a crisis. This happened everywhere, not least in Israel, though in different forms: a kind of primitive Enlightenment in which being human is highlighted in a new way.

Only in this context can one understand the specific intention of Plato's thought. In Homer's human, all *too* human, depiction of the gods there is a touch of irony, and a suggestion of rebellion against the peevish caprices of the higher powers. In Greek tragedy this incipient revolt is actually declared. The tragedians' *deus ex machina* gives dramatic form to a contestation or denial of the actual world and its gods. Were they truly divine, they would intervene as saviors and establish justice in the city. Such attitudes, thus anticipated in a mythopoeic world view, took on the explicit expression of a rational critique in the work of the Sophists. Those attitudes also generated a program for human emancipation from the traditional powers-that-be. What took the place of the latter was natural law—understood, however, simply as the right to self-assertion of the stronger party. This development was to some extent prefigured in the Homeric figure of Odysseus.

But when trust in being and community is undermined in this way, and the individual's own advantage becomes the only lodestar, the bonds of community cannot hold. The spiritual crisis of the fifth and sixth centuries before Christ was also the political crisis of ancient Hellas. It was to this crisis, at once political and spiritual, that Plato and Aristotle tried to respond: not by turning back the wheel of history and putting together again the broken pieces of the world of myth but in a way that might lead to a new future. They entered into the spirit of the Enlightenment, drew on the procedures of the Sophists, tried by this very means to find anew those guiding powers which make community possible. Plato, taking his inspiration from Socrates, set over against the natural law of the strong and the cunning a natural law of being itself, wherein the individual finds his place in the whole. Taking up the concept of natural law, he interprets it not in an individualistic and rationalistic way, but as the justice of being which grants to the individual, and to the whole, their possibility of existing. For Plato, what is important is that justice is truth and so reality. The truth of justice is more real than mere biological life or individual self-assertion. In comparison with justice and truth, mere biological existence appears as outright unreality, a shadow cast by the real, whereas the person who lives by justice lives by the really real.

Such a thought provides a fresh foundation for politics and so a new possibility for the *polis* as community. At the same time, Plato gives it a grounding of a religious kind. In developing this insight by reference to religious tradition, he wishes to identify primordial springs of wisdom which may take the place of the shallow religiosity of the by-now-faded myths. The philosophical martyrdom of Socrates belongs in this context. It is both a political martyrdom and a testimony to the greater degree of reality to be found in justice as opposed to simply biological existence.[5]

These reflections appear to be taking us far from our theological problem. Nevertheless, they are necessary. They show how untenable is that caricature of Platonism on which many current theological stereotypes depend. The real goal of Plato's philosophy is utterly misconceived when he is presented as an individualistic, dualistic thinker who negates what is earthly and advocates a flight into the beyond. The true fulcrum of his thought is the new ground of possibility for the *polis*, a fresh foundation for politics. His philosophy finds its center in the idea of justice. It developed in a political crisis, and derives from the conviction that the *polis* cannot stand wherever justice is something other than reality and truth. The recognition of the living power of truth, which includes the thought of immortality, is not part of a philosophy of flight from the world, but is in an eminent sense political philosophy. These are insights which remain fundamental for an evaluation of contemporary "political theology" and political eschatology. If these movements do not confront the problem of death in its relation to justice at that level of depth which Plato opened up for us, they can in the end only obscure the heart of the matter.

If we try to capture the core of Plato's discovery we can formulate it by saying that man, to survive biologically, must be more than *bios*. He must be able to die into a more authentic life than this. The certainty that self-abandonment for the sake of truth is self-abandonment to reality and not a step into the night of nothingness is a necessary condition for justice. But justice is the condition on which the life of the *polis* endures. In the final analysis, therefore, justice makes possible biological survival itself. When we turn to consider directly the questions of the immortality of the soul and the resurrection of the dead, we shall have to discuss the mythopoeic and political instruments whereby Plato chose to express these insights. It will then become plain to what degree Christian faith had to intervene here, correcting and purifying. There is indeed a profound divergence between Plato and Christianity. Yet this should not blind us to the possibilities of a philosophical unfolding of the Christian faith which Platonism offers. These possibilities are rooted in a deep affinity on the level of fundamental formative intention.

3. THE DEVELOPMENT OF THE QUESTION IN BIBLICAL THOUGHT

(a) The Old Testament

At first, Israel's concept of death simply exemplified the common views of an archaic world sheltered in the conditions of tribal awareness. But from the denial of the gods of myth, and from faith in the unicity of Yahweh, there gradually came about distinct changes in the Israelite picture of reality. Those changes are debated in the crisis of the Wisdom schools, a kind of Jewish parallel to the Greek "Enlightenment." They were in question again in that crisis of Jewish consciousness connected with the figure of Jesus Christ which led to the formation of Christianity.

In the early period, the fulness of life consisted in dying "old and filled with years." What that meant was tasting the full richness of earthly life, seeing one's children and one's children's children so as to participate through them in the future of Israel, Israel's promise. Only childlessness or premature death were felt as inexplicable in natural terms, death's malign intrusion, a punishment falling on man and shattering his proper share in life. Such events were explained by means of a connection between one's actions and one's destiny. That is, they were considered to be results of sin. So here too life, and the idea of life's essential justice, remained in principle intact.

Part of this widespread primitive concept of death, to which Israel has not yet made any distinctive contribution of her own, is that death is not simply annihilation. The dead man goes down into Sheol, where he leads a kind of un-life among the shades. As a shade, he can make an appearance in the world above, and is thus perceived as dreadful and dangerous. Nonetheless, he is essentially cut off from the land of the living, from dear life, banished into a noncommunication zone where life is destroyed precisely because relationship is impossible. The full extent of Sheol's abyss of nothingness is seen from the fact that Yahweh is not there, nor is he praised there. In relation to him too, there is a complete lack of communication in Sheol. Death is thus an unending imprisonment. It is simultaneously being and nonbeing, somehow still existence and yet no longer life.

When one looks at this nonbeing which is, curiously, something other than complete nothingness, one cannot just accept death as an event of the natural order. From this realization, and above all in her life of prayer, Israel developed a phenomenology of sickness and death wherein these things were interpreted as spiritual phenomena. In this way Israel discovered their deepest spiritual ground and content, wrestled with Yahweh as to their import, and so brought human suffering before God and with God to a new pitch of intensity.

Sickness is described with the epithets that belong to death. It pushes man into a realm of noncommunication, apparently destroying the relationships that make life what it is. For the sick person, the social fabric falls apart just as much as the inner structure of the body. The invalid is excluded from the circle of his friends, and from the community of those who worship God. He labors in the clutches of death, cut off from the land of the living. So sickness belongs in death's sphere; or, better, death is conceived as a sphere whose circumference reaches deep into human living. Essentially, this sphere is dereliction, isolation, loneliness, and thus abandonment to nothingness.

The phenomenology of sickness does not only generate a phenomenology of death, and an elucidation of death's spiritual content. It also comprises a phenomenology of life. Not every mode of existence is necessarily what we can call really living. Some life is definitely nonlife. To extend it would be not immortality but rather the eternalizing of a torture, a contradiction. Human life does not become real living simply by its mere presence. Genuine living is something we continually touch, yet in touching it experience how distant we still are from it. Life in the authentic sense of that word is present where sickness, loneliness and isolation are not, and where richness of fulfilment, love, communion, contact with God actually are. Life is identical with blessing, death with a curse. Life means communion, whereas the heart of death is the absence of relationship. The purely physical facts of existing or perishing form only the background of that distinctive human, social and—in the last resort—theological phenomenon which is the life of a man in its heights and depths.

Because of this, the question was simply bound to arise eventually as to whether this state of affairs does not point in two directions. If on the one hand the physically still living and breathing human being can be "dead" in a state of noncommunication, must it not also be true that the power of communion, of divine communion at any rate, is something stronger than physical dying? May there not be life beyond physical perishing?

Yahwistic faith, therefore, makes its own potent contribution to belief in that life which is eternal since God's power is its support and stay. In the light of these connections, it becomes apparent that the acceptance of faith in a resurrection was no mere alien intrusion in Israel.[6] On the contrary, Israel's archaic understanding of Sheol is what, if anything, would link her to the nations. That understanding simply illustrates a stage of awareness found in all cultures at a certain point in their development. As yet, Israel's faith in Yahweh had not unfolded in all its inner consistency. For the notion that death is a barrier limiting the God of Israel to his own finite sphere manifestly contradicts the all-encompassing claims of Yahwistic faith. There is an inner contradiction in the affirmation that he who is life itself encounters a limitation on his power. The state of affairs which such an affirmation betrays was inherently unstable. In the end, the alternatives were either to abandon faith in Yahweh altogether or to admit the unlimited scope of his power and so, in principle, the definitive character of the communion with man he had inaugurated.

This thesis that the indestructability of communion with God, and therewith our eternal life, follows in strictly theo-*logical* terms from Israel's concept of God is of course open to no little objection at the historical level. A number of Old Testament texts show clearly how popular piety in Israel lovingly sought communication with the dead in just the way found in the pagan religions of the ancient Near East. People were familiar with the belief in the afterlife characteristic of Israel's neighbors and, what is more, they cultivated it. The official religion of Israel, as expressed in the Law, the prophets and the historical books of the Hebrew Bible, did not accept these beliefs and practices. It no more denied all existence to Sheol than, at first, it denied the existence of other gods than Yahweh.[7] But it chose not to deal with this area. Indeed, it classified everything to do with the dead as "impure," that is, as disqualifying one for a share in Yahweh's cultus, since, after all, death was synonymous with noncommunication between the Israelite and Israel's God. But in this case, are we not dealing here with a specific option of Yahwistic faith, deliberately setting itself over against the *religio humana et pagana* and excluding belief in immortality in any form? A twofold answer may be given to this question.

In the first place, the classification of the entire sphere of "death" as cultically impure is a rejection of the cult of the dead in whatsoever form. The refusal to admit the legitimacy of a cult of the ancestors—still, of course, widely practiced in that society—was the real reason for the naturalizing of death. In a wide segment of the history of religion, the ancestor cult absorbed people's religious attention to an ever greater degree, finally pushing the high god of a given tradition to the margins of consciousness where he eked out a miserable existence as a *deus otiosus*, dethroned and useless. The ancestor cult presented an attraction which Israel was obliged to resist if her concept of God was not to be destroyed. Thus the comprehensive, exclusive claims of Yahweh, while incorporating the idea of the indestructability of divine communion, demanded in the first instance an absolutely uncompromising ruling out of the cultus of the dead in whatever form. A certain demythologizing of death was needful before Israel could bring out the special way in which Yahweh was himself Life for the dead.

But secondly, the classification of the entire sphere of death as cultically impure was not without its theological consequences. For it had the effect of highlighting the connection between death and sin. Death, being linked with a turning away from Yahweh, throws light on what such separation entails. We shall meet this motif again, as, from its humble beginnings in the primitive logic of "as you act, so shall you be," it becomes ever purer until at last it arrives at insights which point the way to Christology.

By way of conclusion: the "this-worldliness" of Old Testament faith may be ascribed on the one hand to those archaic life-ways which for great tracts of its history were its own, and on the other, to the special claims of the Israelite concept of God. These claims required the elimination of the cult of the dead and the ideas of immortality which that cult enshrined. Yet at the same time, and inevitably so, the same concept of God made it impossible for such "this-worldliness" to have the last word. What we are confronted with is, therefore, an inherently unstable and open historical process. It is a misconception to regard it as a static dogmatic structure. The apparently contradictory demands of the concept of God in Israel made the long journey a taxing one. The final crisis of the traditional doctrine erupted at last in the Wisdom books, those monuments to the Israelite "Enlightenment." In their different ways, Qoheleth and Job express and canonize the collapse of the ancient assumptions.

Both books offer a radical critique of the long-established connection between action and destiny. They hold that the assertion of such a connection is false. Human life and death have no manifest logic.[8] In Qoheleth this realization precipitates a profound scepticism. Everything is nonsensical: all is vanity. These statements are but parried in a half-hearted way by the author's half-skeptical, half-believing resignation. Though he is ready to live without meaning and to trust in a meaning as yet unknown, he can hardly suppress the question whether it might be better not to have been born at all. Life enters a crisis-condition.

Job gives even more dramatic expression to the internal conflict within the Wisdom schools and the resultant repudiation of their classic "action-destiny" schema. The book's climax appears to be the appeal to God as Redeemer over against the God of senseless destruction found in ordinary experience.[9] Job puts his hope in the God of faith over against the God of such experience, entrusting himself to the One who is Unknown. There may be a glimmer of hope here for an abiding life to come, but the textual tradition is too uncertain to allow any worthwhile judgment about the form such hopes might have taken.

Job and Qoheleth, then, document a crisis. With their

aid, we can feel the force of that mighty jolt which brought the traditional didactic and practical wisdom to its knees. Yet before this *dénouement*, something of a breakthrough to a new level of insight had occurred in the spiritual experience of the prophets and other pious individuals in Israel, and this proved able to sustain faith in the crisis of Wisdom. In the first place, we have the interpretation of the painful experience of the Exile in the Servant Songs of Second Isaiah. There, sickness, death, abandonment are understood as vicarious suffering, and in this way the realm of death is filled with a novel, positive content. Death and deprivation through illness are not simply the duly apportioned punishment for sins. They can be the proper path of someone who belongs to God, and, treading that path in suffering, the servant of God can open for others the door to life as their savior. Suffering for God's sake and that of other people can be the highest form of allowing God to be present, and placing oneself at the service of life. Disease and death are no longer now that threshold beyond which a person becomes useless, a thing without meaning, not least for God whom he can no longer praise. These apparently wholly negative things are no longer forms of subjection to the absolute void of Sheol. Rather are they a new possibility of not only doing but *being* more than one ever could do or be through the holy war, or the cultic service of the Temple. The key to this new possibility is mercy, declared as early as Samuel to be more than sacrifice. The reason why these insights are so important is that sickness, death and Sheol remain phenomenologically identical. Thus death no longer appears as the end, as irreversible falling into nothingness and doom. Rather does it stand out as a purifying and transforming power. Sickness and death are now the way and lot of the just wherein justice becomes so profound that it turns into the mercy of vicarious service. The question, then, as to whether or not resurrection in the proper sense of that word is already spoken of in such a text as Isaiah 53, 9–12 is really secondary. Resurrection is objectively implied there. Sheol does not hold the one who suffers in the way of the Servant. Contrariwise, it is by his suffering that the surface of our seeming life is pierced by life in all its authentic plenitude.

In its own fashion, the troubled personal piety of many of the psalms contributed depth and maturity to this emerging experience. After the return from Babylon, the ancient tribal situation, supportive as it was, could not be reestablished. The pious were often reduced to a minority vis-à-vis cynics and sceptics. In a personal wrestling with God, and deprived of the support of the clan, they had to endure the question of the meaningfulness of their own spirituality. I would like to refer here to just two psalms which became important for Christian reflection. First, brief mention should be made of a psalm-text which provided one of the principal supports for the early Christian proclamation of the resurrection: Psalm 16. In a profound trust in God's saving power, the psalmist dares to say:

> . . . my body also dwells secure.
> For thou dost not give me up to Sheol,
>   or let thy godly one see the Pit . . .
>   in thy presence there is fulness of joy,
> In thy right hand are pleasures for evermore.[10]

Even if this text expresses no explicit faith in the overcoming of death, we hear nevertheless the accents of a ringing certitude that Yahweh is stronger than Sheol. The psalmist is aware that he has found shelter in the hands of God, whose life-giving power endures for ever. Even so cautious an interpreter as H. J. Kraus notes:

That living Ground which is God bears up the body of man even in the midst of death. Will not God's life-giving power also bring man through death into new life? This assurance remains as yet concealed within the words of the Old Testament text. Still, no one could mistake the mysterious luminosity of these verses.[11]

Psalm 73—one of Augustine's favorites, by the way—leads us into still deeper waters.[12] Here the psalmist confronts the same problem which had exercized the authors of Qoheleth and Job. Of course, Kraus is perfectly right in pointing out that the psalm is not a scientific treatise but the expression of an existential anguish amounting almost to despair, and of an experience which answers to this necessity.[13] The psalmist notes the happiness of sinners secure in their good fortune. They seem to be supermen who succeed in everything.[14] The world appears to be so perverse that the only rational course is to live like them, to have done with God and to make common cause with the cynical potentates of the earth, the successful people, those human "gods" who seem hardly mortals at all. "They set their mouths against the heavens, and their tongue struts through the earth."[15] Piety seems meaningless and utterly in vain. And in point of fact, so long as one's starting point is the connection between action and destiny, and one's vantage point a concept of religion as earthly utility and justice, the only courses open are indeed either despair or apostasy. The psalmist finds the answer he is seeking in the Temple, that is, not in reflection, nor in the observation of other people, comparing one set with another, nor in an analysis of the course of history which might simply lead to a religion of envy, but in looking at God. In such contemplation he recognizes the phantasmal quality of the happiness of the wicked, its nothingness and pitiableness. The envious man is a fool, no better than a beast.[16] And at this point there arises an experience which,

with truly explosive power, breaks out of everything that
came before:

> Thou dost guide me with thy counsel,
>   and afterward thou wilt receive me to glory.
> Whom have I in heaven but thee?
>   And there is nothing upon earth that I desire besides thee.
> My flesh and my heart may fail,
>   but God is the strength of my heart and my portion for
>   ever.[17]

Adolf von Harnack remarked justly that the force of this
last verse is overwhelming.[18] Without any borrowing from
external sources, without the assistance of any philosophical or mythological structure, the certitude arose quite
simply from the psalmist's deeply experienced communion with God that such communion is more potent than
the decay of the flesh. Communion with God is true reality, and by comparison with it everything, no matter how
massively it asserts itself, is a phantom, a nothing. As
Kraus puts it:

> The void is filled by a communion with God which shatters all
> this-worldliness into smithereens.[19]

As we have seen, communication is life, and its absence
death. From this thoroughly empirical assertion the psalmist now draws out, thanks to his experience, an inference
of decisive importance: communication with God *is* reality. It is true reality, the really real, more real, even, than
death itself. The psalmist neither describes nor elaborates.
He does not ground his statement in reflection, nor explain it. That is the strength and the weakness of this text.
It offers no theory of immortality, simply expressing a certitude of experience which thought must elaborate and
interpret using its own resources. Not that any speculative
model could ever take the place of this central experience

in all its profound originality. For this is one of those texts where the Old Testament stretches forth to touch the New, and most fully possesses its own deepest implications. It develops a really original idea about the overcoming of death which cannot be slotted into Greek or Iranian categories. It operates neither with the concept of soul nor with the idea of resurrection, being derived from the concept of God and the idea of communion, or, rather, from the experience of communion itself. Looking on God, being with God: this is recognized as the point from which the ever-present, all-devouring menace of Sheol may be overcome.

Before concluding this brief survey of the Old Testament, we must not fail to mention a third group of texts, the martyr literature. Through the experience of martyrdom comes a new assurance of life, and a new way of enduring death. Daniel 12,2 belongs to this context:

And many of those who sleep in the dust of the earth shall awake, some to everlasting life, and some to shame and everlasting contempt.

Here we have the clearest formulation of resurrection-faith that the Old Testament contains. Its context is the Hellenistic age when, in the course of persecution of the Jews, some of the finest testimonies to Israel's faith took shape. Call to mind the image of the three young men in the fiery furnace, that timeless symbol of the suffering people of God, praising God in the midst of the flame.

Besides Daniel, two of the latest books of the Old Testament, Wisdom and Second Maccabees, also belong here. The accounts of martyrdom offered by the latter illustrate very graphically the wider context of thought and experience. Confronted with persecution, the believer faces the question as to which he prefers, the righteousness of Yahweh or his own life, his *bios*. Placed before this option be-

tween righteousness and life, no presumed connection between action and destiny can avail. It is faith itself, a
righteousness mirroring that of God, which brings about
the cruelly premature loss of life. The problematic of the
seventy-third psalm takes on its sharpest intensity. In this
situation, the believer comes to recognize that Yahweh's
righteousness is greater than his own biologically conditioned presence to life. He who dies into the righteousness
of God does not die into nothingness, but enters upon authentic reality, life itself. It becomes clear that God's truth
and justice are not just ideas or ideals but realities, the
truth of authentic being. The Book of Wisdom expresses
its author's certitude that the just die into life, not into
nothingness, with the help of ideas borrowed from Greek
thought.[20] But it would be foolish to speak here of a con-
quest of Hebrew thinking by Hellenism. What the third
chapter of Wisdom gives us, at its heart, is that selfsame
spirituality of martyrdom which runs from Isaiah 53 to
Psalm 73. All these texts, even those from the Book of Job,
stem from a situation which was at any rate "martyrdom-
like." In the path followed by the men who wrote the Old
Testament, it was suffering, endured and spiritually borne,
which became that hermeneutical vantage point where
real and unreal could be distinguished, and communion
with God came to light as the locus of true life. By comparison with this crucial departure-point, the utilization
of an Oriental thought pattern about resurrection in Second Maccabees and Daniel, or a Greek one concerning the
fate of the soul in the Book of Wisdom, is altogether secondary. Though such patterns are indeed drawn on to fill
out the picture, the real point lies deeper, in the experience that communion with God means a life stronger than
death. A parallel suggests itself here between an insight
gained on the basis of faith-experience and the experience

of a Socrates dying for justice's sake, as recounted by Plato.
Here we hit upon the real connecting link between biblical thought and Platonic philosophy, the factor which
made possible the meeting of these two traditions.

(b) The Interpretation of Death and Life in the
New Testament

Surveying the dramatic struggle of the Old Testament in
its entire development, the unity of the two Testaments
stands out in clear relief. The New Testament has no need
to formulate any new ideas. Its newness consists in the
new *fact* which gathers acceptingly to itself all that went
before and gives it its wholeness. This new fact is the martyrdom of Jesus, the faithful witness, and his resurrection.
The martyrdom and raising to new life of the Just One *par
excellence* clothes in flesh and blood the vision of the
author of Psalm 73 and the hope-filled confidence of the
Maccabees. In the risen Christ, the cry of troubled faith
has at last found its answering response.

How is death evaluated in this new light? The first thing
to note is that the New Testament quite clearly preserves
the basic thrust of the Old. In the Sign of the Cross, too,
there is no apotheosis of death which would supplant an
earlier joy in life. At the end of the internal development
of the New Testament in the Book of Revelation, the "yes"
to life and the assessment of death as something contrary
to God put in yet another decisive appearance. At the end,
the sea, that mythopoeic image of the underworld of death,
must yield up its dead. Death and Hades, that is, the state
of being dead, are now cast into the lake of fire and burned
for evermore.[21] Death has vanished: only life remains.

We hear the same note sounded in First Corinthians 15.
Death, the "last enemy," is conquered.[22] Its destruction
signifies the definitive and exclusive rule of God, the vic-

tory of life invincible, where the shadow of death cannot fall. The basic Christian attitude to death is thus in continuity with that of the Old Testament, while both are sharply differentiated from such alternative great religious interpretations of reality as that evolved in India by Buddhist piety. There, the highest principle is the abolition of the thirst for being, a thirst conceived as the profoundest source of suffering. Christianity moves in precisely the opposite direction. It gives to our thirst for being the dramatic significance of a thirst for God himself, and sees therein the fulness of our salvation.

At the same time, the New Testament is also determined by a fact discussed earlier which seems (but only seems) to dislodge this fundamental option. Christ himself, the truly Just One, is in his very innocence he who undergoes suffering and abandonment even unto death. The Just One descended into Sheol, to that impure land where no praise of God is ever sounded. In the descent of Jesus, God himself descends into Sheol. At that moment, death ceases to be the God-forsaken land of darkness, a realm of unpitying distance from God. In Christ, God himself entered that realm of death, transforming the space of noncommunication into the place of his own presence. This is no apotheosis of death. Rather has God cancelled out and overcome death in entering it through Christ.

This is nothing less than the inversion of all previous values. Hitherto, life itself had counted as salvation. Now it is in very truth a death which becomes life for us. With the proclamation that the Cross is our redemption, death comes to occupy the central point in the confession of faith. But, one may ask, is not this a way of casting suspicion on life and thus of glorifying death? To find an answer to this question, we need to recall that phenomenology of life and death which had emerged from the inner travail of the Old Testament. It can easily be verified in our own experience of living. We noted that day-to-day living is for the most part merely a shadow existence, a form of Hades, in which we have only the most occasional inkling of what life should truly be. This is why, in general, people have no immediate desire for immortality. The continuance *ad infinitum* of life as it is cannot appear desirable to anybody. And yet what seems to be the obvious conclusion—namely, that death ought to be arranged as painlessly, if also as belatedly, as possible, being perfectly normal and quite properly preceded by the maximum exploitation of life—this approach does not appear to work either. It is resisted by that quite primordial sensation which Nietzsche expressed in the words, "All joy wills eternity, wills deep, deep eternity." There are some moments that should never pass away. What is glimpsed in them should never end. That it *does* end, and, even more, that it is only experienced momentarily anyway: this is the real sadness of human existence.

How can we describe that moment in which we experience what life truly is? It is the moment of love, a moment which is simultaneously the moment of truth when life is discovered for what it is. The desire for immortality does not arise from the fundamentally unsatisfying enclosed existence of the isolated self, but from the experience of love, of communion, of the Thou. It issues from that call which the Thou makes upon the I, and which the I returns. The discovery of life entails going beyond the I, leaving it behind. It happens only when one ventures along the path of self-abandonment, letting oneself fall into the hands of another. But if the mystery of life is in this sense identical with the mystery of love, it is, then, bound up with an event which we may call "death-like." Here we come back once more to the Christian message of the Cross with its

interpretation of life and of death. That message interprets death by teaching us to see in dying more than the
end point of our biological existence. Death is ever present
in the inauthenticity, closedness and emptiness of our
everyday life. The physical pain and disease which herald
death's onset threaten our life less than does the failure to
be with our true being. It is this failure which allows the
promise of life to evaporate, leaving only banalities and
leading to final emptiness.

Can we express our reflections up to this juncture in
rather more ordered form? The phenomenon of death
makes itself known in three very different dimensions.
Firstly, death is present as the nothingness of an empty
existence which ends up in a mere semblance of living.
Secondly, death is present as the physical process of disintegration which accompanies life. It is felt in sickness, and
reaches its terminal point in physical dying. Thirdly, death
is met with in the daring of that love which leaves self behind, giving itself to the other. It is likewise encountered
in the abandonment of one's own advantage for the sake of
justice and truth. How are these three forms of death interrelated? And how are they connected to the death of
Jesus? It is by answering this twofold question that the
Christian understanding of death must attain its own clarity. The starting point must surely lie in the second meaning of "death": namely, that proper and primary sense of
"death" found in the biological component of human
reality.

Pain and disease can paralyze one as a human being.
They can shatter one to pieces, not only physically, but
also psychologically and spiritually. However, they can
also smash down complacency and spiritual lethargy and
lead one to find oneself for the first time. The struggle
with suffering is the place of human decision-making *par*

excellence. Here the human project becomes flesh and blood. Here man is forced to face the fact that existence is not at his disposal, nor is his life his own property. Man may snap back defiantly that he will nevertheless try to acquire the power that will make it so. But in so doing, he makes a desperate anger his basic attitude to life. There is a second possibility: man can respond by seeking to trust this strange power to whom he is subject. He can allow himself to be led, unafraid, by the hand, without *Angst*-ridden concern for his situation. And in this second case, the human attitude towards pain, towards the presence of death within living, merges with the attitude we call love.

As we know, people run up against the fact that life is not at their disposal in more forms than those of such physical limitations as sickness bring home to us. The same thing happens in the central region of the human landscape: our intimate ordination towards being loved. Love is the soul's true nourishment, yet this food which of all substances we most need is not something we can produce for ourselves. One must wait for it. The only way to make absolutely certain that one will *not* receive it is to insist on procuring it by oneself. And once again, this essential dependence can generate anger. One can attempt to shake it off, and reduce it to the satisfaction of those needs that require no adventure of the spirit or the heart for their filling. Conversely, we can accept this situation of dependence, and keep ourselves trustingly open to the future, in the confidence that the Power which has so determined us will not deceive us.

And so it turns out that the confrontation with physical death is actually a confrontation with the basic constitution of human existence. It places before us a choice: to accept either the pattern of love, or the pattern of power. Here we are at the source of the most decisive of all questions. This claim of death upon us which we come across time and again *in media vita*—are we able to receive it in the attitude of trust which will usher in that fundamental posture of love? Or would this just be to throw up life's glittering prizes in exchange for "Waiting for Godot": a something that either does not exist at all or, at any rate, does not exist in the form in which we imagine it? Up to this point, our reflections have shown the interconnection of three distinguishable meanings of "death." But now the relevance of the Christological question begins to become apparent. The God who personally died in Jesus Christ fulfilled the pattern of love beyond all expectation, and in so doing justified that human confidence which in the last resort is the only alternative to self-destruction. The Christian dies into the death of Christ himself. This formula which has come down to us from Tradition now takes on a very practical sense. The uncontrollable Power that everywhere sets limits to life is not a blind law of nature. It is a love that puts itself at our disposal by dying for us and with us. The Christian is the one who knows that he can unite the constantly experienced dispossession of self with the fundamental attitude of a being created for love, a being that knows itself to be safe precisely when it trusts in the unexacted gift of love. Man's enemy, death, that would waylay him to steal his life, is conquered at the point where one meets the thievery of death with the attitude of trusting love, and so transforms the theft into increase of life. The sting of death is extinguished in Christ in whom the victory was gained through the plenary power of love unlimited. Death is vanquished where people die with Christ and into him. This is why the Christian attitude must be opposed to the modern wish for instantaneous death, a wish that would turn death into an extensionless moment and banish from life the claims of the metaphysical. Yet it is in the transforming acceptance of death, present time and again to us in this life, that we mature for the real, the eternal, life.

If we juxtapose these thoughts with the picture we gained from a consideration of the biblical development of the theme of martyrdom, yet another window opens. Just as the dying of a human being cannot be confined to the moment of clinical death, so also sharing in the *martyria* of Jesus is not something that starts when a person lets his name go forward for imminent execution. Here too, the fundamental form of our participation is not spectacular, but perfectly ordinary. It consists in the daily readiness to give greater weight to faith, to truth and to what is right than to the benefits of not getting involved. It is surely evident that what makes human intercommunication possible at all is just this subordination of individual advantage to truth. How is it that human beings can communicate? It is because above them, common to them all yet proper to each of them, is a third factor: righteousness and truth. Certainly, trust in truth is only fully possible where there is conviction that truth exists and has spoken to us. But this simply brings us back to what we said before: martyrdom with Christ, the repeated act of granting truth more importance than self, is nothing other than the movement of love itself. If death be essentially the closing-off of the possibility of communication, then the movement which leads to communion is at the same time the inner movement of life. The process of dispossession of self uncovers the abyss of Sheol, the depth of nothingness and abandonment to nothingness which is present in our self-glorying, our desire to survive at the cost of what is right. Consequently, this process which seems death-dealing is really life-giving in the fullest sense.

In the light of this one can reach some understanding of

the Christian language of "justification" through baptismal faith. The doctrinal assertion that justification is by faith and not by works means that justification happens through sharing in the death of Christ, that is, by walking in the way of martyrdom, the daily drama by which we prefer what is right and true to the claims of sheer existence, through the spirit of love which faith makes possible. Conversely, to seek justification by works means trying to save oneself through one's own efforts in isolated concentration on the principle that finds the inevitable fruits of one's actions in one's destiny. As worked out in detail in particular cases, this attempt can take very subtle forms, but the basic pattern is always the same. Justification by works means that man wants to construct a little immortality of his own. He wants to make of his life a self-sufficient totality. Such an enterprise is always sheer illusion. This is true no matter on what level it is undertaken, whether in a primitive fashion or with the utmost scientific sophistication in the attempt to overcome death by means of medical research. Such self-assertion is at root a refusal of communication, which issues in a misjudgment about reality at large and the truth of man's existence in particular. For man's own truth is that he passes away, having no abiding existence in his own right. The more he takes a stand on himself, the more he finds himself suspended over nothing. He falls a prey to that nothingness which, taken by himself, he will assuredly enter everlastingly. Only by handing oneself over to truth and rightness does one find that communication which is life. It is intrinsic to my life that I find life only in endless receiving from others, being powerless to achieve it through my own active efforts. It is not works that are vivifying, but faith.

Now this way lit up for us by the theology of the Cross,

especially in the form of the Pauline doctrine of justification, in no way implies a *Weltanschauung* of passivity.
Turning to truth, to rightness and to love, precisely as a
process of receiving is at the same time the highest human
activity of which we are capable. Similarly, it is surely
clear that the rejection of "works" does not signify a rejection of the moral task but, on the contrary, a full assent to
life as communication in that truth which has found its
personal form in the risen martyr Jesus Christ.

Here we have reached a point at which the innermost
unity and simplicity of Christianity show themselves for
what they are. I may declare that the heart of Christianity
is the Paschal mystery of death and resurrection. Or I may
say that this midpoint really consists in justification by
faith. Or, again, I may affirm that the center of it all is the
triune God, and, therefore, love as the alpha and omega of
the world. These three statements are, in fact, identical. In
all three the self-same truth is indicated: sharing in the
martyria of Jesus by that dying which is faith and love.
Such faith and love are simultaneously God's acceptance
of my life and my will to embrace the divine acceptance.
And all this is from the God who can be love only as the
triune God and who, in thus being love, makes the world
bearable after all.

One last thought. By reflecting on that most personal
event of our own dying, we become aware that Christian
eschatology does not sidestep the shared tasks of the
world, shifting the focus of human concern to the beyond,
or making us retreat into a private salvation for individual
souls. The starting point of Christian eschatology is precisely commitment to the common justice guaranteed in
the One who sacrificed his life for the justice of mankind
at large and thus brought it justification. Moreover, eschatology encourages us, nay, challenges us in most com-

pelling fashion, to dare to realize in our own lives that justice and truth whose claims upon us—along with those of love—are eschatology's very own content.

4. SOME CONCLUSIONS ON THE ETHOS OF DEATH IN CHRISTIANITY

(a) Assent to Life as a Whole

Christian faith favors life. It believes in that God who is the God of the living. Its goal is life, and so it assents to life on all its levels as a gift and reflection of the God who is Life itself. It assents to life even in its overshadowing by suffering. For even then life remains a gift of God, opening up for us new possibilities of existence and meaning. For Christian faith there is no such thing as a life not worth living. Life, with all its shadow side, remains the gift of God, entrusted to us as companions who by loving service one of another acquire true riches and liberty.

(b) The Meaning of Suffering

Christian faith knows that human life is life in a higher and more comprehensive sense than mere biology grants. Spirit is not the soul's enemy but a richer and greater life. Man finds himself only in that measure in which he accepts truth and justice as the locus of real living, even though the opening-up of life to these wider dimensions always takes on, in human history, the character of *martyria*. While faith does not deliberately seek out suffering, it knows that without the Passion life does not discover its own wholeness, but closes the door on its own potential plenitude. If life at its highest demands the Passion, then faith must reject *apatheia*, the attempt to avoid suffering, as contrary to human nature.

In view of the importance of this attempt to avoid suffering, we must here for a moment reflect further. The avoidance of suffering can take place in one of two directions. In the first place, there is an upward *apatheia* which has found impressive elaboration in Stoicism and in Asian piety. On the basis of his spiritual convictions, the Stoic gains such sovereignty over self that suffering, the twists and turns of external fortune, are left behind as something alien. Epicurus, on the other hand, stands for a downward avoidance of suffering when he teaches a technique of enjoyment which would put suffering into a parenthesis. Both ways can achieve a certain virtuosity of practice, and succeed in their ambitions more or less perfectly. However, both ways are reducible to a pride which denies the fundamental character of being human. Both make a secret claim to divinity which contradicts the truth of man. What thus goes against truth is a lie, and so in the last resort is nothingness and destruction. In the end, such techniques close themselves off from the true greatness of life—though in saying this I must not be taken as ignoring that great gulf which separates Epicurus from a spiritually achieved *apatheia* whose highest forms presuppose a passage through suffering.

It is from this vantage point (and not on the basis of a facile contrast between Biblical and Greek thought) that we can understand why the death of Christ is so different from the death of Socrates. Christ does not die in the noble detachment of the philosopher. He dies in tears. On his lips was the bitter taste of abandonment and isolation in all its horror. Here the hubris that would be the equal of God is contrasted with an acceptance of the cup of being human, down to its last dregs.[23]

Owing to the increasing technical powers that man has at his disposal, this theme of the avoidance of suffering has taken on an almost unparalleled importance. The attempt to do away with suffering through medicine, psychology, education and the building of a new society has grown into a gigantic bid for the definitive redemption of mankind. Of course, suffering can and should be reduced by these means. But the will to do away with it completely would mean a ban on love and therewith the abolition of man. Such attempts constitute a pseudotheology. They can lead only to an empty death and a vacuous life. The person who does not confront life refuses his life. Flight from suffering is flight from life. The crisis of the Western world turns not least on a philosophy and program of education which try to redeem man by bypassing the cross. In acting against the cross, they act against the truth. Let us not be misunderstood: the *relative* value of actions of this kind is undoubted. They become a help to man when they see themselves as part of a greater whole. But taken by themselves, absolutely, they lead into the void. The only sufficient answer to the question of man is a response which discharges the infinite claims of love. Only eternal life corresponds to the question raised by human living and dying on this earth.

V

The Immortality of the Soul and the Resurrection of the Dead

I. THE STATE OF THE QUESTION

In the last few decades, a basic question has arisen about the immortality of the soul and resurrection. The ensuing discussion has increasingly transformed the panorama of theology and devotion. Oscar Cullmann put it cursorily, if dramatically:

If today one asks an average Christian, no matter whether Protestant or Catholic, whether intellectually inclined or not, what the New Testament teaches about the destiny of the individual human being after death, in almost every case one will receive the answer, 'The immortality of the soul'. In this form, this opinion is one of the greatest misunderstandings of Christianity there can be.[24]

Today, few would venture to offer the answer that was earlier a matter of course, since the idea that this answer was based upon a misunderstanding has spread with astonishing speed among the congregations of Christendom. However, no new answer of any concreteness has taken its place. The way to this change of attitudes was paved by two men: the Protestant theologians Carl Stange (1870–1959) and Adolf Schlatter (1852–1938), to some extent aided and abetted by Paul Althaus whose eschatology was first published in 1922. Appealing to the Bible and to Luther, these men rejected as Platonic dualism the notion

of a separation of body and soul in death such as the doctrine of the immortality of the soul presupposes. The only
truly biblical doctrine is that which holds that when man
dies "he perishes, body and soul." Only in this fashion can
one preserve the idea of death as a judgment, of which
Scripture speaks in such unmistakable accents. The proper
Christian thing, therefore, is to speak, not of the soul's immortality, but of the resurrection of the complete human
being and of that alone. The piety currently surrounding
death, impregnated as it is with an eschatology of going to
heaven, must be eliminated in favor of the only true form
of Christian hope: expectation of the Last Day. In 1950,
Althaus tried to enter some caveats against this view
which had meanwhile gained so much ground. He pointed
out that the Bible was perfectly familiar with the "dualistic scheme." It too knew not only the expectation of
the Last Day, but a form of individual hope for heaven.
Althaus also tried to show that the same was true for
Luther. And so he reformulated his position in the following words:

Christian eschatology must not fight against immortality as
such. The scandal which in recent times we have frequently given
by this fight is not the *skandalon* that the Gospel speaks of.[25]

Though the discussion which followed Althaus' article
produced a broad consensus in his favor,[26] his "retracta-
tions" had no impact on the continuing debate as a whole.
The idea that to speak of the soul is unbiblical was accepted to such an extent that even the new Roman Missal
suppressed the term *anima* in its liturgy for the dead. It
also disappeared from the ritual for burial.

How was it possible to overthrow so quickly a tradition
firmly rooted since the age of the early Church and always
considered central? In itself, the apparent evidence of the

biblical data would surely not have sufficed. Essentially, the potency of the new position stemmed from the parallel between, on the one hand, the allegedly biblical idea of the absolute indivisibility of man and, on the other, a modern anthropology, worked out on the basis of natural science, and identifying the human being with his or her body, without any remainder that might admit a soul distinct from that body. It may be conceded that the elimination of the immortality of the soul removes a possible source of conflict between faith and contemporary thought. However, this scarcely saves the Bible, since the biblical view of things is even more remote by modern-day standards. Acceptance of the unity of the human being may be well and good but who, on the basis of the current tenets of the natural sciences, could imagine a resurrection of the body? That resurrection would presuppose a completely different kind of matter, a fundamentally transformed cosmos which lies completely outside of what we can conceive. Again, the question of what, in this case, would happen to the dead person until the "end of time" cannot simply be pushed aside. Luther's idea of the "sleep of the soul" certainly does not solve this problem. If there is no soul, and so no proper subject of such a "sleep," who is this person that is going to be really raised? How can there be an identity between the human being who existed at some point in the past and the counterpart that has to be re-created from nothing? The irritated refusal of such questions as "philosophical" does not contribute to a more meaningful discussion.

In other words, it soon becomes obvious that pure biblicism does not take us very far. One cannot get anywhere without "hermeneutics," that is, without a rational rethinking of the biblical data which may itself go beyond these data in its language and its systematic linkage of ideas. If we leave aside those radical solutions which try to solve the problem by forbidding all "objectifying" statements and permitting only "existential" interpretations, we find ourselves confronted with a twofold attempt to take the matter further. This twofold attempt turns on a new concept of time, and a fresh understanding of the body. The first set of ideas is related to the reflections we glanced at in III.1 above in the context of the question of imminent expectation. There we saw that some writers tried to solve the problem of the imminently expected Kingdom by noting that the end of time is itself no longer time. It is not a date which happens to come extremely late in the calendar but rather non-time, something which, since it is outside of time, is equally close to every time. This idea was easily combined with the notion that death itself leads out of time into the timeless. In Catholic circles, these suggestions received some support in the discussion about the dogma of Mary's assumption into glory. The scandal attaching to the assertion that a human being, Mary, has already risen in the body was a challenge to rethink more generally the relation between death and time as well as to reflect on the nature of human corporeality. If it is possible to regard the Marian dogma as offering a model of human destiny at large, then two problems at once evaporate. On the one hand, the ecumenical and speculative scandal of the dogma disappears, while on the other the dogma itself helps to correct the traditional view of immortality and resurrection in favor of a picture at once more biblical and more modern. Although this new approach received no very clear or consistent elaboration, it became generally accepted that time should be considered a form of bodily existence. Death signifies leaving time for eternity with its single "today." Here the problem of the "intermediate state" between death and resurrection turns out to be a problem only in seeming. The "between" exists only in our perspective. In reality, the "end of time" is timeless. The person who dies steps into the presence of the Last Day and of judgment, the Lord's resurrection and parousia. As one author put it, "The resurrection can thus be situated in death and not just on the 'Last Day'."[27] Meanwhile, the view that resurrection takes place at the moment of death has gained such widespread acceptance that it is even incorporated, with some qualifications, into the *Dutch Catechism*, where we read:

Existence after death is already something like the resurrection of the new body.[28]

This means that what the dogma of the assumption tells us about Mary is true of every human being. Owing to the timelessness which reigns beyond death, every death is an entering into the new heaven and the new earth, the parousia and the resurrection.

And here two questions suggest themselves. First, is this not merely a camouflaged return to the doctrine of immortality on philosophically somewhat more adventurous presuppositions? Resurrection is now being claimed for the person still lying on his deathbed or on the funeral journey to his grave. The indivisibility of man and his boundness to the body, even when dead, suddenly seems to play no further role, even though it was the point of departure of this whole construction. Indeed, the *Dutch Catechism* asserts:

Our Lord means that there is something of man, that which is most properly himself, which can be saved after death. This 'something' is not the body which is left behind.[29]

G. Greshake formulates the claim even more incisively:

Matter as such (as atom, molecule, organ . . .) cannot be perfected. . . . This being so, then if human freedom is finalised in death, the body, the world and the history of this freedom are permanently preserved in the definitive concrete form which that freedom has taken.[30]

Such ideas may be meaningful. The only question is by what right one still speaks of "corporeality" if all connection with matter is explicitly denied, and matter left with a share in the final perfection only insofar as it was "an ecstatic aspect of the human act of freedom." Be this as it may, in this model the body is in fact left to death, while at the same time an afterlife of the human being is asserted. Just why the concept of the soul is still disowned now ceases to be intelligible. What we have here is a covert assumption of the continuing authentic reality of the person in separation from his or her body. The idea of the soul meant to convey nothing other than this. In this amalgam of notions of corporeality and soulhood we have a strange mishmash of ideas which can hardly count as a definitive solution of our problem.

The second component in the characteristic modern approach to the idea of death and immortality is the philosophy of time and of history which constitutes its true lever. Are we really confronted with a choice between the stark, exclusive alternatives of physical time on the one hand, and, on the other, a timelessness to be identified with eternity itself? Is it even logically possible to conceive of man, whose existence is achieved decisively in the temporal, being transposed into sheer eternity? And in any case, can an eternity which has a beginning be eternity at all? Is it not necessarily non-eternal, and so temporal, precisely because it had a beginning? Yet how can one deny that the resurrection of a human being has a beginning, namely, after death? If, coerced by the logic of the position, one chose to deny this, then surely one would have to suppose that man has always existed in the risen state, in an eternity without beginning. But this view would abolish all serious anthropology. It would fall, in fact, into a caricature of that Platonism which is supposed to be its principal enemy. G. Lohfink, an advocate of the thesis that resurrection is already achieved in death, has noticed these difficulties. He tries to deal with them by invoking the mediaeval concept of the *aevum*, an attempt to describe a special mode of time proper to spiritual creatures on the basis of an analysis of angelic existence. Lohfink sees that death leads not into pure timelessness but into a new kind of time proper to created spirits. The purpose of his argument is primarily to give a defensible sense to biblical imminent expectation which he takes to be the central theme of the message of Jesus. His concern is not with the body–soul problematic from which such speculations emerged but with the necessity, at least as he reads the Gospels, of a discourse that would throw light on the permanent temporal closeness of the Parousia. Such imminence is feasible, according to Lohfink, if the human person may be said to enter through death into the peculiar time of spirits and so into the fulfilment of history. The idea of the *aevum* thus becomes the hermeneutically respectable way of saying that the parousia and resurrection take place for each person in the moment of death. Imminent expectation can now be identified with the expectation of death itself, and so warranted for everybody.

. . . we have now seen that a reflective concept of time, which eschews the naive assumption that time in the beyond is commensurable with earthly time, necessarily leads to our locating the last things—and not simply those concerning the individual, but the end of the world itself—in the moment of death. The last things have thereby become infinitely close to us. Every human being lives in the 'last age'. . . .[31]

This proposal for a differentiated concept of time entails genuine progress. Yet the queries listed above are in no way rendered redundant by it. Looking more closely, one discovers that this concept of the *aevum* has simply been added on, in somewhat external fashion, to a predetermined conceptual construct. The point of this construct is the claim that on the other side of death history is already complete. The end of history is ever waiting for the one who dies. But this is just what can hardly be reconciled with the continuation of history. History is viewed as simultaneously completed and still continuing. What remains unexplained is the relationship between, on the one hand, the ever new beginnings of human life in history, both present and future, and, on the other, the state of fulfilment not only of the individual but of the historical process itself, a state said to be already realized in the world beyond death. The idea of the *aevum* is helpful when we are considering the condition of the individual person who enters into perfection while remaining a creature of time. In this domain the concept has a precise meaning. But it says nothing at all which could justify the statement that history as a whole, from whatever point of view, can be seen as already fulfilled.

It is odd that an exegete should appeal in support of this speculation to the "primitive Christian view" for which, in the case of Jesus, "resurrection from the dead follows immediately upon death," a view which supposedly supplies the "real model of Christian eschatology" which the early Church somehow forgot to apply more widely.[32] For, to begin with, one can hardly ignore the fact that the message of resurrection "on the third day" posits a clear interim period between the death of the Lord and his rising again. And, more importantly, it is evident that early Christian proclamation never identified the destiny of those who die before the Parousia with the quite special event of the resurrection of Jesus. That special event depended on Jesus' unique and irreducible position in the history of salvation. Moreover, there are two respects in which one must bring the charge that all this is a case of aggravated Platonism. First, in such models the body is definitively excluded from the hope for salvation. Secondly, the concept of the *aevum* as here employed hypostatises history in a way which only falls short of Plato's doctrine of the Ideas by virtue of its logical inconsistencies.

Perhaps we have lingered overlong on these theses. That seemed necessary because at the present time they have been almost universally received into the general theological consciousness. Such a consensus, it should now be clear, rests on an extremely fragile foundation. In the long run, theology and preaching cannot tolerate such a quirky theological patchwork, full of logical leaps and ruptures. As quickly as possible we should bid farewell to this way of thinking which deprives Christian proclamation of an appropriate discourse and thus cancels its own claim to be taken seriously as a form of Christian understanding.

2. THE BIBLICAL DATA

Having thus sketched the present state of the question, we can now turn to an investigation of the Bible's teaching about these two questions: resurrection and immortality.

(a) The Resurrection from the Dead

In our reflections on the theology of death we have already considered the approach of Old Testament faith to the idea of resurrection. So we can begin here with the witness of the *New* Testament. The doctrine of the resurrection had not been generally accepted in intertestamental Judaism. If we are looking for an explanation of why it became the fundamental confession of Christians we shall find it easily enough in the fact of Jesus' resurrection as experienced and communicated by the witnesses. The risen Lord became, so to speak, the canon within the canon: the criterion in whose light tradition must be read. In the illumination which he brought, the internal struggles of the Old Testament were read as a single movement towards the One who suffered, was crucified and rose again. The travail of Old Testament faith became itself a testimony to the resurrection.

This new fact, which brought about the passage from the Old Testament to the New, was prepared for by the words of Jesus which interpreted it before it took place. Only because its intelligibility was prepared beforehand could the resurrection of Jesus gain any historical significance at all. Mere facts without words, without meaning, fall into nothingness as fully as do mere words to which no reality corresponds. To this extent we can say with complete certainty that the origin of the Easter proclamation is unthinkable without some corresponding announcement by Jesus himself. In this context, the crucial text is Jesus' discussion with the Sadduccees about the resurrection as given in the gospel according to Mark.[33] In his debate with the Sadduccees who argued in fundamentalistic fashion that only the Pentateuch might be acknowledged as Scripture, and took it as the exclusive rule of faith, *sola scriptura*, Jesus is obliged to prove his thesis on the basis of the books of Moses. He does so in a way which is both exciting and wonderfully simple. He points to the Mosaic concept of God, or more precisely to the divine self-presentation in the burning bush as reported by Moses: "I am the God of Abraham, and the God of Isaac, and the God of Jacob."[34] That means: those who have been called by God are themselves part of the concept of God. One would turn God into a God of the dead and thus stand the Old Testament concept of God on its head if one declared that those who belong to him who is Life are themselves dead. This text shows that, in principle, Jesus adopted the Pharisaic, over against the Sadducean, variety of Jewish teaching which included, then, the confession of the resurrection. However, there is also something new in Jesus' presentation. The resurrection moves into a central position in the expression of faith. It is no longer one tenet of faith among many others, but rather is identified with the concept of God itself. Resurrection faith is contained in faith in God. The massive simplicity of Israel's early faith is not obscured by the addition of other obligatory items but is deepened by a more acute seeing. Faith remains simple. It is simply faith in God. Yet it becomes both purer and richer by being thus deepened. All that business of demythologization is taken care of from the outset. Cosmological, anthropological, speculative, psychological and chronological aspects of religion: all these are set aside. What is affirmed is that God himself, and the communion he offers, are life. To belong to him, to be called by him, is to be rooted in life indestructible.

The nascent Church had the task of rethinking the earlier Pharisaic tradition, as applied to the words and actions of Jesus, in the light of the new fact of the Lord's resurrection. On the basis of the original insights, this process would flow on in the stream of the Church's faith through all succeeding generations. Within the limits of this book it would be impossible to catalogue every relevant text. We shall consider simply the two main witnesses within the New Testament corpus, namely Paul and John. In what follows we shall be looking at some characteristic texts in which the further development of the doctrine of the resurrection is already indicated.

Two Pauline texts especially important for our enquiry are Romans 6, 1–14 and First Corinthians 15. In the Letter to the Romans, baptism is interpreted as being engrafted onto the death of Christ. By baptism we enter on a common destiny with that of Jesus and so with the death which was his fate. But that death is ordered intrinsically to the resurrection. Of necessity, then, suffering and dying with Christ means at the same time a participation in the hope of the resurrection. One permits oneself to be inserted into the passion of Christ since that is the place at which resurrection breaks forth. The theological concept of resurrection which we discovered in Mark 12 suddenly becomes quite concrete. It becomes, in fact, theo-christological in a suitable correspondence with the christological extension of the concept of God which had taken place in the period between the historical ministry and Paul's calling to the apostolate. Communion with God, which is the native place of life indestructible, finds its concrete form in sharing in the body of Christ. Through the sacramental dimension of this idea, the Church's Liturgy and the Church herself as the bearer of the Liturgy become part of the same doctrine. Theo-christology also possesses an ecclesiological aspect. In comparison with the simple grandeur of the words of Jesus things may seem to have become rather complicated. It is more correct to say that they have become, rather, more concrete. What is now described in more detail is *how* the belonging to God that Jesus spoke of actually takes place. The fundamental structure of the doctrine is not impaired but remains fully intact. Faith in the resurrection is not part of some speculation in cosmology or the theology of history but is bound up with a person, with God in Christ. Thus the theologizing of resurrection faith is also its personalization.

In the other Pauline text, First Corinthians 15, we find the apostle engaged in controversy with spiritualizing reinterpretations of faith in the resurrection. In such rein-

terpretation, resurrection as a future bodily event touching both the cosmos and our own destiny is called into
serious question. What precisely was being put in its place
the text hardly permits us to say. But some light is thrown
thereon by Second Timothy 2,18 where the author mentions a view of the Gospel for which "the resurrection has
already happened." Here the sacramental foretaste of the
resurrection hope has been misconceived. The resurrection event is robbed of its futurist character, and identified
with the event of becoming or being a Christian. Resurrection thus undergoes a "mystical" or "existential" reduction. It is probably ideas of this kind which lie behind the
Corinthian denial of the resurrection as well. In opposing
them, the apostle has to emphasize that the resurrection
is not simply a mystical or existential assurance to the
Christian in the present. In the last analysis, this would
mean nothing: your faith would be vain.[35] Rather is the
resurrection a pledge to the future of man and the cosmos,
and in this sense a pledge to space, time and matter. History and cosmos are not realities alongside spirit, running
on into a meaningless eternity or sinking down into an
equally meaningless nothingness. In the resurrection, God
proves himself to be the God also of the cosmos and of history. To this extent, the temporal and cosmic elements in
the Jewish belief in the resurrection take their places
within Christian confesson. Yet they are strictly related to
the new theological and christological structure, and in
this way the inner simplicity of that structure remains un-
touched. The point is still the same. If the dead do not rise,
then Christ has not arisen.[36] The resurrection of Christ
and the resurrection of the dead are not two discrete realities but one single reality which in the end is simply the
verification of faith in God before the eyes of history.

We should look as well at two monuments to Johannine

theology: John 6 and John 11. The story of Lazarus in John 11 leads up to the affirmation, "I am the resurrection and the life."[37] The theo-christological conception of the resurrection met with in Paul finds here its purest and most consistent form. The evangelist has found his way back to the utter simplicity of that vision in Mark 12. He has translated its theology into christology in a systematic fashion. "He who believes in me, though he die, yet shall he live."[38] The bond with Jesus is, even now, resurrection. Where there is communion with him, the boundary of death is overshot here and now. It is in this perspective that we must understand the Discourse on the Eucharist in John 6. Feeding on Jesus' word and on his flesh, that is, receiving him by both faith and sacrament, is described as being nourished with the bread of immortality. The resurrection does not appear as a distant apocalyptic event but as an occurrence which takes place in the immediate present. Whenever someone enters into the 'I' of Christ, he has entered straight away into the space of unconditional life. The evangelist does not raise the question of an intermediate state between death and resurrection, a rupture in life, precisely because Jesus is himself the resurrection. Faith, which is the contact between Jesus and myself, vouchsafes here and now the crossing of death's frontier. The entire Old Testament inheritance is thus presented in the new mode of christological transformation. In the Old Testament, it had become clear that death is the absence of communication in the midst of life. Similarly, it had become evident that love is a promise of life. But now it becomes manifest that a love stronger than death actually exists. The borderline between Sheol and life runs through our very midst, and those who are in Christ are situated on the side of life, and that everlastingly.

Bultmann took this Johannine theology to be the perfect

expression of authentic Christianity. As we know, this means for him that resurrection is to be interpreted exclusively and without remainder in an "existential" sense. He is obliged to treat St. John's references to the Last Day[39] as the interpolations of a later ecclesiastical redactor, whose effect is to drag down the lofty insights of the evangelist to the crude level of the Church populace. Yet in reality, when the work of the evanglist is thus snapped into two fragments, not even the aspect which Bultmann favors can survive. If the passage into the christological sphere be not an entry into that unconditional life that abides even beyond earthly dying, then it is not a real passover at all. It is nothing more than a gyration in the inescapable futility of a private existence whose fundamental nothingness is not overcome but rather reconfirmed.

Just one more comment on the biblical data as a whole will be in order here. For the New Testament, the resurrection is a positive event, a message full of hope. By contrast, we know from the Old Testament, with its phenomenological analysis of "life" and "death," that when human existence issues in opposition to God, in the nothingness of spiritual shipwreck, it cannot itself be called "life." On the contrary, such a fate is really the definitive presence of "death." Even for resurrection faith this possibility— which of course must not be confused with the sheer annihilation of the human existent—still remains open. We will have to look at it in greater detail somewhat later.

Meanwhile, let us try to formulate a conclusion. Faith in the resurrection is a central expression of the christological confession of God. It follows, indeed, from the concept of God. Its emphasis is placed not on a particular anthropology, whether anti-Platonic or Platonic, but on a theology. This is why we may reasonably expect it to have the capacity to make a variety of anthropologies its own and find appropriate expression by means of them. But at the same time, and equally, we must expect that this theology will confront all anthropologies with its own critical measuring rod. From its thought of God it draws forth a number of affirmations about man. On the one hand, the new life has already begun and will nevermore be snuffed out. On the other hand, that *vita nuova* is ordered to the transformation of all life, to a future wholeness for man and for the world.

(b) The "Intermediate State" Between Death and Resurrection

If the "Last Day" is not to be identified with the moment of individual death but is accepted as what it really is, the shared ending of all history, then the question naturally arises as to what happens "in-between." In Catholic theology, as that received its systematic form in the high Middle Ages, this question received its answer in terms of the immortality of the soul. To Luther, such a solution was unacceptable. For him it was a result of the infiltration of faith by philosophy. Yet his own enquiry into the matter produced an ambiguous report. In great majority, the relevant texts of Luther take up the biblical term for death, "sleep," seeing in it a description of the content of the intermediate state. The soul sleeps in the peace of Christ. It is awakened, along with the body, on the last day. Elsewhere one finds Luther in a different state of mind, for instance in his comments on the story of Lazarus.[40] There he remarks that the distinction between body and soul whereby hitherto people had tried to explain Lazarus' life "in the bosom of Abraham" was *ein Dreck*, "a load of rubbish." As he explains: "We must say, *totus Abraham*, the whole man, is to live. . . ."[41] The impression one takes away from this is that Luther's concern was not so much with the denial of the life of the dead, but with an attack on the body-soul distinction. Luther does not succeed in replacing that distinction by any clear or even recognizable new conception. In our survey of the *status quaestionis*, we discovered that recent theology rules out an "intermediate state." By doing so, it gives systematic expression to a point of view first developed by Luther.

i. *Early Judaism.* What does the Bible have to say? In the light of our investigation into the ideas of the New Testament about the resurrection we can already make one fairly general statement. To posit an interruption of life between death and the end of the world would not be in accord with Scripture. In fact, the texts permit a much more precise set of assertions than this, as the exemplary work of P. Hoffmann in particular has shown in careful detail.[42] The first point to notice is that both the primitive community and St. Paul belonged with the Jewish traditon of their time, just as had Jesus himself. Naturally, they situated themselves vis-à-vis the internal debate within that tradition by reference to the fundamental criterion found in Jesus' own image of God.[43] This produced in time a gradual transformation of the preexisting tradition, by way of its thorough-going assimilation to the demands of Christology. Our first task, therefore, is to get acquainted with the data of intertestamental Judaism—a complicated affair for which I must rely on Hoffmann's study.

Let us look at some characteristic documents. The book of Enoch in its Ethiopian recension, datable to c. 150 B.C., offers in its twenty-second chapter an account of the abode of the spirits or souls of the departed. Here the ancient idea of Sheol, earlier taken as the realm of shadow-life, receives more articulated and differentiated description. Its "space" is characterized in greater detail. The world in which the dead are kept until the final judgment is no longer located simply in the earth's interior, but, more specifically, in the West, the land of the setting sun, in a mountain where it occupies four different regions (pictured as caves). The just and the unjust are now separated. The unjust await the judgment in darkness whereas the just, among whom the martyrs occupy a special position, dwell in light, being assembled around a life-giving spring of water. We already get a glimpse of how such "early Jewish" notions lived on in unbroken fashion in the early Church. The memento of the departed in the Roman Canon (now the "First Eucharistic Prayer") prays that God may grant to those who have died marked with the sign of faith and now "sleep the sleep of peace" a place of light, "fresh water" (*refrigerium*) and repose. The prayer thus identifies the three conditions which inhabitants of the Mediterranean world consider the proper expression of all good living. Patently, the idea coincides in all respects with the destiny of the just as described in *Enoch*.

A further stage of development can be observed in the Fourth Book of Ezra, written somewhere around the year 100 A.D. Here too the dead dwell in various "chambers," their "souls" the bearers of a continuing life. As in *Enoch*, the just have already entered upon their reward. But whereas the author of *Enoch* defers the start of the punishment of sinners until the final judgment, in *Ezra* the pains of the Godless begin in the intermediate state, with the result that at a number of points their position seems to be that of a definitive Hell. In Rabbinic Judaism, the dividing line between two kinds of human destiny is even more consistently observed. From the moment of judgment, which follows immediately upon death, two paths open up. One leads into the paradise garden of Eden, conceived either as lying in the East or as preserved in heaven. The other goes to the alley of Gehenna, the place of damnation. But, besides the idea of paradise, the destiny of the just is represented by other images and motifs as well. Thus we hear of the "treasury of souls," of waiting "beneath the throne of God," and of the just—and especially martyrs—being received into Abraham's bosom.[44] Here again the continuity between Jewish and early Christian conceptions is striking. The idea of paradise;[45] the image of the bosom of Abraham;[46] the thought of the tarrying of souls beneath the throne of God[47]: all these are present in the New Testament tradition.

But before we turn to the New Testament itself, something should be said about the writings bequeathed to us from Qumran. So long as the community represented under this name, the Essenes, were known only from Josephus, scholars were obliged to regard them as belonging to the Hellenizing strand within early Judaism, at any rate where our question in this present section was concerned. Josephus had summed up their views in the following words:

For their doctrine is this: that bodies are corruptible, and that the matter they are made of is not permanent; but that the souls are immortal, and continue for ever, and that they come out of the most subtile air, and are united to their bodies as to prisons, into which they are drawn by a certain natural enticement; but that when they are set free from the bands of the flesh, they then, as released from a long bondage, rejoice and mount upward.[48]

But with the discovery of the original Qumran manuscripts, our image of the Covenanters has necessarily undergone revision. As K. Schubert, in his study of the Dead Sea community, commented on the text just cited:

In all probability, this description is nothing more than a concession by Josephus to his Greek readership. . . . The Essenes were not a Hellenistic-syncretistic group, but a Jewish apocalyptic movement.[49]

However, we are dealing here with ideas of the afterlife conceived in markedly material terms, so much so that this same writer can say that the Essenes of Qumran "believed in a continuation of bodiliness, even though they accepted the passing-away of their bodies in the first instance."[50] To this extent, Josephus' description is perhaps not too far removed from the truth. He too ascribes to the sect a materialist understanding of the soul of the kind common in Stoic philosophy.[51] This shows how complex in this period the reciprocal interpenetration of the Hellenistic and Jewish worlds could be. The much-favored dichotomy between "Greek" and "Hebrew" simply does not stand up to historical examination. The discussion of the Qumran texts also indicates that the mere maintaining of strictly material notions about the life to come does not in itself guarantee fidelity to the spiritual inheritance of the Old Testament. The heart of that option which entered history in Abraham's faith cannot be grasped without finer differentiation than this. In this perspective, a number of contemporary contributions seem to belong to a continuing "Essene" tradition, in that the issue of materiality has overshadowed every other consideration.

ii. *The New Testament.* It should be clear by now that the New Testament belongs to that Jewish world whose fundamental contours have been sketched in the preceding section. As a general methodological assumption, it is legitimate to suppose that Jesus and the earliest Church shared Israel's faith in its (then) contemporary form. The acceptance of Jesus' awareness of his own mission simply gave to this faith a new center, a nucleus by whose power the individual elements of the tradition were step by step transformed: first and foremost, the concept of God, but then following it, and in a graduated order of urgency, all the rest.

The Synoptic tradition preserved two sayings of Jesus on the topic of the "intermediate state." These are Luke 16, 19–31 and Luke 23, 43, and they were briefly touched on above. So far as the first, the story of Lazarus, is concerned, we may admit that the parable's doctrinal content lies in its moral, a warning against the dangers of wealth, rather than in the descriptions of Lazarus in Abraham's bosom and Dives in Hell. And yet, manifestly, the teller of the parable does regard these evocations of the afterlife as appropriate images of the real future of man. In this, the text clearly testifies to the fact that the earliest Christianity shared in the faith of contemporary Judaism about the beyond. So much we can say without even entering into the (quite independent) question of whether in the parable we are overhearing the *ipsissima vox* of Jesus himself.

Something along the same lines must be said about the second text, the dialogue of the Crucified with the good thief. Here too the Jewish background is palpable. Paradise is the place where the Messiah, concealed, awaits his hour, and whither he will return.[52] But it is in this self-same text that we begin to see the Christian transformation of the inherited Jewish tradition at work. That destiny reserved by Jewish tradition to the martyrs and the privileged "righteous ones" is now promised by the Condemned Man on the Cross to a fellow condemnee. He possesses the authority to open wide the doors of paradise to the lost. His word is the key which unlocks them. And so the phrase "with me" takes on a transformative significance. It means that paradise is no longer seen as a place standing in permanent readiness for occupation and which happens to contain the Messiah along with a lot of other people. Instead, paradise opens in Jesus. It depends on his person. Joachim Jeremias was right, therefore, to find a connection between the prayer of the good thief and the petition of the dying Stephen: "Lord Jesus, receive my spirit."[53]

With impressive unanimity, ... the New Testament presents communion with Christ after death as the specifically Christian view of the inter-mediate state.[54]

Here is the dawning realization that Jesus himself is paradise, light, fresh water, the secure peace toward which human longing and hope are directed. Perhaps we may remind ourselves in this connection of the new use of the image of "bosom" which we find in John's Gospel. Jesus does not come from the bosom of Abraham, but from that of the Father himself.[55] The disciple who is to become the type of all faithful discipleship rests on the bosom of Jesus.[56] The Christian, in his faith and love, finds shelter on the breast of Jesus and so, in the end, on the breast of the Father. "I am the resurrection": what these words mean emerges here from a new angle.

Let us move on to the Pauline writings. It has become customary to distinguish two phases in the development of Paul's eschatological thought: an early phase, in which he expects to experience the resurrection and the parousia personally,[57] and a later phase, in which such expectations are gradually eliminated while the question of the intermediate state becomes all the more urgent and meaningful. There is much to be said in favor of such an evolution in Paul's thinking. However, Hoffmann has shown that Paul's ideas about the intermediate state and the resurrection were not affected by it, but remained the same throughout. Because the image of sleep which appears in these texts crops up time and again from Luther to the Dutch Catechism, Hoffman's analysis of the semantic field of the language of sleep is especially important. Sleep was a euphemism for dying, and for being dead. Found in both the Jewish and the Hellenistic sphere, it was capacious enough a metaphor to find room for a variety of somewhat different contents. It comprised the idea of unconsciousness, as well as the more positive notion of the peace enjoyed by the just as distinct from sinners. So far as Paul is concerned, Hoffmann shows that his use of the word is uncommitted as between those various contents. So no inferences can be drawn about his views of the condition of the dead.[58]

In his correspondence with the church at Thessalonica, the only eschatological issue Paul addresses is that of the future resurrection. In writing to Philippi, on the other hand, Paul, faced with imminent danger of death, looks steadily at his own destiny and at what will follow death. Yet Philippians is familiar with the same mode of thinking as that in First Thessalonians and, most importantly, both letters argue from the same foundational premise, namely, from Christ, who guarantees the life of those who belong to him. A careful examination of the formula "the dead in Christ," found in First Thessalonians 4, 16, leads Hoffman to the following judgment:

To me it seems by no means improbable that the idea of communion with Christ as the determining factor in the death of Christians, found in Philippians 1,23, is already adumbrated here.[59]

Neither in Philippians nor in First Thessalonians are resurrection and intermediate state mutually exclusive. Judaism had bound both firmly together.[60] It seems to me that the profound link between these two Pauline letters in this regard is even clearer in First Thessalonians 5, 10 where the apostle refers to Christ as he who died for us so that "whether we wake or sleep we might live with him." Evidently, then, it is not "waking" or "sleeping," earthly "life" or "death" which make the decisive difference but life in communion with Christ or in separation from him.

The hardest nut to crack among the texts debated in this context is Second Corinthians 5, 1–10:

For we know that if the earthly tent we live in is destroyed, we have a building from God, a house not made with hands, eternal in the heavens. Here indeed we groan, and long to put on our heavenly dwelling, so that by putting it on we may not be found naked. For while we are still in this tent, we sigh with anxiety; not that we would be unclothed, but that we would be further clothed, so that what is mortal may be swallowed up by life. He who has prepared us for this very thing is God, who has given us the Spirit as a guarantee. So we are always of good courage; we know that while we are at home in the body we are away from the Lord, for we walk by faith not by sight. We are of good courage, and we would rather be away from the body and at home with the Lord. So whether we are at home or away, we make it our aim to please him. For we must all appear before the judgment seat of Christ, so that each one may receive good or evil, according to what he has done in the body.

None of the numerous interpretations can be called satisfactory in every respect. However, although a number of detailed points will probably always remain controversial, the meticulous textual analysis found in both Hoffmann's work[61] and in Bultmann's commentary on this Letter,[62] agreeing as they do in all essentials, seems to offer a reliable guide to the general thrust of the text. These writers hold that Paul is not offering an express judgment of either a positive or a negative kind about the intermediate state. Rather is he emphasizing the Christian hope for salvation as such, a hope which lies in the Lord and has its focus in our own resurrection. The foil to Paul's remarks must be located in the "afflictions" suffered by the disciples and listed in chapter 4 of the Letter. What this means is that the text has nothing of direct relevance to contribute to our discussion. However, the scholars we are following also arrive at a second conclusion which is of indirect importance for us. Despite what a number of exegetes allege,

Paul does not say that he is afraid of dying—afraid of dying, that is, before the Parousia. It is true that he rejects the Gnostic idea that "nakedness" of soul is a salvific good, pushing it aside without a word of discussion as inhuman and untrue. But fear of the intermediate state as a time of nakedness is notable by its absence. As Bultmann puts it:

Tharrein means we face death with confidence, and *eudokoumen mallon* that we even welcome it! Nothing better could happen to us! . . . The intrepid zeal to serve the Lord not only knows no more fear of death; there is even a touch of longing for death.[63]

How can such an attitude be explained without invoking Paul's certitude, expressed in Philippians 1, 23, that, even now, to die means to "be with Christ." A profound isomorphism unites Second Corinthians 5, 6–10 to Philippians 1, 21–26, something especially clear if one concentrates in particular on v. 8 of the Corinthian text and v. 21 of the Philippian. In both cases, the truly desirable thing is being at home with the Lord: already, now, as soon as possible. Yet in both cases, to speak in the accents of Bultmann, it is also clear that faith banishes not just fear of death, but its opposite, the growing yearning for death, as well. For faith can give even to the burden of "wasting away . . . daily"[64] the radiance that belongs to being allowed to "please him."[65]

What makes all these texts, but notably Second Corinthians, so opaque from our viewpoint today is the fact that Paul makes no attempt to develop an anthropology which might clarify this hope in its diverse stages but simply argues from the side of references to Christ. It is Christ who is life: both now and at any point in the future. In the presence of such a certainty, the anthropological "substrate" of Paul's thinking lies necessarily outside his focus of attention, in shadow. To Paul this must have been un-problematic, since he shared the common presuppositions of his fellow Jews. His task was simply that of formulating the novel element, the reality of Christ and relationship with him, in all its dramatic importance.

In consequence of these reflections, we can afford to be brief in dealing with Philippians 1, 23. For Paul, life in this world is "Christ," but death is gain, since in the "disso-lution" of all that is earthly, death means "being with Christ." An inner freedom springs from this knowledge, a fearless openness in death's regard and also an uncom-plaining—no, more—a joyful readiness for further service. In an earlier generation of scholars, it was believed that this text was inexplicable save by the intrusion of "Hel-lenisation" into the apostle's thought processes. Today we understand that there is no break whatsoever vis-à-vis Paul's earlier affirmations.

What he says in Philippians 1 he could already have proclaimed in First Thessalonians, had he seen an opportunity for doing so.[66]

What is happening before our very eyes is not that Hebrew "monism" is yielding to Greek "dualism," but that a preexistent Jewish heritage is receiving its proper christo-logical center. The transformation went so far that it already reached the idea which John would express so graphically: "I am the resurrection and the life."[67]

(c) Conclusions and Implications

The first point we can make by way of an attempt at a conclusion is that the decisively new element which per-mitted Christianity to emerge from Judaism was faith in the risen Lord and in the present actuality of his life. The presence of the risen Christ transforms faith into a real-ized claim on the future, filling it with the certitude of the believer's own resurrection. More partial, individual aspects are taken over, without break of continuity, from Judaism, and assimilated piecemeal to this christological foundation. Through faith in the risen Lord, the intermediate state and the resurrection are linked to each other in a more thoroughgoing way than could have been the case before. Nevertheless, they remain distinct. In the New Testament and the fathers, all the images generated by Judaism for the intermediate state recur: Abraham's bosom, paradise, altar, the tree of life, water, light. We shall see in a moment how conservative the early Church was to be in this very area of eschatological representation. So far from undergoing the sea-change from "Semitism" to "Hellenism," the Church remained fully within the Semitic canon of images, as the art of the catacombs, the Liturgy and theology combine to show. It simply became ever more lucidly clear that these images do not describe places but transcribe Christ himself, who is true light and life, the very *arbor vitae.* In such a fashion, these images lost their more-or-less cosmological status and became the vehicles of assertions about God in Christ. In thus floating free, they took on new depth.

In the light of these insights, it should be evident that the Bible did not turn a particular anthropology into dogma. Rather did it offer the christology which flows from the resurrection as the one foundation for eschatology truly appropriate to faith. This foundation confers on thought the right and duty to draw on its own potential in order to illuminate the anthropological presuppositions and implications contained in the foundation itself. Starting out from this perception, the patristic age haltingly and the Middle Ages more self-confidently used the instruments provided by Greek thinkers so as to grasp the meaning of the statement that we will not be stored up after death in

caves and chambers like chattels, but clasped by that person whose love embraces us all.

From these mullings, we can extract four implications
which sum up the significance of our reflections hitherto
for systematic theology, and give us an idea of the task
which lies ahead.

1. First, the idea of a sleep of death, in the sense of an
unconscious state spanning the period between death and
the end of the world is an unfounded piece of archaizing
which no New Testament text warrants. Paul's thinking
always proceeds on the basis of the Pharisaic and Rab-
binical teaching to which he gives a christological heart
and depth without ever rejecting it. That those who have
died in Christ are alive: this is the fundamental certitude
which was able to exploit contemporary Jewish conceptions for its own purposes.

2. Secondly, not only in the New Testament period but
throughout the life-span of the early Church, this fundamental certitude was expressed in images made available
by Judaism—and, naturally enough, by closely related images from the treasury of forms that was Mediterranean
culture. The mediaevals tried to throw fresh light on the
essential claim found in the ground-conception of a life
deriving from the presence of Christ. It is obvious, I suppose, that the status of a pictorial representation or a conceptual expression is not to be judged by its antiquity but
in terms of its correspondence with the thought which it
embodies. A later analysis, such as that undertaken in the
Middle Ages, may do more justice to some fundamental
idea than any of its predecessors.

3. Thirdly, whilst on the one hand a host of images
underwent a kind of christological simplification and integration, it must be recognized that human beings, in
their need for an object to contemplate, felt compelled to

unfold images once again. There is nothing perverse in such a re-creation of iconic forms. Indeed, it would be foolish to strive for a completely imageless piety, in blatant contradiction of human nature. However, precisely this consideration makes it all the more imporant to evaluate images in terms of their true measure, to keep them faithful to this measure, and to prevent them from shooting off into the realms of mythology. Here there are certainly legitimate grounds for criticizing the history of spirituality in which such measuring against the authentic standard was hardly ever carried out with the requisite degree of thoroughness. It is not the business of those entrusted with preaching the faith to expel the images from the Church. But it is very much their business to purify them again and again.

4. Fourthly and finally, to the degree that christology's full significance was realized, the individual eschatological images became filled with christological meaning. The importance of their temporal constituents, including those concerned with the history of the cosmos, quite naturally shrank accordingly. But then the question which gained in urgency, and which in our time is once again a central feature in discussion of the problem of eschatology, became this: to what extent can that temporal and cosmic aspect be excluded, and rightly excluded, without abolishing the realistic and universal content of the Gospel promise? It is to this dilemma that we will be devoting special attention in the pages that follow.

3. THE DOCUMENTS OF THE CHURCH'S MAGISTERIUM

Three stages can be discerned in the formation of the Church's doctrine. Characteristically enough, the early

Church formulated no dogma about the immortality of the soul. There was no occasion for such a formulation. On the one hand, the Jewish matrix of Christianity provided the Church with a tradition which held it to be self-evidently certain that the dead do not return to nothingness but await the resurrection in "Hades," in a manner appropriate to their form of life. On the other hand, since Christian faith had made no specific statement about immortality, there was no reason to give it its own special slot in the Church's rule of faith, wherein only the chief articles of Christianity in its particularity and novelty were set forth. Historians of doctrine have shown that in the Christian East Clement and Origen represent something of a turning point, the full extent of whose implications remain to be investigated.[68] Yet even for these two Alexandrians and their intellectual posterity, the condition of the dead remains an intermediate state. Although they shook up the kaleidoscope, they by no means obliterated the fundamental pattern, Jewish-oriented as that was, of the community's faith. In the West, even a modest caesura of this kind was lacking, though, this said, more work needs to be done on developments from the fourth century onwards. In accordance with Jewish tradition, it was customary to distinguish the destiny of the martyrs from that of the rest of the dead. The martyrs alone enjoyed the final and definitive glory. The influence of Hellenistic symbolism on funereal art and in the libation rituals for the dead did not wipe out this state of things but rather gave it more solid, if coarse-grained, form. While the theological thinking of the great patristic divines began to modify the concept of Hades under the pressure of the architectonic connections between christology and anthropology, this movement of ideas remained fairly fluid. As yet there was no development sufficient to render new dogmatic formulations possible. Nor did the theological enterprise affect the general consciousness of the faithful so nearly that such formulations could be thought of as necessary.

Against a background of imperfectly clarified convictions, distinct enough, however (thanks notably to the story of Lazarus), to constitute genuine convictions of faith, there shone that central star in the firmament of Christian confession: belief in the resurrection of the body. All the creeds and *regulae fidei* speak of it, with pride of place among them the Creed of Nicaea-Constantinople. (But note also, for instance, the *Quicumque vult* or Pseudo-Athanasian Creed.)[69] In the West, as distinct from both the Greek East and Egypt, the churches confessed the resurrection of the *flesh*, rather than of the dead. It has been shown that what we have here is a continuation of the Jewish terminology for the resurrection, which by means of the venerable formula "all flesh" denoted mankind as a whole.[70] At the same time, the phrase was indebted to Johannine theology with which, in early patristic times, Justin and Irenaeus had a special affinity. The idiom expresses, therefore, a concern not, in the first place, with corporeality, but with the universality of the resurrection hope. However, in the second place, since "all flesh" signifies the entire creature, called "flesh" in contrast to the divine Creator, the phrase also connotes the bodiliness of the creature, understanding it, we may be sure, by reference to that life-giving "flesh" of the Lord of which John had spoken.

During the first few centuries of the Church's existence, what was needed was the sheer confrontation of the Christian creed and its basic truth-claims with the *Lebensgefühl* of the world of that time and its scientific consciousness—not forgetting those aberrant reinterpretations of

Christianity which had let themselves be absorbed by such ideas. Towards the end of the late antique period, when the nettle of Origenist theology had to be grasped, the going got somewhat rougher. A controversy broke out as to the kind of materiality which the risen body possessed and its relation to the earthly body. We shall have to return to this later, in connection with some present-day controversies. Here it must suffice to draw attention to the later credal formularies with their distinctly uncompromising language. The *Fides Damasi*, originating probably in the southern Gaul of the late fifth century, has this to say:

We believe that we who have been purified in his death, and in his blood, will be raised on the Last Day in that flesh in which we now live.[71]

Or again, the Council of Toledo of 675 declared:

The true resurrection of all the departed will take place after the example of our Head. Not in an ethereal or in any other widely different flesh, as some assert in their foolishness, will we rise again, but, as our faith teaches, in this self-same flesh in which we live, exist and move.[72]

Fifth century Gaul also bequeathed us the *Statuta Ecclesiae Antiqua* which laid down rules for an examination of faith prior to the consecration of a new bishop. The candidate must be asked "whether he believes in the resurrection of that flesh in which we now live, and of no other: *quam gestamus et non alterius.*[73] Pope Leo IX made use of this text in 1053 when he was asked for his confession of faith by the Antiochene patriarch Peter: "I believe in the true resurrection of precisely that flesh which is now mine, *quam nunc gesto*, and in the life everlasting."[74] The same dogmatic tradition was confirmed by the Fourth Lateran Council of 1215 in its repudiation of the teaching of the Albigensians and Cathars: "All will rise with their own bodies, the bodies which they bear here. . . ."[75]

Whereas these earliest doctrinal statements of the mediaeval Church in the area of eschatology remain fully within the problematic of patristic Christendom, a new stage of development in the Church's teaching was brought about by the dogmatic bull *Benedictus Deus* which Pope Benedict XII promulgated on 29 January 1336. In this bull the Pope taught that, in the time after Christ's passion, death and ascension into heaven, the souls of those departed persons who stand in no further need of purification do not have to linger in an intermediate state. Rather, "even before their reunification with their bodies and the general judgment . . . they are and will be in heaven," so that they "see the divine nature in an immediate vision, face-to-face, without the mediation of any creature."[76] What was the occasion of this definition, and what is its relation to the heritage of the early Church? As regards the public events which prepared the way for the papal bull, it should be noticed that as early as 1241 the University of Paris— then acting as a kind of magisterial mouthpiece for the Church—had made a similar determination of doctrine. Moreover, the kernel of the teaching had been incorporated into the confession of faith drawn up in 1274 by the Second Council of Lyons for the reception into Catholic communion of the Byzantine emperor Michael Palaeologus.[77] Pope John XXII, who reigned from 1316 to 1334, had himself early regarded such formulae as self-evidently right and proper. But in his later years, as a result of extensive study of the fathers, he came to doubt their validity. In the texts of the fathers he discovered the doctrine of waiting for heaven which, as we have seen, dominated the entire patristic period and could still be found, in living continuity with that period, at more than one point in the works of Bernard of Clairvaux (c. 1090–1153).[78] This led the Pope to present, in a series of sermons, his newly formed conviction that there is a strictly christological intermediate phase in the destiny of the dead. Only after the final judgment and the resurrection is this intermediate state replaced by a definitive Trinitarian condition. Until the Last Day, the saints lie, as the Book of the Apocalypse suggests, "beneath the altar"[79]: that is, under the consoling protection of Jesus' humanity. Not till the final judgment will they come from beneath the cover of that humanity to receive the direct vision, "over the altar," of God himself. The transition from one state to the other is the event whereby Jesus hands over the Kingdom to the Father, as announced by St. Paul in First Corinthians 15, 24.

Such an archaizing conception of the life beyond proved a tremendous scandal to the faith-consciousness of believers at large, since that consciousness had meanwhile been formed in a very different manner. The scandal was exploited for political ends in the accusation of heresy brought by the Pope's Franciscan opponents in the circle of William of Ockham at the court of the emperor Louis of Bavaria. On his deathbed, the Pope issued a carefully formulated recantation. His Franciscan successor, who had come to the papal chair from life in academe, decided some few years after his accession to put an end to the uncertainty by giving the Church's current faith-consciousness binding expression in the bull mentioned above. When we look more closely at the nature of the theological developments involved in all this, we shall have to return to the question of the inner logic contained in this process. But even at this stage, we can say that the papal text of 1336 implies in its teaching a certain distancing from the fathers. Yet in our evaluation we must not overlook the fact that its core assertion derives from christology, being in the last resort an interpretation of the meaning of Christ's ascension in all its objectivity with a view to determining at the same time the meaning of Christ's passion, disclosed in the ascension. According to this text, then, the Lord's ascension is essentially an event of a kind which may be called "anthropological-historical." It signifies that now, after Christ, there is no longer a closed heaven. Christ is in heaven: that is, God has opened himself to man, and man, when he passes through the gate of death as one justified, as someone who belongs to Christ and has been received by him, enters into the openness of God. Thus the difference between John XXII and Benedict XII lies above all in their varying estimates of christology. This suggests how inadequate a mere material comparison with the patristic formulae would be in guiding our judgment in this area. As we saw, the ideas of the New Testament and the Fathers about the life of the dead between death and resurrection were borrowed from the variegated conception of Sheol in early Judaism. The Christian authors placed such ideas in a relationship with the christological center, through which step they underwent a process of "christologizing." At first, this process took second place behind the more urgent task of clarifying and defending the message of the resurrection. The ideas inherited from Judaism could not, however, remain permanently self-enclosed and self-sufficient. They were subject to a process of christianization, of being drawn into the sphere of christology, along a trajectory whose basic direction was already visible in the patristic age but whose journey was far from completed then.

In this perspective, the dogmatic texts which have come down to us from the thirteenth and fourteenth centuries mean that the still indeterminate connection between intertestamental Judaic conceptions and Christian confession is at last receiving a more sharply etched form. Only one picture of the intermediate state survives this transformation, and that is purgatory. After the various Jewish accounts of Sheol had been thrown into the melting-pot, purgatory was grasped as a distinct theological quantity in its own right, being defined with the assistance of the idea of purification. Because this development took place after the separation from the churches of the East it was ever afterwards impossible to reach a common view on the matter in both East and West. The traditional view, for which the righteous and the sinners had their respective abodes, collapsed and was replaced by a scheme of preliminary and final states, itself indebted to a christological reflection on the ascension. According to this scheme, hell's portals are now open for the sinner, just as heaven's gate is for the just.[80] Confronted with the ascension of Christ in all its definitive quality, the notion of a preliminary stage in the attainment of eternal destiny loses something of its importance yet is by no means abandoned altogether. According to *Benedictus Deus*, there is still something provisional about the state of the separated soul inasmuch as the *resumptio corporis*, reunification with the body, and the final judgment are still to come. What existence under these conditions might consist in is not, however, further clarified. Luther, on the other hand, in his swing away from the idea of the immortality of the soul towards that of resurrection, adopted a thoroughly antagonistic posture vis-à-vis the notion of a preliminary stage. In the context of the story of Lazarus he stresses, against the Scholastics, in a text we have already touched on:

Totus Abraham: the whole man shall live! What you do is to tear me off a bit of Abraham and say, 'This is what shall live.' . . . A soul which is in heaven and desires the body: it must be a crazy soul we are talking about.[81]

The mediaeval dogmatic text we have been considering, by contrast, maintained the idea of an intermediate state by distinguishing between the personal and the cosmic-historical definitiveness of christology (and so, in christology, of human destiny). In this sense, it can be seen, in fact, as a synthetic statement of the spiritual and intellectual movement of the patristic age.

A rather different controversy has left its mark on the last text to be treated here, the bull *Apostolici regiminis* which came out of the eighth session of the fifth Lateran Council (19 December, 1513). Over against the Renaissance Aristoteleanism of Pietro Pomponazzi (1464–1525), this document affirms that one cannot call the spiritual soul mortal, or assert that it is something non-individual, impersonal, a collective reality in which the single human being merely participates. This is an instructive text, since it highlights the confrontation between, on the one hand, the patrisic and mediaeval synthesis of Greek and Christian elements, and, on the other, the spirit of the Renaissance which rejected this synthesis, seeking Greek thought in its pre-Christian purity and in that way pointing on towards the modern age. It is significant that Pomponazzi's reconstruction of Greek thought in its historical originality did not lead to a stress on the immortal soul as opposed to the resurrection of the body. Rather did it produce a very un-Greek denial of the Christian doctrine of the soul and the soul's hope.

4. THEOLOGICAL UNFOLDING

(a) The Heritage of Antiquity

Were we to take as our unquestioned starting point currently fashionable views in the history of theology, we should be obliged to say that *Benedictus Deus* marks the triumph of Hellenic body–soul dualism—even if the fathers may be judged more leniently. Yet, given the considerable distance in both time and spiritual experience which separates the fourteenth century from the Hellenic world, we have the right to ask whether such a diagnosis can lay claim to any probability, especially after noting the distorting effect of fresh encounter with the original Greek heritage during the Renaissance. To assess the real significance of Greek influence on Christianity, and so to describe justly the development which Christianity underwent, we must carry out some reflection of our own on the attitudes of the Greeks to the body and the soul.

In looking at the history of thought about death, we already had occasion to mention the turning point which lies between the archaic world of Homer, where body and person coincide, and the thought of Plato. The new view is generally held to have originated in the Orphic mystery religion, crucial for the life of the Greek spirit through the mediation of such figures as Pythagoras and Empedocles. Here it is that one comes across the separation of body and soul and the concept of the body as the soul's tomb or prison. The soul appears as the locus of the knowledge of truth while such ideas as guilt, purification and judgment play an important ancillary role.

There can be no doubt that this religious tradition was important for Plato in his attempt to rebuild the Greek polis. But at the same time, it is equally certain that the Orphic tradition remained more or less esoteric and cannot simply be identified with what is "Greek" *tout court*.[82] By origin, it was far from Greek. Moreover, Plato transformed this religious tradition philosophically, directing it to his own principal *Leitmotiv*, justice. This is especially clear in the form which little by little his doctrine of the soul took on. Plato saw a threefoldness at work in man: there is

something multiply animal-like in us with the many
heads of beasts both wild and tame; there is also something more specifically lion-like; and finally, there is
something distinctively human. The last aspect he calls
the "inner man,"[83] thus coining an expression which will
recur in the writings of St. Paul.[84] This threefold division
is a projection into the individual of the three estates of
Aryan society: priests and scholars; warriors; peasants and
merchants.[85] The human being is thus interpreted in political terms, by reference to the life of the polis. At the
same time, these three aspects of man coincide with the
three fundamental virtues: wisdom, courage, temperance.
As determinations of the individual person in his concreteness they are also related to ancient medical traditions which sought to localize the active centers of the
human totality, body together with soul. For Plato, the human task consists in drawing these three into a unity. The
result is the fourth cardinal virtue, justice. At this key
point, therefore, anthropology points once more in the direction of political philosophy from which it can indeed
hardly be separated. Simultaneously, we also become
aware that Plato knows no primordial dualism among the
powers of the human soul. His goal is, rather, the inner
unity of man, the gathering together and purification of all
our powers in "justice." His goal is to breed and ennoble
the stock of the tame animals, to hinder the development
of their savage counterparts and to make the lion in us use
his strength in the struggle for unity. Similarly, in the context of the interrelation of body and soul, Plato's supreme
aim is the "integration of dualistic elements in a unity-in-
multiplicity."[86]

Moreover, Plato consciously acknowledged the element
of mystery in all this. From the fruitful ground of this
mystery he was able to gather numerous insights for anthropology. Yet he always respected the metaphorical na-

ture of its characteristic discourse wherein the aspect of mystery is faithfully retained, since it cannot be decanted into some purely philosophical position. Typical here is the conclusion of that section of the *Phaedo* which deals with our theme: There Plato wrote:

A man of sense ought not to say, nor will I be very confident, that the description which I have given of the soul and her mansions is exactly true. But I do say that, inasmuch as the soul is shown to be immortal, he may venture to think, not improperly or unworthily, that something of the kind is true. The venture is a glorious one, and he ought to comfort himself with words like these.[87]

Accordingly, Plato time and again shifts his register of images,[88] accentuating them differently in dependence on the different occasions when they are brought into play. We cannot pursue here the complex questions which exegesis of the Platonic corpus demands. Nevertheless, certain things of importance for our investigation have already become clear. First, immortality is never a purely philosophical doctrine. It could be asserted only where a religious tradition with its own due authority entered onto the scene, was suitably acknowledged and subsequently given philosophical interpretation. In Plato, the doctrine of immortality belongs to a religious context that is at the same time a departure point for a philosophy of justice, itself, in the perspective of his political thought, his principal concern. Dualistic elements inherited from tradition are placed at the service of a positive mode of thinking whose lodestars are the cosmos and the polis, and in this way those elements lose their dualistic edge. So far as we can tell, Plato did not develop, however, a unified philosophical account of the nature of the soul both in itself and in its relation to the body. His successors thus found themselves wandering in the philosophical landscape pitted with problems. Plato left no "Hellenic schematization" just lying at the wayside for any interested passer-by to pick up.

With Aristotle, as the heritage of mythopoeic ideas is stripped away, the portrait of the soul becomes rather two-dimensional. The definition of the soul which he bequeathed is that of the soul as "entelechy" or act, that is, "substance in the sense of the form of a natural body which has life through its own potentiality."[89] The soul is understood as an organic principle, bound as form to its matter, and likewise perishable along with it. The truly spiritual element in man resides in *nous*, "mind," regarded not as something individual and personal, but as a participation of man in a divine, transcendent principle.[90] Here we find ourselves confronted with a rigorously non-dualistic unity of the human being as a body–soul composite. At the same time, we are faced with an impersonal, spiritual principle whose irradiating power includes man, without belonging to him as a person.

It has already been mentioned above that the Stoics reverted to a materialistic view of the world. For them, the soul consisted of the lightest of the elements, namely fire. As such, it is able to give life to the "mixture" of body and soul which is man. After death, it returns into the great fire, in accordance with the law whereby every element returns to its own place. Individuality has no future beyond death.[91]

Finally, let us steal a glance at that great renovator of Platonist philosophy in the third century, Plotinus. Here too we find nothing that corresponds to the current textbook schematization of "Greek thought." For Plotinus, the whole world consists of three substances: the One, the *nous*, and soul. This doctrine of three substances is simultaneously his cosmology and his theology, the Neo-Platonist "Trinity." It constitutes the essential framework of his anthropology. To the extent that the soul peers down into the recessive stream of the cosmic process it appears multiplied in the mirror of matter. The more it looks down, the more it forgets its own unity. But the more it turns back, the more it returns from the ephemeral appearances of the play of images into unity, and so into both reality and divinity. Plotinus' doctrine of three substances is at the same time, and indeed first and foremost, a spiritual doctrine which, by situating the contrasting movements of descent and ascent within man himself, bids him withdraw his being from its dissipation by looking towards unity. Plotinus calls on man to re-climb the ladder of reality whose top rests in the unitary divine origin. In that crucible the appearance of individuality simply melts away.

These few hints may suffice to show that the frequently encountered notion of a Hellenic–Platonic dualism of soul and body, with its corollary in the idea of the soul's immortality, is something of a theologian's fantasy. Certainly, there were mystery cults which held out to their initiates the promise of immortality. But some supposed universal Greek conviction of this kind is a will-o'-the-wisp. If anything, the fundamental mood of antiquity at the time when Christianity was spreading could be described as stamped by despair.

It is above all the burial inscriptions of that age which testify so vividly to the hopelessness of pagan people. Either they believed in no after-life, or they thought of it as a sepulchral shadow-existence in Hades.[92]

By way of postscript, a text from Origen of Alexandria's commentary on the Song of Songs may bring out the confusion which reigned amid the welter of opinions about the soul:

For the soul (appropriate understanding) will include a certain
self-perception, by which she ought to know how she is constituted in herself, whether her being is corporeal or incorporeal, and
whether it is simple, or consists of two, three or several elements;
also, as some would enquire, whether the substance of the soul
has been made, or has definitely not been made, by anyone; and, if
it has been made, how it was made; whether, as some opine, its
substance is contained in the bodily seed and originates together
with the first beginning of the body; or whether it is introduced
from the outside into the womb of a woman, and there united, as
a perfect thing, to the body already prepared and formed for it.
And, if this be the case, whether it comes as a new creation that
has only just been made when the body is seen to have been
formed; . . . or whether we should think that, having been created
some time earlier, it comes for some reason to assume a body. . . .
And there is the further question whether the soul puts on a body
only once and, having laid it down, seeks for it no more; or
whether, when it once has laid aside what it took, it takes it yet
again; and, if it does so a second time, whether it keeps what it
has taken always, or some day puts it off once more.[93]

(b) The New Concept of Soul

The ancients did not communicate to their successors
any clear concept of human destiny beyond the grave.
The early Church could not derive its answers from this
source. On the basis of the results our enquiry has produced so far, we can formulate with some confidence our
principal thesis on this question. The view of the afterlife,
the span of time between death and resurrection which developed in the early Church, is based on Jewish traditions
of the life of the dead in Sheol, traditions transmitted and
given christological focus by the New Testament. Any
other position than this is in conflict with the historical
facts. The doctrine of immortality in the early Church had
two sides to it. First, it was determined by the christological center, whence the indestructibility of the life gained
through faith was guaranteed. Second, it linked this theo-

logical insight to the idea of Sheol, utilizing that idea as an anthropological foundation, and in this way it found anchorage in a basic belief which is, as we have seen, of a universal human kind. This fundamental belief had certainly developed beyond the archaic, yet its anthropological implications had not been worked out in any consistent or precise manner. This explains why the early Church lacked a unified terminology in this realm. In the Jewish tradition, that being of the human person which survives death, and thus, in the Christian perspective, the bearer of existence with Christ, is most frequently called the soul or spirit. (The terms stand side by side in, for example, the Ethiopian book of Enoch.[94]) Unfortunately, both concepts were obscured by the fast spreading Gnostic systems in which *psyche*, soul, is classified as the lowest rung of human existence, by contrast with the more elevated condition of the men of spirit, the "pneumatics." The ballast thus taken aboard by these terms had its effect far beyond the ambit of those sympathetic to Gnostic thought.

Clearly, then, what the Church had to maintain was, on the one hand, the central certainty of a life with Christ that not even death can destroy, and, on the other hand, the incompleteness of that life in the time before the definitive "resurrection of the flesh." For this very reason, some clarification in the anthropological means of expression of this teaching was highly desirable. Moreover, the Christian faith itself made certain demands upon anthropology, and these demands were not met by any of the pre-existing ways of understanding what it is to be human. Nevertheless, the conceptual tools of such earlier anthropologies could and must be placed in the service of the Gospel by way of an appropriate transformation. What needed to be developed was an anthropology which in the first instance recognized that man is, in his unified totality, the creature of God, conceived and willed by him. But at the same time, this anthropology was also obliged to distinguish within man between an element that perishes and an element that abides—though in such a way that the path towards the resurrection, the definitive reunification of man and creation, remained open. In sum, the anthropology desired should weld together Plato and Aristotle precisely at the points where their doctrines were mutually opposed. There was a need to take over Aristotle's teaching on the inseparable unity of body and soul, yet without interpreting the soul as an entelechy. For, in the latter case, the soul of man would be just as much bonded to matter as is organic life at large: dependent on matter for being what it is. Instead, the special, spiritual nature of the soul had to be highlighted, without letting the soul drop into some murky ocean of an *anima mundi*. Granted the inherent difficulty of such an undertaking, it is scarcely surprising that the synthesis was so long in the making.

It found its final and definitive form only in the work of Thomas Aquinas. Following Aristotle, Thomas defines the nature of the soul by means of the formula *anima forma corporis:* the soul is the "form" of the body. But in reality, this definition embodied a complete transformation of Aristoteleanism. To Aristotle, this formula meant that the soul, just like the entelechy—the formative principle of material reality in general—is tied to matter. Matter and form for him are strict correlatives. Without "form," matter remains a mere potency, while form becomes reality only in its union with matter. If the soul is form, then it belongs to the world of bodies, marked by coming to be and passing away again. And this in turn means that the spirit, which does not belong to the world, cannot be individual or personal. Indeed, only as being neither is it immortal. Thomas' twofold affirmation that the spirit is at once something personal and also the "form" of matter would simply have been unthinkable for Aristotle. Anton Pegis, whose researches contributed greatly to a correct understanding of the relation between Thomas and Aristotle, has this to say on just this topic:

From this point of view, the Thomistic doctrine of an intellectual substance as the substantial form of matter must be seen as a moment in history when an Aristotelean formula was deliberately used to express in philosophical terms a view of man that the world and tradition of Aristoteleanism considered a metaphysical impossibility.[95]

And so we come at last to a really tremendous idea: the human spirit is so utterly one with the body that the term "form" can be used of the body and retain its proper meaning. Conversely, the form of the body is spirit, and this is what makes the human being a person.

The soul is not two things: substance, and the form of the body. Rather, is it substance *as* the form of the body, just as it is the form of the body *as* substance. . . . The separation of the soul from its body goes against its nature and diminishes its likeness to God, its Creator. Being in the body is not an activity, but the self-realisation of the soul. The body is the visibility of the soul, because the soul is the actuality of the body.[96]

What seemed philosophically impossible has thus been achieved. The apparently contradictory demands of the doctrine of creation and the christologically transformed belief in Sheol have been met. The soul belongs to the body as "form," but that which is the form of the body is still spirit. It makes man a person and opens him to immortality. Compared with all the conceptions of the soul available in antiquity, this notion of the soul is quite novel. It is a product of Christian faith, and of the exigencies of faith for human thought. Only the downright ignorance of history could find this contestable. Since this point is so central, permit me to make it again in a different way. The idea of the soul as found in Catholic liturgy and theology up to the Second Vatican Council has as little to do with antiquity as has the idea of the resurrection. It is a strictly Christian idea, and could only be formulated on the basis of Christian faith whose vision of God, the world and human nature it expresses in the realm of anthropology. For this reason the Council of Vienne in its third session (May 6, 1312) was right to defend this definition of the soul as appropriate to the faith.

We reject . . . as erroneous . . . any teaching . . . which rashly . . . doubts that the substance of the rational . . . soul is truly and essentially the form of the human body.[97]

The bull *Benedictus Deus* discussed above presupposed this anthropological clarification in its doctrine of the final vision of God. Once this insight had matured, the doctrine of Sheol had perforce to be seen in a new light. What had been meaningful before necessarily became dated and archaistic.

(c) The Dialogical Character of Immortality

It might be objected against everything that has been said up to this point that the central issue of the contemporary debate has still not been confronted. What is at stake is not the defense or rejection of a particular anthropology, a given concept of the soul. The challenge to traditional theology today lies in the negation of an autonomous, "substantial" soul with a built-in immortality, in favor of that positive view which regards God's decision and activity as the real foundation of a continuing human existence. As Paul Althaus wrote:

Whether believers or not, it is God who makes us endure. He it is who enables us to persist, through all the reality of death in which we are lost to ourselves. He makes us endure and, in resurrection, gives us back to ourselves once more so that we may stand before his judgment-seat and live.[98]

We have seen that, where the Christian concept of soul is concerned, the accusation of dualism is misplaced. Yet an objection to the soul might be raised in a somewhat different way. It might be said that, as soon as one begins to speak of a soul one renders immortality "substantialistic," grounding it upon the indivisibility of spiritual substance in a theologically inappropriate manner. It may indeed be the case that somewhat simplistic notions have gone the rounds in popular thinking. However, in none of the great theological teachers have I found a purely substantialist argument for immortality. Not even Plato argues on this basis.

Let me offer a classic example of the basic conception of both patristic and mediaeval theology, a homily by Gregory of Nyssa on the beatitudes. It is a magnificent witness to continuity with antiquity, but also to the transmutation of the thought of the ancient world. Gregory is commenting on a saying of the Lord preserved in St. Matthew's gospel: "Blessed are the pure in heart, for they shall see God."[99] Behind this beatitude, a favorite among the fathers, we can discern another saying of Jesus, this time from his high-priestly prayer: "This is eternal life, that they may know you. . . ."[100] The Greek longing for vision, the Greek awareness that vision is life—that knowledge, being wedded to the truth, is life—this mighty outreach of the Greek spirit towards the truth here finds its confirmation and final resting-place. Yet this word filled with hope and promise at first strikes man as we know him with a sense of despair, of the absurdity of his existence. Seeing God: *that* is life! But the ancient wisdom of the peoples, echoed by the Bible from the Pentateuch to Paul and John, tells us that no one can see God. He who would see God dies. Man wants to see God, for only then can he live. But his strength cannot bear such a sight.

If God be Life, then anyone who does not see God does not see life. However, the prophets and the apostle testify: no one can see God. . . .

And so the human situation may be compared with that of Peter trying to walk upon the waters of Gennesareth. He wants to get across to the Lord, but he cannot. The philosopher, we might say, is Peter on the lake, wishing to step beyond mortality and glimpse life but not succeeding, indeed sinking beneath the waves. For all his capacity to speculate about immortality, in the end he cannot stand. The waters of mortality bear down his will to see. Only the Lord's outstretched hand can save sinking Peter, that is, humankind. That hand reaches out for us in the saying, "Blessed are the pure in heart, for they shall see God." Philosophical understanding remains a walking on the waters: it yields no solid ground. Only God incarnate can draw us out of the waters by his power and hold us firm. Only he can make us stand up straight on the breakers of the sea of mortality. His promise is that we will attain the vision of God, which is life, not through speculative thinking but by the purity of an undivided heart, in the faith and love which take the Lord's hand and are led by it. Here, then, owing to a christological transformation, the Platonist notion of the life which flows from truth is rendered more profound, and made the vehicle of a "dialogical" concept of humanity: man is defined by his intercourse with God. At the same time, this new concept makes absolutely concrete claims about the things which will set us right on the path of immortality, and so changes a seemingly speculative theme into something eminently practical. The "purification" of the heart which comes about in our daily lives, through the patience which faith and its offspring, love, engender, that purification finds its mainstay in the Lord who makes the paradoxical walking on the waters a possibility and so gives meaning to an otherwise absurd existence.[101]

This quite basic conception has remained characteristic of Christian thought in the tradition, though it may be presented with a variety of different nuances. In Thomas, it is integrated into an account of the dynamic movement of all creation towards God. The *anima*, as we have seen, belongs completely to the material world, yet also goes beyond this world in going beyond itself. It is in that movement that the material world, indeed, comes into its own, by stretching forth towards God in man. In man's turning to God "all the tributaries of finite being in all its variety of level and value, return to their Source."[102] Man is conceived as a being "capable of the knowledge and love of God and called thereto."[103] In this way, the dialogical conception of humankind which emerged from the christological perspective is linked up with a resolution of the problem of matter, in terms of the dynamic unity of the entire created world. Anton Pegis put it beautifully when he described the fundamental continuity of Christian anthropological thought in these terms:

What St Augustine expressed with the help of Platonic elements was not a philosophical teaching about man. Quite directly, and first and foremost, he described a spiritual Odyssey . . . the story of the awakening of faith in a Christian man called to truth and blessedness. . . . St Thomas remained faithful to such a man. . . .[104]

(d) Immortality and Creation

Up to this point we have taken it for granted that the "substantialistic" grounding of human immortality was to be rejected out of hand. Looking more closely, however,

a problem raises its head, and we must address ourselves
to it. So far we have established that human life beyond
the grave must be understood "dialogically," which means,
in the concrete, in christological terms. But in saying as
much, have we not committed ourselves to a supernatural-
ism which, when faced with the questionings of human
beings at large is either dumb or, alternatively, finds itself
having to extend the concept of christology so far that it
becomes quite indeterminate, deprived of whatever makes
it specific? When immortality is thought of simply as
grace, or, indeed, as the special destiny of the pious, then it
takes flight into the realm of the miraculous and loses its
claim on the serious attention of thinking people. So we
must face the question of just how the understanding of
the issue we have gained up to now should be related to
the God-made being of man at large. How far is what we
are dealing with sheerly a matter of the affirmations of
faith? And how far can faith make an impression on the
rationality which all men share, and so on philosophical
reflection?

In fact, the answer to these questions is already indicated in what we have covered. Being referred to God, to
truth himself, is not, for man, some optional pleasurable
diversion for the intellect. When man is understood in
terms of the formula *anima forma corporis*, that relationship to God can be seen to express the core of his very essence. As a created being he is made for a relationship
which entails indestructibility. Teilhard de Chardin once
remarked that it is in the nature of evolution to produce
ever better eyesight. If we take up this thought, we can describe man accordingly as that stage in the creation, that
creature, then, for whom the vision of God is part and parcel of his very being. Because this is so, because man is capable of grasping truth in its most comprehensive mean-

ing, it also belongs intrinsically to his being to participate in life. We agreed earlier that it is not a relationless being oneself that makes a human being immortal, but precisely his relatedness, or capacity for relatedness, to God. We must now add that such an opening of one's existence is not a trimming, an addition to a being which really might subsist in an independent fashion. On the contrary, it constitutes what is deepest in man's being. It is nothing other than what we call "soul." We could also come at the same insight from another angle and say, A being is the more itself the more it is open, the more it is in relationship. And that in turn will lead us to realize that it is the man who makes himself open to all being, in its wholeness and in its Ground, and becomes thereby a "self," who is truly a person. Such openness is not a product of human achievement. It is given to man; man depends for it on Another. But it is given to man to be his very own possession. That is what is meant by creation, and what Thomas means when he says that immortality belongs to man by nature. The constant background here is Thomas' theology of creation: nature is only possible by virtue of a communication of the Creator's, yet such communication both establishes the creature in its own right and makes it a genuine participator in the being of the One communicated.[105]

One naturally asks, then, how it is possible for human beings to live in a fashion that goes counter to their own essence: closed off from, rather than open to, the rest of being. How can they deny, or simply fail to perceive, their relationship to God? The foregoing gives us the basis of an answer, but following up the question will help us to see the true breadth and depth of the theology of creation, as well as to identify the point where the special, novel feature of christology enters into the picture. If we recall our reflections on the theology of death, we remember that biblical thought spirals constantly around that question. Man as we know him wants to generate his own immortality. He would like to fabricate it out of his own stuff: *non omnis moriar*, not everything about me will perish. The *monumentum aere perennius*, the achievements I bequeath, these will immortalize a part of me. But in this attempt to manufacture eternity, the vessel of man must, at the last, founder. What endures after one is not oneself. Man falls headlong into the unreal, yielding up his life to unreality, to death. The intimate connection of sin and death is the content of the curse we read of in the book of Genesis:

You shall not eat of the fruit of the tree which is in the midst of the garden, neither shall you touch it, lest you die.[106]

An existence in which man tries to divinize himself, to become "like a god" in his autonomy, independence and self-sufficiency, turns into a Sheol-existence, a being in nothingness, a shadow-life on the fringe of real living. This does not mean, however, that man can cancel God's creative act or put it into reverse. The result of his sin is not pure nothingness. Like every other creature, man can only move within the ambit of creation. Just as he cannot bring forth being of himself, so neither can he hurl it back into sheer nothingness. What he can achieve in this regard is not the annulment of being, but lived self-contradiction, a self-negating possibility, namely "Sheol." The natural ordination towards the truth, towards God, which of itself excludes nothingness, still endures, even when it is denied or forgotten.

And this is where the affirmations of christology come into their own. What happened in Christ was that God overcame this self-contradiction from within—as distinct from destroying human freedom by an arbitrary act from without. The living and dying of Christ tell us that God himself descends into the pit of Sheol, that in the land of absolute loneliness he makes relationship possible, healing the blind[107] and so giving life in the midst of death. The Christian teaching on eternal life takes on, once again, a thoroughly practical character at this point. Immortality is not something we achieve. Though it is a gift inherent in creation it is not something which just happens to occur in nature. Were it so, it would be merely a *fata morgana*. Immortality rests upon a relationship in which we are given a share, but by which, in sharing it, we are claimed in turn. It points to a *praxis* of receiving, to that model for living which is the self-emptying of Jesus,[108] as opposed to the vain promise of salvation contained in the words "Ye shall be as gods," the sham of total emancipation. If the human capacity for truth and for love is the place where eternal life can break forth, then eternal life can be consciously experienced in the present. It can become the *forma corporis*, not in the sense of estranging us from the world, but, rather, in that of saving us from the anarchy of formlessness, shaping us into a truly human form instead.

(e) Summary: The Principal Features of the Christian Faith in Eternal Life

At the conclusion of our analysis of the various aspects, both historical and doctrine, of Christian faith in the life everlasting, we are in a position to attempt a description of the proper or specific physiognomy which distinguishes the Christian view from other conceptions. It may be summed up in three key phrases:

Firstly, the determinative starting point of the Christian understanding of immortality is the concept of God, and from this it draws its dialogical character. Since God is the

God of the living, and calls his creature, man, by name, this creature cannot be annihilated. In Jesus Christ, God's action in accepting humanity into his own eternal life has, so to speak, taken flesh: Christ is the tree of life whence we receive the food of immortality. Immortality cannot be accounted for in terms of the isolated individual existent and its native capacities, but only by reference to that relatedness which is constitutive of human nature. This statement about man returns us once again to our image of God, throwing light as it does so on the Christian understanding of reality at its central point. God too possesses immortality, or, more correctly, he *is* immortality, being that actuality of relationship which is Trinitarian love. God is not "atomic": he is relationship, since he is love. It is for this reason that he is life. In this perspective, the relationship of two people which is human love shines with the radiance of the eternal mystery. The signal we derive from this view of being tells us: relation makes immortal; openness, not closure, is the end in which we find our beginning.

Secondly, from belief in creation there follows the integral character of Christian hope. What is saved is the one creature, man, in the wholeness and unity of his personhood as that appears in embodied life. "Even the hairs of your head are all numbered."[109] This does not mean that nothing in man is transient. But it does mean that in the transfiguration of the transient, what takes shape is the abiding. Matter as such cannot provide the underpinning for man's continuing identity. Even during our life on earth it is changing constantly. Thus a duality distinguishing the constant from the variable factors in the make-up of man is necessary, being demanded, quite simply, by the logic of the question. Hence the indispensability of the body-soul distinction. Nevertheless, the Christian tradition, with an ever increasing consistency of purpose, which reached its climax, as we have seen, with the work of Thomas and the Council of Vienne, has conceived this duality in such a way that it is not dualistic but rather brings to light the worth and unity of the human being as a whole. Even in the continuous "wasting away" of the body, it is the whole man in his unity who moves towards eternity. It is in the life of the body that God's creature grows in maturity in expectation of seeing God's face.

Thirdly, part of the Christian idea of immortality is fellowship with other human beings. Man is not engaged in a solitary dialogue with God. He does not enter an eternity with God which belongs to him alone. The Christian dialogue with God is mediated by other human beings in a history where God speaks with men. It is expressed in the "We" form proper to the children of God. It takes place, therefore, within the "body of Christ," in that communion with the Son which makes it possible for us to call God "Father." One can take part in this dialogue only by becoming a son with the Son, and this must mean in turn by becoming one with all those others who seek the Father. Only in that reconciliation whose name is Christ is the tongue of man loosened and the dialogue which is our life's true spring initiated. In christology, then, theology and anthropology converge as two strains in a conversation, two forms of the search for love. In all human love there is an implicit appeal to eternity, even though love between two human beings can never satisfy that appeal. In Christ, God enters our search for love and its ultimate meaning, and does so in a human way. God's dialogue with us becomes truly human, since God conducts his part as man. Conversely, the dialogue of human beings with each other now becomes a vehicle for the life everlasting, since in the communion of saints it is drawn up into the dialogue of the Trinity itself. This is why the communion of saints is the locus where eternity becomes accessible for us. Eternal life does not isolate a person, but leads him out of isolation into true unity with his brothers and sisters and the whole of God's creation.

All of these statements turn in the last analysis upon the insight which holds that the place where true life is found is the risen Christ. As Heinrich Schlier has beautifully shown, Christ brings time to its completion by leading it into the moment of love. When human life is lived with Jesus it steps into the "time of Jesus": that is, into love, which transforms time and opens up eternity.[110]

One important question remains. Over against the theories sketched out in the opening section of this chapter, we were able to show that the idea of a resurrection taking place in the moment of death is not well-founded, either in logic or in the Bible. We saw that the Church's own form of the doctrine of immortality was developed in a consistent manner from the resources of the biblical heritage, and is indispensable on grounds of both tradition and philosophy. But that leaves the other side of the question still unanswered: what, then, about the resurrection of the dead? Is there such a thing as resurrection understood as a material event? Is there something of this kind which is genuinely an *event*, which resists transposition into the timelessness of eternity, but is to be connected with the end of history instead. Is it asking too much of thought to make it cope with such ideas? Would it not be wiser to look for ways to render them redundant? Such questions make us realize that, despite their contrary starting points, the modern theories we have met seek to avoid not so much the immortality of the soul as the resurrection, now as always the real scandal to the intellectuals. To this extent, modern theology is closer to the Greeks than it cares to recognize.

In attempting to face these problems we move into what is, from a methodological viewpoint, a new field. So far, in dealing with the questions of death and resurrection we have been moving in an area where fundamental anthropological experience and insight are a great support, even if purely human knowledge is no adequate yardstick there. We found that, at any rate to some extent, we could extrapolate from the present life to the existence if not the character of the life to come. Yet the content of eternal life, its *Was* as distinct from its *Dass*, lies completely outside the scope of our experience, being quite simply unknowable from our perspective. And so, in the concluding chapter of this book, as we reflect on the hints which divine revelation offers about this *Was*, in its fundamental possibilities, we must be alert to the limitations of what we can say. The tradition of the faith is not given to us for the satisfying of idle curiosity. Where it exceeds the proper limits of human experience, its aim is to *direct* us, not to *divert*, that is, to entertain us. This is why it opens up what lies beyond only to the extent that this will be a helpful signpost for those in the here and now. We must bear this in mind as we turn now to the final theme of eschatology.

Part Three

The Future Life

VI

The Resurrection of the Dead and the Return of Christ

I. WHAT DOES "THE RESURRECTION OF THE DEAD" MEAN?

(a) The State of the Question

At the end of the last chapter, we approached the question of the resurrection by counterposing the ideas of "resurrection" and "immortality." In that context, it became clear that the point of departure for the more recent theological developments lay in an abrupt rejection of "immortality," combined with a passionate plea for "resurrection." However, we also saw that, as the discussion unfolded, the content of the idea of "resurrection" suddenly shifted. Resurrection was stripped of time, and was relocated at the moment of death. Such elimination of time necessarily implied the elimination of matter, since it is obvious that in the moment of death a human being does not rise bodily. We criticized the new approach on the basis of these internal contradictions, and rehabilitated a genuinely Christian concept of immortality from the resources provided by tradition.

So now, the other side of the question, hitherto lingering in the background, must at last be taken up. What is the resurrection? On the foundation of our reflections up to this point, this still very general question can find more focused expression in two very concrete problems. First of all, Is there such a thing as the end of time? Beyond the "being with Christ" which awaits the believer after death, should one posit something more? This is the paramount question: Must faith assert that there will be an end to history, to history *comme tel* and as a whole, a truly "Last Day"? And secondly, does the resurrection have anything to do with matter? Does faith expect a transformation of matter, and thus something very like corporeality in the risen state?

The contemporary positions which we encountered in the previous section answer both of these questions with a resounding "No." In a comprehensive study, A. Vögtle tried to show, with an impressive panoply of scholarship, that the New Testament teaches nothing about the future of the cosmos.

It cannot be demonstrated that so much as one of the texts relevant in this context means to offer a prediction of a didactic kind about the future destiny of the universe. It cannot even be shown to be probable. Nor can it be argued that Jesus himself, or the bearers of the primitive Christian proclamation, believed that the Christ-event would effect change in the future state of the universe. . . . The New Testament makes no claim to offer a didactic statement about the cosmological dimension in the proper sense of that phrase.[1]

Two questions arise here. First, what is the "cosmological dimension in the proper sense of that phrase"? Secondly, when is a statement "didactic" and when not? Both questions depend on systematic presuppositions and so cannot be answered by any purely historical, exegetical analysis. On closer inspection, then, it transpires that Vögtle has succeeded in demonstrating only one conclusion: given a certain concept of what constitutes a "didactic state-

ment," there is in the New Testament an absence of statements which correspond to this concept. For such a result
to be of any historical or doctrinal use, Vögtle would first
have to clarify how he arrived at this concept of "didactic
statements." Moreover, he would also have to satisfy us
that he was justified in applying it as a criterion in the case
of the literary forms of the New Testament writings. Since
he has not done either of these things, his enquiry rests on
the superimposition of historical and systematic categories whose own methodological foundation is distinctly
murky. This is not to deny, however, that much of the
book's detailed discussion is valuable. One tentative conclusion we might draw from the argument as a whole is
that New Testament images should not be interpreted in a
naively direct fashion as objective statements. Between
the linguistic schema and the objective intention there is
a difference—something we had occasion to look at fairly
thoroughly in connection with the idea of imminent expectation of the End. Vögtle's book is valid insofar as it
points to this difference, without which his systematizing
analysis would surely have found no foothold in the texts.
However, his apodeictic negation of the presence of "cosmological" statements in the New Testament goes beyond
the limits which a sound methodology would quite properly set. This is all the more so given that he does not ask
himself what the terms "cosmological" and "eschatological" mean.

The point which Vögtle tries to make on grounds of exegesis is really the same as that formulated before him by
Greshake writing as a systematic theologian. Three characteristic texts from the latter's study of resurrection may
serve to bring out this identity:

Matter 'as such' (as atom, molecule, organism . . .) cannot be perfected. Matter's only meaning and goal is to be the ecstatic aspect

of man's free action. Accordingly, it reaches perfection only as what makes that action concrete.[2]

If we understand that resurrection of the body which happens in death in terms of God's life-giving faithfulness to a *concrete* existence which has reached, in death, its definitive condition, then we may say that a 'piece' of the world, of history, has been gathered up into that concreteness. . . . When a hitherto unimaginable future of new life in communion with Christ opens up before us, then what is fulfilled is not just an 'individual subjectivity' but also the very history of the world.[3]

If one regards perfection as an infinite, dynamic process of transition from 'this' aeon to another, then one does not need to postulate an End.[4]

(b) The Tradition

i. *The New Testament.* What, then, has tradition to say on this issue? In order to involve as few of our own presuppositions as possible in the answer to this question, we shall do well to approach it in a simple and modest manner. The inner logic of the texts themselves suggests two promising starting points. We have already seen that the New Testament as a whole, in consonance with the Jewish world of belief in the period, yet transforming the inherited faith by a christological revolution, maintained that there is an "intermediate" state of being with Christ, something to be expected immediately after death as a continuation of life with Christ. We can ask, therefore, Are there any indications that this intermediate state is itself the resurrection? Or, by way of contrast, is the resurrection distinguished from that state as a further stage, as yet unrealized and so the proper object of fresh expectation? We must also ask whether there exist explicit statements about bodiliness in the risen state, statements which are not simply linguistic devices lingering on from traditional eschatological discourse, but are consciously formulated in a novel way on the basis of the Christian reality.

The second question necessarily draws our attention to First Corinthians 15, 35–53. In that text, Paul faced an opponent who had attempted a *reductio ad absurdum* of resurrection faith by asking, "How are the dead raised? With what kind of body do they come?"[5] In dealing with this question of the bodily character of the resurrection, Paul transposes the experience of the new corporeality of the risen Lord into an understanding of the resurrection of all the dead.[6] And this means that Paul was decidedly opposed to the prevailing Jewish view whereby the risen body was completely identical with the earthly body and the world of the resurrection simply a continuation of the world of the present. Such ideas were utterly shattered by encounter with the risen Lord who in his total otherness had withdrawn himself from earthly perception and knowledge, being emancipated from subjection to the laws of matter and yet visible after the manner of theophany—in his appearing from out of the world of God.

I tell you this, brethren: flesh and blood cannot inherit the kingdom of God, nor does the perishable inherit the imperishable.[7]

Here all naturalistic or physicalistic ideas of the resurrection are set aside. At a stroke, all speculation about how the perishable might become imperishable is rendered superfluous. According to Paul, this is precisely what will *not* happen. Yet Paul's unconditional rejection of the naturalistic approach does not stop him from continuing to speak of the resurrection of the body, different though this is from the resuscitation of corpses as the world would conceive it. For Paul, the rejection of naturalism does not mean abandoning the resurrection but illuminating it. To his mind, body exists not only in the Adamic mode of the

ensouled body but also in the christological mode prefigured in the resurrection of Jesus, a corporeality stemming from the Holy Spirit. In other words, what Paul opposes to a physicalist realism is not spiritualism but a
pneumatic realism. In this dialectical quality, Paul's text
reminds one not only of the accounts of the Lord's resurrection in all the gospels, but also of the inner tension
which characterizes the Eucharistic Discourse in the gospel of John. Any spiritualistic evaporation of faith, Church,
sacrament is countered by the hard realism of the affirmation that

my flesh is food indeed, and my blood is drink indeed. He who
eats my flesh and drinks my blood abides in me, and I in him.[8]

On the other hand, a purely naturalistic understanding of
the risen Lord and his presence in the Church's Liturgy is
ruled out by the abrupt statement, seemingly cancelling
outright what has gone before but in reality teaching one
to grasp it in its true meaning, "It is the spirit that gives
life; the flesh is of no avail."[9] It is within this tension that
the novel and distinctive realism of the risen Lord becomes apparent beyond all naturalism and spiritualism
alike.

Will the New Testament yield any further, and more
concrete, kind of enlightenment about the nature of the
risen body? One might be inclined to infer from Second
Corinthians 5, 1 that, for Paul, our risen body is even now
waiting in heaven, being, so to speak, already prepared in
the body of Christ. Such an idea would seem to enjoy
some support from Ephesians 2, 6, where the resurrection
and ascension of the Christ are described as an event
which has already taken place. Colossians 3, 1–3 moves
in the same direction, for that letter's exhortation that
believers should set their minds on the things above is

grounded in the statement that their true life already exists in a hidden form with Christ, whereas their earthly life has really already died, lying behind them like a cast-off garment. Because the authentic life of believers lies, in its authenticity, outside them, they must live excentrically, finding the true self elsewhere than in its empirical counterpart. However, these texts are not clear enough to offer any certainty in advancing additional statements over and above what is contained in First Corinthians 15. They underscore the newness of the risen life which comes from above, not from below. They stress the christological character of that life. But they offer no theory about the relation between Christ's body and the risen bodies of believers.

One must be very cautious when using biblical data in systematic theology. The questions which we ask are *our* questions. Our answers must be capable of holding up in biblical terms, but it would be false to treat them as exegetical conclusions because the way we have decided in their favor is that appropriate to systematic thought. This complicating factor in the theological appropriation of Scripture is in any case something demanded by the structure of the Bible's own affirmations. As in the case of the topic of immortality, what the New Testament offers to reflection is a beginning, not an end. Through christology, it gives a new focus to both of these questions. Yet this new center is itself in search of suitable anthropological means of expression. The Bible itself forbids biblicism.

It is clear that neither Paul nor John identify the resurrection with that current existence with Christ which they ascribe to the dead. Despite this immediate hope, and over against all the *aporiai* of human speculation, they emphatically assert the resurrection in its bodiliness, thus excluding such a solution. But where the materiality of such a resurrection is concerned, nearly everything remains open. That the resurrection state is quite different from our present conditions of life is resoundingly affirmed. What, in more actual terms, such anti-spiritualist pneumatic realism may mean is less immediately obvious. And yet the claim that the whole of God's creation, in whatever form, will enter upon its definitive salvation at the end of time is so palpable that any reflective systematization of the biblical data must do it justice.[10]

ii. *The Clarification of the Formula "The Resurrection of the Flesh" in the First Three Centuries.* The first phase in the theological appropriation of the apostolic heritage in the early Church can be traced by following the early history of the resurrection formula in the Western creed. That creed does not speak of the "resurrection of the dead," but of the "resurrection of the flesh." G. Kretschmar has shown that this formula was taken over, in quite serene fashion, from Judaism.[11] It is attested, for example, in the Apocalypse of Moses, composed as that was before the destruction of the temple, and is likewise found in the Greek translation of Job 19, 26 as used in the *Prima Clementis.*[12] We meet it in Tertullian, where it appears as an aspect of the tradition handed down in the Roman see, and indeed can trace its fortunes there from Hippolytus to the Apostles' (or 'Old Roman') Creed. Thanks to its Jewish roots, this phrase indicates the salvation of the human creature, or of creation, in its entirety. However, since no explicit distinction had yet been made between man's being a creature and his being embodied, there could at this stage be no direct or express answer to the question of whether the resurrection of the human creature necessarily extended to his bodiliness. In the controversies which marked the life of the early Church, this Jewish usage, taken over thus unquestioningly, came up against the new meaning which the word "flesh" acquired in

Paul. Using his own conceptuality, Paul had insisted that "flesh and blood cannot inherit the kingdom of God."[13] In this way early Christian debate turned into a wrestling match between Pauline and Johannine terminology, an altercation over the concrete content of Christian realism.

Typical of this battle about the scope and limits of the apostolic teaching are two "Gnostic" texts which show a remarkable resemblance to modern positions. The Valentinian gospel of Philip, originating in the Egypt of the second or third centuries, is an interesting attempt to harmonize the biblical claims with ideas favored by the dominant rationality of the period. The text does not deny the resurrection of the flesh, yet interprets it in such a way that its scandal disappears.

The one who is risen is indeed not 'naked'. However, he no longer bears his own flesh, but the flesh of Christ.[14]

Here resurrection faith is reduced to its strictly christological component. The resurrection of Christ is already our own resurrection. In logion 23 of the gospel of Philip the flesh and blood of Christ, which alone will be our only "clothing" and which should fully justify the expression "resurrection of the flesh," are identified with the Logos and the Holy Spirit.[15] Only this "flesh" is the abode of salvation, all other flesh being excluded therefrom by appeal to First Corinthians 15, 50. Thus not only is pneumatic realism reduced to christology, but the span of christology itself is narrowed to that of a Logos- and Pneuma-christology. What this might imply becomes clearer from another Valentinian source, the second century Letter of Rheginos. On the basis of the Corinthian text just cited, together with Colossians 3, 1ff., the writer claims that we have already ascended with Christ into the heavens. The resurrection is now.

Valentinus exhorts the reader of his letter to 'look at himself as already risen. . .': i.e. the resurrection 'in the flesh' is a new self-understanding.[16]

This surprising development is argued for in Valentinus not just on the basis of Scripture but by reference to systematic considerations: it is supported by appeal to the timelessness which reigns once we leave the sphere of historical change. Since the truth lies beyond history, that is, since the definitive reality which awaits us on the far side of death is timeless, the resurrection must be understood as ever-present there. To the extent that we understand both ourselves and reality aright, we transcend the flux of historical becoming and participate in that true present, in the already realized resurrection. By selecting a particular catena of biblical texts and combining it with a philosophy of time and eternity, the Valentinians were able to preserve the formula "the resurrection of the flesh" and yet spiritualize totally the Christian hope.

It seems to me highly significant that the early Church did not accept this offer of a synthesis that would reconcile to perfection the requirements of Greek thought and the scandalous language of a fleshly resurrection. By contrast, we find in the treatise *De Resurrectione*—probably the work of Justin Martyr—this glorious sentence:

If the gospel of salvation is proclaimed to humanity, then salvation is also proclaimed to the flesh.[17]

Similarly, Irenaeus unhesitatingly rejects the view that after death there takes place an immediate ascension to heaven.[18] Again, Justin makes splendid use of First Corinthians 15, 50, placing that controversial text in a completely new context:

Paul wished to say that whatever corresponds to the flesh is death. The flesh has nothing else to hope for: least of all, the kingdom of God. For in this process of inheritance, God's Kingdom is always a subject, never an object. The kingdom of God is life, and this life also inherits the body, the flesh.[19]

So it is not the mortal which does the inheriting. Rather, by a paradox of God's mighty mercy, is it inherited instead. As Justin puts it, "Life now takes the mortal as its inheritance."[20] Like Irenaeus, he finds the deepest ground of necessity for this fact in the earthly activity of Jesus as God incarnate, an earthly activity directed precisely towards the suffering flesh of mankind. But Jesus' activity and indeed very being are due on their part to the fact that no part of God's creation is too insignificant to be made perfect.

Those who lay the charge against the flesh that it has come from the dust of the earth, and forces the soul into sin do not know the 'whole working of God'.[21]

The Church's rejection of Valentinus resulted from her conviction that God is faithful to his *whole* creation. In the healing activity of Jesus, this faithfulness was made known as a fidelity not least towards the body, towards this earth which God has made.

Let us try to formulate a conclusion from this somewhat taxing analysis of the earliest development of our faith in these matters. At the end of the subapostolic period it had become clear that "the resurrection of the flesh" can mean that resurrection of the creature only if it also means the resurrection of the body. The apparent biblicism of Valentinus turned out to be the narrowing down of faith to a handful of Pauline passages which, yanked into a new context, offered leverage to those who wanted to spiritualize the Christian hope. The real content of Paul's teaching had to be defended on the basis of John and the Synoptics. An experiment in what seemed to be radical Paulinism led to the conclusion that, where "all flesh" is misunderstood as the creature minus his corporeality, the realism intended by the apostle cannot stand. It also became manifest that the removal of corporeality brought into question the continued significance of temporal existence, leaving in the end nothing more exciting than a new "self-understanding." Once a deliberate enquiry into the scope of the word "flesh" is undertaken, "body" cannot be excluded, even if it is not the primary meaning of "flesh." Kretschmar tried to relativize the value of his conclusions by claiming that the position of Justin and Irenaeus was inseparable from their chiliasm. But T. H. C. van Eijk has convincingly shown that this claim is false.[22] The clarification of the theological mind which the debate with Valentinus produced in the Church of the second and third centuries was founded on nothing other than the exclusion of *a priori* speculative construction in the interests of maintaining the inner logic of the New Testament itself. The difficulties which the New Testament presented were resolved by reading it consistently as a whole. The "philosophy," if one may call it that, of these Church writers consisted in their confidence that the entire Bible constitutes a unity and in their practice of an exegesis which let itself be guided by this conviction.

iii. *The Debate About the Risen Body in the History of Theology.* After people had reached a modicum of clarity on the point that the resurrection of the flesh must include that of the body in some form as yet undetermined, the next question they naturally asked was, What is a risen body? A first attempt at an answer, though its exact bearing is disputed, was offered by Origen. Origen distinguished between two principles within the body. On the one hand, there is matter, in continuous flux and failing to retain its full identity from one day to the next. On the other hand, there is the persisting form in which the individual gives himself permanent expression. The identity of the risen body cannot possibly lie in what in any case is ever-changing. It must, then, be sought in the "form" or "character" which a human being displays.[23] These somewhat indeterminate statements were systematized—rather naively so—in the Origenist school. For that school, what counts is not the preservation of the former body or its mimetic re-creation but rather the continuation of the essential factor within it. The final state our bodies will attain will not be based upon the caprice of earthly circumstance. We shall have "essential" bodies, "ideal" bodies. Here we see Greek minds accepting that embodiment is definitive, albeit in ideal form. The result was the conversion of the question about the risen body into the mathematical conundrum of the ideal form of the body, identified as that of the sphere.

The mind of the Church resisted this solution so typical of Scholastic procedures with their combination of intellectual acuteness and the sheerly obtuse. It found that the humanity of man had its identity erased in such a mathematically constructed ideal world. It felt that the meaning of faith in the resurrection had been misunderstood. The results that came from this reaction were those granite formulations on the self-identity of the earthly and risen body in the various creeds we cited above in 5. iii. In retrospect, these formulae are quite a textbook case in the hermeneutics of dogma. They give us a clear view of the inescapable task which the Church's magisterium had to carry out under the pressure of, quite simply, faith itself. The magisterium had to protect a human resurrection over against a mathematical one. But in formulating this defense it had no appropriate conceptual tools of expression to hand, because reflection had itself been led down the wrong path. So it could only express itself in the language of a naive sensualism which was incapable of counting as the last word on the subject. Something rather similar happened in the early Middle Ages during the controversy about the presence of Christ in the Eucharistic species. The Church held to a Eucharistic realism, yet thought had not found a way between spiritualism on the one hand and naturalism on the other. Thus the Church's confession of faith was obliged to adopt naturalism in order to remain realistic. The only permanent element in this solution was the intention to maintain "realism." Granted that these two themes, Eucharistic realism and the realism of resurrection faith, are intimately connected, indeed scarcely intelligible except in terms of each other, it comes as no surprise that the decisive step towards a solution of each of the two dilemmas was found in the same context of thought.

The crucial factor in reaching this solution was the entry of Aristotle into Christian thinking during the course of the thirteenth century. The Platonic heritage, in many ways so useful for taking up the intellectual challenge of the biblical message, had led to the dilemma between spiritualism and naturalism just described. Of itself, it was unable to clear a path through the thicket. With the help of Aristotle, however, a non-sensualist realism could be formulated and in this way a philosophical counterpart to the pneumatic realism of the Bible could be found. The decisive step was the new understanding of the soul which Thomas Aquinas achieved through his daring transformation of the Aristotelean anthropology. We saw above that the picture of the soul which developed in definitive fashion from Christianity implied at the same time a new view of the body. In Thomas' interpretation of the formula *anima forma corporis*, both soul and body are realities only thanks to each other and as oriented towards each other. Though they are not identical, they are nevertheless one; and as one, they constitute the single human being. As both expression and being-expressed they make up a dual unity of a quite special kind. For our purposes, this insight carries with it a twofold consequence of a remarkable sort. First, the soul can never completely leave behind its relationship with matter. Greshake's idea that the soul receives matter into itself as an "ecstatic aspect" of the realization of its freedom, while leaving it for ever to the clutches of the necessarily imperfectible precisely in its quality as matter, would be unthinkable for Thomas. If it belongs to the very essence of the soul to be the form of the body then its ordination to matter is inescapable. The only way to destroy this ordering would be to dissolve the soul itself. What is thus emerging is an anthropological logic which shows the resurrection to be a postulate of human existence. Secondly, the material elements from out of which human physiology is constructed receive their character of being "body" only in virtue of being organized and formed by the expressive power of soul. Distinguishing between "physiological unit" and "bodiliness" now becomes possible. This is what Origen was getting at with his idea of the characteristic form, but the conceptual tools at his disposal did not allow him to formulate it. The individual atoms and molecules do not as such add up to the human being. The identity of the living body does not depend upon them, but upon the fact that matter is drawn into the soul's power of expression. Just as the soul is defined in terms of matter, so the living body is wholly defined by reference to the soul. The soul builds itself a living body, a self-identical living body, as its corporeal expression. And since the living body belongs so inseparably to the being of man, the identity of that body is defined not in terms of matter but in terms of soul.

In Thomas, these insights find their determinate expression through the Aristotelian understanding of prime matter and the role of form connected with this. Matter which does not belong with some form is *materia prima*, pure potency. Only in virtue of form does this *materia prima* become matter in the physical sense. If the soul be the only form of the body, then the ending of this form-relationship by death implies the return of matter to a condition of pure potency. This reversion should not, of course, be thought of as occupying a distinct moment in time: we are making an assertion in ontology. In point of fact, the place occupied by the old form is at once taken over by a new one, so that physical matter remains as it was. However, since this physical matter is now actualized by a different form, it is something fundamentally different from that which existed before when the soul was the form in question. Between the living body and the corpse there lies the chasm of prime matter. Consistently maintained, therefore, the Thomistic teaching cannot preserve the self-identity of the body before and after death.

This might seem to be an advantage in the case of the question of resurrection. Yet it has anthropological and ontological consequences which are strange, to say the least. For this reason, Aquinas' new anthropology, summed up in the formula *anima unica forma corporis*, called forth stiff opposition and ecclesiastical condemnations. At the philosophical level, it denied the identity of the corpse of Jesus with him who was crucified. Incidentally, if the body derives its identity in no way from matter but entirely from the soul, which is not passed on by a man's parents, there would also be another problem here concerned with conception, with the genuineness of parenthood.[24] This was why Thomas himself held back from embracing the consequences of his own theory and, in the question of the resurrection, fenced it in with additional considerations meant to supply for its deficiencies. Only Durandus of Saint-Pourçain (c. 1275–1334) dared to accept all the consequences entailed in Aquinas' starting point, basing the identity of the risen body exclusively upon the identity of the soul. His remained a somewhat isolated voice in the mediaeval period. During the nineteenth century, the thesis was taken up again by such men as Laforêt, Hettinger and Schell. In the twentieth century it was adopted by Billot, Michel, and Feuling. In its original shape, the Aristotelian concept of matter and form underlying Durandus' thesis is no longer conceivable to us: the simple repristinization of a thoroughgoing Thomism is not the way we seek. The synthesis which Thomas formulated with such brilliance in the conditions of his century must be re-created in the present, in such a way that the authentic concerns of the great doctor are preserved. Thomas does not offer a recipe which can just be copied out time and again without further ado; nevertheless, his central idea remains as a signpost for us to follow. That idea consists in the notion of the unity of body and soul, a unity founded on the creative act and implying at once the abiding ordination of the soul to matter and the derivation of the identity of the body not from matter but from the person, the soul. The physiology becomes truly "body" through the heart of the personality. Bodiliness is something other than a summation of corpuscles. At this point, then, where historical discussion points on beyond itself to a systematic treatment of the subject, let us interrupt our reflections in order to deal with two interrelated questions of systematic theology: the end of time and the "materiality" of the resurrection.

(c) What Is "Resurrection on the Last Day"?

It goes counter to the logic of both Scripture and tradition to locate the resurrection in the moment of the individual's death. So much has become clear. Let us remind ourselves once more of the main reason for this. An eternity with a beginning is no eternity at all. Someone who has lived during a definite period of time, and died at a definite point in time, cannot simply move across from the condition "time" into the condition "eternity," timelessness. Nor is recourse to the mediaeval concept of *aevum*, as suggested by Lohfink, a real solution, though it helps to clarify the issue. The idea of *aevum* was developed in order to throw light on the mode of existence of angels, of pure spirits, not that of man. In death, man no more becomes an angel than he becomes a God. Remaining human as he does, concepts which express the being of an angel or of God himself do not suit him. If there is to be any progress here, we must gain a profounder grasp of anthropology, and not take refuge in ontological constructions suitable only for nonhuman modes of being. In other words, we must ask how time belongs to man precisely as man, and so whether it is possible to find here a starting point for conceiving a human mode of existence beyond that which depends on physical conditions of possibility. Pursuing this question, we will find that "temporality" pertains to man on different levels, and so in different ways.

Most valuable in such an analysis is Book X of the *Confessions* where Augustine traverses the varied landscape of his own being and comes across *memoria*, "memory." In memory, he finds past, present and future gathered into one in a pecular way which, on the one hand, offers some idea of what God's eternity might be like, and, on the other, indicates the special manner in which man both is bound to time and transcends time. In these reflections, Augustine comes to realize that memory alone brings about that curious reality we call the "present." This it does, compass-like, by cutting out the circumference of a circle from the continuous flux of things, and demarcating it as "today." Naturally, the present of different people differs, in dependence on the extent of that which consciousness presents as present. Yet in memory, the past is present, albeit in a diverse manner from the presence of that which we take to be "the present." It is a *praesens de praeterito:* the past, present *in its quality as past.* And something similar is true of the *praesens de futuro.*

What does this analysis tell us? It tells us that man, insofar as he is body, shares in physical time measured as that is in terms of the velocity of moving bodies by parameters which are themselves in motion and thus also relative. Man, however, is not only body. He is also spirit. Because these two aspects inhere inseparably in man, his belonging to the bodily world affects the manner of his spiritual activity. Nevertheless, that activity cannot be analyzed exclusively in terms of physical data. Man's participation in the world of bodies shapes the time of his conscious awareness, yet in his spiritual activities he is temporal in a different, and deeper, way than that of physical bodies. Even in the biological sphere, there is a temporality which is not mere physical temporality. The "time" of a tree, expressed in the yearly rings of its trunk, is the manifestation of its specific life cycle, and not a mere unit of rotation around the sun. In human consciousness, the various levels of time are at once assumed and transcended, rendering that consciousness temporal in a way all its own. Time is not just a physical quality ascribed to man but wholly external to him. Time characterizes man in his humanity, which itself is temporal inasmuch as it is human. Man is temporal as a traveller along the way of knowing and loving, of decaying and maturing. His specific temporality also derives from his relationality—from the fact that he becomes himself only in being with others and being towards others. Entering upon love, or indeed refusing love, binds one to another person and so to the temporality of that person, his "before" and "after." The fabric of shared humanity is a fabric of shared temporality.

These fragmentary philosophical reflections may suffice to formulate a conclusion which is quite decisive for our question: a human being lives in time not just physically but anthropologically. Following Augustine's lead, let us call this human time "*memoria*-time." This *memoria*-time is shaped by man's relation to the corporeal world, but it is not wholly tied to that world nor can it be dissolved into it. This means that, when a human being steps out of the world of *bios*, *memoria*-time separates itself from physical time, yet, though left sheerly to its own devices does not for all that become eternity. Herein lies the reason for the definitiveness of what we have done in this life, as well as for the possibility of a purification and fulfilment in a final destiny which will relate us to matter in a new way. It is a precondition for the intelligibility of the resurrection as a fresh possibility for man, indeed as a necessity to be expected for him.

But this puts us in possession of a further insight. When we die, we step beyond history. In a preliminary fashion, history is concluded—for me. But this does not mean that we lose our relation to history: the network of human relationality belongs to human nature itself. History would be deprived of its seriousness if resurrection occurred at the moment of death. If the resurrection occurs in death then, fundamentally, history is indeed in one sense at an end. Yet the continuing reality of history and thus the temporal character of life after death is of quite basic importance for the Christian concept of God as we find that expressed in christology: in God's care for time in the midst of time. Origen has the finest statement of this that I have been able to find:

The Lord spoke to Aaron: 'Wine and intoxicating liquor you shall not drink, you and your sons with you, when you draw near the tent of the covenant or approach the altar'. . . . Now our Lord and Saviour is called by Paul 'the high-priest of the blessings to come'. He himself is thus 'Aaron' and his 'sons' are the apostles. . . . Let us see how we can apply this to our Lord Jesus Christ . . . and to his priests and sons, our apostles. We must first note that this true high-priest, *pontifex*, with his assistant priests, *sacerdotes*, before they 'approach the altar', do drink wine. However, when he begins to 'approach the altar' and enter the tent of the covenant, he abstains from wine. . . . Before he sacrificed, during the time of the earthly economy, *inter dispensationum moras*, he drank wine. But when the moment of the cross drew nigh, and he was about to 'approach the altar' where he would offer the sacrifice of his flesh, 'he took', we read, 'the cup', blessed it, and gave it to his disciples, saying, 'Take this, all of you, and drink from it'. You, he says, may still drink, you who will not in a little while 'approach the altar'. But he, as one who now does 'approach the altar', said, 'Amen, I say to you, I will not drink from the fruit of this vine until I drink it with you in the Kingdom of my Father'.

If someone there is among you who draws near with purified hearing, let him understand an unspeakable mystery. What does it mean when he says, 'I will not drink. . . .?'. My Saviour grieves even now about my sins. My Saviour cannot rejoice as long as I remain in perversion. Why cannot he do this? Because he himself is 'an intercessor for our sins with the Father'. . . . How can he, who is an intercessor for my sins, drink the 'wine' of joy, when I grieve him with my sins? How can he, who 'approaches the altar' in order to atone for me a sinner, be joyful when the sadness of sin rises up to him ceaselessly? 'With you', he says, 'I will drink in the Kingdom of my Father'. As long as we do not act in such a way that we can mount up to the Kingdom, he cannot drink alone that wine which he promised to drink with us. . . . He who 'took our wounds upon himself' and suffered for our sakes as a healer of souls and bodies: should he regard no longer the festering wounds? Thus it is that he waits until we should be converted, in order that we may follow in his footsteps and he rejoice 'with us' and 'drink wine with us in the Kingdom of his Father'. . . . We are the ones who delay his joy by our negligence toward our own lives. . . .

But let us not ignore the fact that it is said not only of Aaron that 'he drank no wine', but also of his sons when they approach the sanctuary. For the apostles too have not yet received their joy: they likewise are waiting for me to participate in their joy. So it is that the saints who depart from here do not immediately receive the full reward of their merits, but wait for us, even if we delay, even if we remain sluggish. They cannot know perfect joy as long as they grieve over our transgressions and weep for our sins. Perhaps you will not believe me on this point . . . but I will bring a witness whom you cannot doubt, the 'teacher of the nations' . . . , the apostle Paul. In writing to the Hebrews, after enumerating all the holy fathers who were justified by faith, he adds, 'These, all of whom received the testimony of faith, did not attain the promise, because God had provided for something better for us, so that they should not be made perfect without us'. Do you see, then? Abraham is still waiting to attain perfection. Isaac and Jacob and all the prophets are waiting for us in order to attain the perfect blessedness together with us. This is the reason why judgment is kept a secret, being postponed until the Last Day. It is 'one body' which is waiting for justification, 'one body' which rises for judgment. 'Though there are many members, yet there is only one body. The eye cannot say to the hand, I do not need you'. Even if the eye is sound and fit for seeing, if the other members were lacking, what would the joy of the eye be?

You will have joy when you depart from this life if you are a saint. But your joy will be complete only when no member of your body is lacking to you. For you too will wait, just as you are awaited. But if you, who are a member, do not have perfect joy as long as a member is missing, how much more must our Lord and Saviour, who is the head and origin of this body, consider it an incomplete joy if he is still lacking certain of his members? . . . Thus he does not want to receive his perfect glory without you: that means, not without his people which is 'his body' and 'his members'. . . .[25]

One can certainly accuse this text of utilizing "mythological" expression. And equally certainly, one can argue that it is also formed by ideas about the intermediate state which the new anthropological insights of the high Middle Ages will later correct. But these undeniable limitations do not cancel out the deep human and theological truth on which it is built. This truth consists, first and foremost, in the indestructible relation which it posits between human life and history. The incarnation of God brings this truth onto a deeper plane where it becomes the theological assertion that in the man Jesus God has bound himself permanently to human history. Of course one cannot speak with any strict appropriateness about this relationship: in a certain sense, one's language must be "mythological." Still, one can speak in such a way that a number of anthropological truths that are not myths come to light.

In trying to do just that, we find that relationship to history can be seen from either of two sides and so in two contrary ways. First, we can ask whether a human being can be said to have reached his fulfilment and destiny so long as others suffer on account of him, so long as the guilt whose source he is persists on earth and brings pain to other people. In its own way, the doctrine of karma in Hindu and Buddhist teaching systematized this fundamental human insight, though it also coarsened it.[26] Nevertheless, it expresses an awareness which an anthropology of relationship would be wrong to deny. The guilt which goes on because of me is a part of me. Reaching as it does deep into me, it is part of my permanent abandoment to time, whereby human beings really do continue to suffer on my account and which, therefore, still affects me. Incidentally, this enables us to grasp the inner connection between the dogmas of Mary's freedom from sin and assumption into Heaven. Mary is fully in the Father's house, since no guilt came forth from her to make people suffer, working itself out unremittingly in that "passion narrative" which tells of the sting of death in this world.

What Origen says about the waiting Christ also obliges us, however, to look at the matter from the opposite perspective. It is not only the guilt we leave behind on earth that prevents our definitive reclining at table for the eschatological banquet, in joy unalloyed. The love that overcomes guilt has the same effect. Whereas guilt is bondage to time, the freedom of love, conversely, is openness for time. The nature of love is always to be "for" someone. Love cannot, then, close itself against others or be without them so long as time, and with it suffering, is real. No one has formulated this insight more finely than Thérèse of Lisieux with her idea of heaven as the showering down of love towards all. But even in ordinary human terms we can say, How could a mother be completely and unreservedly happy so long as one of her children is suffering? And here we can point once again to Buddhism, with its idea of the Bodhisattva, who refuses to enter Nirvana so long as one human being remains in hell. By such waiting, he empties hell, accepting the salvation which is his due only when hell has become uninhabited. Behind this impressive notion of Asian religiosity, the Christian sees the true Bodhisattva, Christ, in whom Asia's dream became true. The dream is fulfilled in the God who descended from heaven into hell, because a heaven above an earth which is hell would be no heaven at all. Christology entails the real relation of God's world to history, even though that relationship takes different forms for God and for man. Nevertheless, as long as history really continues, it remains a reality, even from a vantage point beyond death, and therefore to declare that history is already cancelled and lifted up into an eternal Last Day after death is impossible. Greshake's attempt to reconcile an endlessly continuing history with the hope for Christ's return runs aground on the rocks of such insights. For him, Christ's victory need not be a true end. It can be realized in a dynamic, unlimited succession. . . . Understood in this way, continuing history is both open—its future undetermined, fluid— and yet in God's sight it is the steady procession of a triumphal march.[27]

Such a triumphal march of God would surely have something cruel about it, for it would be in despite of humanity. The God whom we come to know in Christ's cross is different. For him, history is so real that it leads him down to Sheol, so real that heaven can be really and truly heaven only when it forms the canopy of a new earth.

In principle, these insights have decided our answers to the remaining questions which can, therefore, be dealt with briefly. First, on the basis we have established, the true content of the doctrine of Purgatory becomes clear. So does the meaning of the distinction between "heaven" and the final perfecting of the world, and thus between personal judgment and the general judgment. "Purgatory" means still unresolved guilt, a suffering which continues to radiate out because of guilt. Purgatory means, then, suffering to the end what one has left behind on earth—in the certainty of being definitively accepted, yet having to bear the infinite burden of the withdrawn presence of the Beloved. "Heaven," in the period of the postponement of the definitive banquet, in the absence of final perfection, means being drawn into the fulness of divine joy, a joy which infinitely fulfils and supports and which, incapable as it is of being lost, is in its pure fulness ultimate fulfilment. This joy is also the certainty of realized justice and love, the overcoming of suffering with all its question marks, not just one's own suffering but that which persists on earth. All of this is conquered in the visible Love which is almighty and so can do away with every injustice. Proleptically, in anticipation, this Love, the God who has suffered, has become the final victor over all evil. In this sense, truly, heaven already exists. Yet on the other hand, we have also to reckon with the openness of this fulfilled Love for history. History is still real, it really continues and its reality is suffering. Even though, in God's Love made visible, suffering has been overcome by anticipation and the outcome is already certain, such that all anxieties are borne away and all questions have their response, nevertheless, the fulness of salvation is not yet realized so long as that salvation is only certain by anticipation in God, falling short of even so much as one person who still suffers.

Given, therefore, the real interdependence of all men and all creation, it turns out that the end of history is not for any man something extrinsic, something which has ceased to concern him. The doctrine of the body of Christ simply formulates with that final consistency that christology makes possible a truth which was quite predictable on the basis of anthropology alone. Every human being exists in himself and outside himself: everyone exists simultaneously in other people. What happens in one individual has an effect upon the whole of humanity, and what happens in humanity happens in the individual. "The Body of Christ" means that all human beings are one organism, the destiny of the whole the proper destiny of each. True enough, the decisive outcome of each person's life is settled in death, at the close of their earthly activity. Thus everyone is judged and reaches his definitive destiny after death. But his final place in the whole can be determined only when the total organism is complete, when the *passio* and *actio* of history have come to their end. And so the gathering together of the whole will be an act that leaves no person unaffected. Only at that juncture can the definitive general judgment take place, judging each man in terms of the whole and giving him that just place which he can receive only in conjunction with all the rest.

(d) The Risen Body

We left the question of the materiality of the resurrection at the point to which Thomas Aquinas had brought it. The fundamental insight to which Thomas broke through was given a new twist by Rahner when he noted that in death the soul becomes not acosmic but all-cosmic.[28] This means that its essential ordination to the material world remains, not in the mode of giving form to an organism as its entelechy, but in that of an ordering to this world as such and as a whole. It is not difficult to connect up this thought to ideas formulated by Teilhard de Chardin. For it might be said in this regard that relation to the cosmos is necessarily also relation to the temporality of the universe. The universe, matter, is as such conditioned by time. It is a process of becoming. This temporality of the universe, which knows being only in the form of becoming, has a certain direction, disclosed in the gradual construction of "biosphere" and "noosphere" from out of physical building blocks which it then proceeds to transcend. Above all, it is a progress to ever more complex unities. This is why it calls for a total complexity: a unity which will embrace all previously existing unities. From the cosmic standpoint, the appearance of each individual spirit in the world of matter is an aspect of this history in which the complex unity of matter and spirit is formed. For, significantly enough, the exigence for unity found in matter is fulfilled precisely by the nonmaterial, by spirit. Spirit is not, then, the splintering of unity into a duality. It is that qualitatively new power of unification absolutely necessary to what is disintegrated and disunited if ever it is to be one.

The "Last Day," the "end of the world," the "resurrection of the flesh," would then be figures for the completion of this process, a completion which, once again, can happen only from the outside, through the entry onto the scene of something qualitatively new and different, yet a completion which corresponds to the innermost "drift" of cosmic being. This would mean that the search of being for unity in its own becoming arrives at its goal, a goal which it cannot create from its own resources yet one which it ever strives for. The search reaches the point of integration of all in all, where each thing becomes completely itself precisely by being completely in the other. In such integration, matter belongs to spirit in a wholly new and different way, and spirit is utterly one with matter. The pancosmic existence which death opens up would lead, then, to universal exchange and openness, and so to the overcoming of all alienation. Only where creation realizes such unity can it be true that "God is all in all."[29]

And this in turn means that the detailed particularities of the world of the resurrection are beyond our conceiving. First Corinthians 15, 50 and John 6, 63 bar the doors against such misconceived ventures, and to the extent that Greshake opposes such "physicist" conceptual games one can only agree with him.[30] We cannot play them, we need not play them and indeed, we ought not to try. What remains over and above all images is, however, this truth: an everlasting, unrelated and therefore static juxtaposition of the material and spiritual worlds contradicts the essential meaning of history, the creation of God and the word of Scripture. This is why, without any dishonor to Greshake's valuable study, one must reject his statement that "Matter as such . . cannot be perfected."[31] Despite all assurances to the contrary, this would imply a division of the creation and to that degree a definitive dualism in which the entire sphere of matter is removed from the goal of creation and reduced to the level of a secondary reality. It is strange that Christians, who in the Creed confess the resurrection of the flesh, should in this regard lag behind Marxist thinkers like Bloch and Marcuse who certainly do expect from a new world a new condition of matter. For them, this expectation follows on from the insight that historical alienation can only be overcome in such a way. In Marxist thought, such an assertion remains an anthropological postulate[32] which undergoes development in the logical order. The trouble is that the conditions of its realization are not logical, and so compel one to adopt either an alogical politics of destruction or a posture of total resignation. Such a postulate can certainly be offered by anthropology but its fulfilment cannot be conceived on the foundation of its own axioms alone. If it so happens that anthropology gives us the challenge to strive for a new world, natural science can hardly forbid our doing so. Although science cannot bring such a new world within our ken, its discourse does nothing to support the static alternative. The world which the scientist observes is the theatre of a strange conflict. On the one hand, it is a world engaged in self-consumption according to the entropy principle, a world moving towards a lukewarm nothingness. On the other hand, it is a world in steady ascent towards ever more complex unities. The question of where this movement, with its dilemma of decay or plenitude, will end up cannot be answered from within natural science, though more speaks for decay than for plenitude. Fresh evidence is required of a kind that can only come from without. The Christian message expects at one and the same time both decay—in conformity with the way of the cosmos itself, and plenitude—in the new power coming from without, namely, Christ. Of course, faith does not see in Christ something simply external, but the proper origin of all created being which, therefore, while coming "from without" can fulfil what in the cosmos is most deeply "within."

In conclusion: the new world cannot be imagined. Nothing concrete or imaginable can be said about the relation of man to matter in the new world, or about the "risen body." Yet we have the certainty that the dynamism of the cosmos leads towards a goal, a situation in which matter and spirit will belong to each other in a new and definitive fashion. This certainty remains the concrete content of the confession of the resurrection of the flesh even today, and perhaps we should add: especially today.

2. THE RETURN OF CHRIST AND THE FINAL JUDGMENT

(a) The Biblical Data

i. *The Signs of Christ's Return.* The question of the relation of Christ's coming to time as we know it is mirrored in the question of the signs of the End. Deriving from the analogous problematic of Jewish apocalyptic, this issue has arisen again and again in Christianity since the time of the first disciples. A cursory reading of the New Testament gives the impression that two distinct positions competed with each other. On the one hand, there is the resolute rejection of all asking for signs. Christ's coming is quite incommensurable with historical time and its immanent laws of development, so it cannot in any way be calculated from the evidence of history. In so calculating, man works with history's inner logic, and thereby misses Christ, who is not the product of evolution or a dialectical stage in the processive self-expression of reason, but the Other, who throws open the portals of time and death from the outside. In itself, the Parousia has no date. The only answer to the request for "signs" and to every attempt to make Christ's coming a matter of empirical description is the rejection of the question itself and its replacement by the challenge: "What I say to you, I say to all, Be watchful!."[33] The human attitude which corresponds appropriately to the relation of the risen Lord to the time of the world is not the working out of a philosophy or theology of history but rather "watchfulness."

However, a fairly substantial component of tradition seems to be opposed to this perspective, asserting quite distinctly that there *are* signs which announce Christ's coming. Jean Daniélou saw in this contrast of positions the continuation of two Old Testament lines of hope. On the one hand, the Old Testament seeks a human Messiah. On the other hand, it also expects a direct transformation of history through God's very own and absolutely direct intervention. According to Daniélou, the divine–human mystery of Jesus as defined by the Council of Chalcedon permits us to understand the inner unity of these two lines and the particular justification of each. In Jesus Christ, God acts as God, immediately, in a divine fashion. But in Jesus Christ, God also acts as man, mediately, through the mediation of history. As Daniélou puts it in terminology made available by the Greek language, Christ is at once the *telos*, the "end" or "goal" of history, and its *peras*, its "boundary" or "limit." Daniélou means that Christ is the fulfilment, *telos*, of all reality, and so cannot be measured against the continuous time of this world and of history, as well as being the chronological end, *peras*, of historical time. Christ's coming is thus at one and the same time a pure act of God without precedent in history and which no periodization of history can attain, *and also* the liberation of man, a liberation not achieved by man, yet not achieved without him either. And in this latter respect, while the Parousia does not permit of being calculated, it does allow the possibility of signs.[34]

This is a most compelling view which is extremely il-

luminating for the internal unity of christology and eschatology. Its implications become clearer when one takes
a closer look at the signs of the End actually mentioned in
the New Testament. In Mark 13, among the signs which
herald the End we find the appearing of false Messiahs,[35]
wars world-wide,[36] earthquakes and famine,[37] the persecution of Christians,[38] and the "abomination of desolation in
the holy place"[39]—something which, from the sentence
construction involved and the allusions to the book of
Daniel,[40] should probably be understood as a person, a personal subject of an act of desecrating the sanctuary. A positive precondition of the End is also mentioned: the proclamation of the Gospel to all peoples.[41] After this come
images of cosmic catastrophe,[42] but as these belong to the
delineation of the moment of the Parousia itself, we shall
deal with them separately later.

Elsewhere in the New Testament, some of these signs
take on greater concrete content. Most notably, the figure of the antichrist moves into the foreground: anony-
mously, in the first place, in Second Thessalonians 2,
3–10. To understand this apocalyptic figure of the "law-
less man,"[43] we should note that Paul sketches in his character with the aid of two Old Testament texts, Daniel 11,
36 and Ezekiel 28, 2. The first of these two texts describes
the great persecutor of the Jewish faith in the Hellenistic
period, Antiochus Epiphanes. The second offers a pen-
portrait of the legendary Prince of Tyre who committed
hubris and fell through pride. The fact that the future
antichrist is thus described with features which originally belonged to two other figures from the distant past
naturally deprives him of any very well defined uniqueness. It situates the antichrist of the End within a series
where a long line of predecessors have already nursed the
evil that comes to its supreme intensity in him. The same

tendency is even more apparent in I John 2, 18–22 and II John 7 where the actual term "antichrist" at last surfaces. In both of these texts, christological heretics contemporary with the writer are called "antichrist," leading to the conclusion that the "final hour" is now. In truth, however, this "hour" loses thereby its chronological content, becoming the expression for a certain spiritual condition, a certain inner closeness to the End. The book of the Apocalypse offers a comparable perspective. Inner correspondence to the condition of being "antichrist" is there imaged in the two beasts, one rising out of the sea and the other from the earth.[44] Here too the antichrist is envisaged very concretely, in terms of contemporary history. The beasts are identified with the self-deifying Roman state, as embodied in the "divine" emperor and the priesthood associated with him. Linked with the idea of antichrist is a sharper accenting of the motif of persecution: an emphasis, this, which reaches its climax in the Apocalypse. Reference might also be made here to the themes of Gospel proclamation and the universal efficacy of Christ's saving work, which received their supreme deepening in Paul's struggle with the theological reality of Israel. Through that deepening, Paul was able to announce the definitive salvation of Israel as following on the completed formation of the Church of the Gentiles. In the history of interpretation, chapters nine to eleven of the Letter to the Romans were held to require the conversion of Israel to Christ within historical time as a necessary preliminary before the ending of that time.

Is the upshot of such affirmations the "chronologizing" of the End? Has the End turned into a calculable event which just happens to take place at a very advanced point in the temporal process? Or is the balance of the Chalcedonian mystery, as described by Daniélou, in fact preserved, that balance whereby the eschatological event has its human component, and therefore its historical preconditions, yet does not for all that cease to be something "wholly other" in relation to history, to which one can only respond through "watchfulness": openness for the wholly other God? Analyzing somewhat more closely the individual signs of the End, one discovers an answer which displays with great clarity the inner unity of these two aspects of New Testament thought. The first, and more obvious, group of signs can be summed up as war, catastrophe and the persecution of faith by the "world." Two points here call for special attention. First, what prepares the transition to the End is not some consummate ripeness of the historical process. Paradoxically, it is the inner decadence of history, its incapacity for God and resistance to him, which point to the divine "Yes." Secondly, even a cursory glance at the actual reality of every century suggests that such "signs" indicate a permanent condition of this world. The world has always been torn apart by wars and catastrophes, and nothing allows one to hope that, for example, "peace research" will manage to erase this watermark of all humanity. But precisely for this very reason, every generation could feel addressed by these signs and apply them to their own age. Thus Gregory the Great could speak in the sixth century of an aging world:

Nation rises against nation, and we see their distress across the face of the earth—more so in our own time than what we read of in the codices. You are aware that we often hear from other parts of the world how earthquakes undermine countless cities. Plagues we suffer without cease. True, we hardly see openly as yet signs in the sun, the moon and the stars, but that we are not so far away from them we can appreciate from the change in the atmosphere that is already detectible.[45]

And one could also apply the same principle in a converse direction and say with Paul:

When people say "There is peace and security," then sudden destruction will come upon them as travail comes upon a woman with child, and there will be no escape.[46]

What seems to be an extremely ancient text from the Gospel of Luke carries a similar message:

As it was in the days of Noah, so will it be in the days of the Son of man. They ate, they drank, they married, they were given in marriage, until the day when Noah entered the ark, and the flood came and destroyed them all. Likewise as it was in the days of Lot—they ate, they drank, they bought, they sold, they planted, they built, but on the day when Lot went out from Sodom fire and brimstone rained from heaven and destroyed them all—so will it be on the day when the Son of man is revealed.[47]

The signs, at any rate as we have considered them so far, do not permit a dating of the End. They do indeed relate the End to history—but by compelling every age to practise watchfulness. They indicate that the time of the End is ever present, for the world never ceases to touch that "wholly other" which, on one occasion, will also put an end to the world as *chronos.*

This fundamental pattern is maintained by the other signs mentioned above. Even in his own age, Paul believed that he had in fact offered the Gospel to the whole inhabited world. The demand that the Gospel should be preached to all the world seemed thus already fulfilled in the generation of the apostles, what the Markan Jesus calls "this generation."[48] Nevertheless, that demand remains at the same time an uncompleted task so long as there are human beings left on this earth. As far as the antichrist is concerned, we have seen that in the New Testament he always assumes the lineaments of contemporary history. He cannot be restricted to any single individual. One and the same, he wears many masks in each generation. Gerhoh of Reichersberg, who lived from 1093 (or 1094) to 1169, was right to regard the antichrist as a sort of Church-historical principle which

is rendered concrete not in one but in many figures. . . . In radical fashion, he sweeps away the traditional image: this image, he insists, must be understood allegorically, not in some literal historical way. What 'the antichrist' means is grasped philologically: everyone who is *Christo Filio Dei contrarius* deserves this name. . . . In other words, anyone who destroys *ordo* and furthers *confusio* is an antichrist.[49]

Although the pessimistic Augustinian provost may have overstepped the mark in this final conclusion, he was basically correct in his theory that the antichrist is one only in the multiplicity of his historical appearances, each of which threatens in its own way the period in which it occurs.

The overall thrust of these signs disqualifies any interpretation of the conversion of Israel after the coming-in of the fulness of the Gentiles, announced by Paul in Romans,[50] as an empirical event which would allow a simple calculation of the date of the End. Paul himself did not count Israel's conversion among the "signs." Yet he described it in prophetic terms, from the heart of his own faith in salvation, as a reality belonging to the very center of the christological mystery.[51] This inevitably rules out any attempt at an empirical explanation which would denature prophecy by turning it into empty speculation. Here we see, finally, that the two distinct lines of expectation that belong to the Jewish hope have merged together through christology. In the man Jesus, God comes at one and the same time in a human and in a divine way. His coming transcends the logic of history, yet concerns all history. Human activity carries on with its own kind of objectivity,[52] but a new dimension is opened up pertinent to human existence and thus to all the world. The divine coming compels man to adopt an attitude of watchful readiness which looks out for the Parousia of Jesus and thus prevents history from falling into a self-enclosure which would condemn human existence to meaningless-ness and purposelessness.

In an interview which forms a kind of last will and tes-tament, Martin Heidegger remarked that, in the face of the situation into which humankind has blundered, only a god could save us. Our one possibility, he considered, was "to prepare the way for the readiness to receive the appear-ing of the god." In this dictum of a post-Christian pagan, there is a genuine insight into the depths of our subject. The "readiness to expect" is itself transforming. The world is different, depending on whether it awakens to this readiness or refuses it. Readiness, in its turn, is differ-ent, depending on whether it waits before a void or goes forth to meet the One whom it encounters in his signs such that, precisely amid the ruin of its own possibilities, it becomes certain of his closeness.

ii. *The Return of Christ.* Of its nature, the return of the Lord can be described only in images. The New Testament drew its imaginative material in this connection from Old Testament descriptions of the Day of Yahweh, themselves a treasury of ancient forms from the history of religion. Other material was added by way of borrowing from the cultus of civil society (the motif of the ruler's epiphany, for example),[53] and from the Liturgy. In this fashion, the day of Yahweh took on concrete shape as the day of Jesus Christ. At the same time, the all-encompassing nature of the rule of Christ was stressed, in opposition to the cosmic and universal claims of political power: practically speaking, of the Roman empire. Christ is not the cultic deity of some private religious association, but the true *imperator* of all the world. On this basis, we can offer a faithful evaluation of the language of cosmic symbolism in the New Testament. This language is liturgical language because the imperial liturgy of the Roman polity expressed itself in cosmic symbols. For that liturgy, the emperor is, as the tradition of the Ancient Near East would have it, a cosmic figure. He is the *cosmocrator*, the summit of the world and its point of contact with the divinity.[54] The Old Testament Liturgy also spoke and thought in cosmic terms. One of the key phrases of eschatological imagery is the "cry," mentioned in, for instance, Matthew's parable of the ten maidens at the marriage-feast.[55] This belonged not only to the civil cultus in the *polis* but also to the Liturgy of the Old Testament, where, along with the "trumpet-blast," it played a decisive role at the New Year or New Moon festival of Rosh Hashonoh.[56] Thus the evocation of the Parousia draws simultaneously on the ruler's epiphany and the Liturgy of the New Year celebrations. In this two-fold way, Christ is shown here as the One who overturns the ancient powers of this world. His breaking-in on the world is the arrival of the true *imperator*. His coming means the collapse of the "elements" of the world,[57] elements which "constituted the material for the venerable feasts of new moon and new year."[58] It signifies, then, the beginning of the new "year" of God, the eternal wedding-feast which he celebrates with his own.

This analysis allows us to draw two conclusions. The cosmic imagery of the New Testament cannot be used as a source for the description of a future chain of cosmic events. All attempts of this kind are misplaced. Instead, these texts form part of a description of the mystery of the Parousia in the language of liturgical tradition. The New

Testament conceals and reveals the unspeakable coming of Christ, using language borrowed from that sphere which is graciously enabled to express in this world the point of contact with God. The Parousia is the highest intensification and fulfilment of the Liturgy. And the Liturgy is Parousia, a Parousia-like event taking place in our midst. This helps us to realize that whereas in the Liturgy the Church appears to be engaged in self-contemplation, in reality she enters into the heart of the world, and works actively for the latter's liberating transformation. Just as one must not misinterpret the liturgical symbols as naturalistic description, so also one must not eliminate the truth-claims about the cosmos that they carry. Such claims are not rococo ornamentation, but belong to the heart of the matter.

And so light falls on a further aspect: the interweaving of present and future which constitutes the specific mode of Christianity's presence in the world and its openness to what is to come. The dethronement of the world elements, the fading of sun, moon and stars, has already taken place,[59] and yet it is still to come. The trumpet of the Word is already summoning us, and yet it is still to be sounded. Every Eucharist is Parousia, the Lord's coming, and yet the Eucharist is even more truly the tensed yearning that he would reveal his hidden Glory. That deepening of the idea of the Parousia achieved in the Fourth Gospel is not, therefore, when compared with the Synoptic tradition, something different and strange. Rather does it clarify the relation of the Parousia to the worldly time, something only lightly sketched in the Synoptics. It would take a careful analysis of the concepts of "going" and "coming" in the Farewell Discourse to display the idea of the Parousia in that mature form which was reached at the close of the New Testament development and passed on from there to the Church. Such an analysis would go beyond the scope of this book. We can simply note here that "going," related to the Cross, and "coming," related to the Resurrection, interpenetrate in an inward way. As the Crucified, Jesus continues to be the One who goes away. As the Pierced One with the outstretched arms he continually comes. For the loving person who keeps his commandments, his coming occurs as an "eschatological event" in the midst of the world.[60] In touching the risen Jesus, the Church makes contact with the Parousia of the Lord. She prays and lives, so to speak, into that Parousia whose disclosure will be the definitive revelation and fulfilment of the mystery of Easter.[61]

Seen in this perspective, the theme of the Parousia ceases to be a speculation about the unknown. It becomes an interpretation of the Liturgy and the Christian life in their intimate connection as in their continual going beyond themselves. The motif of the Parousia becomes the obligation to live the Liturgy as a feast of hope-filled presence directed towards Christ, the universal ruler. In this way, it must become the origin and focus of the love in which the Lord can take up his dwelling. In his Cross, the Lord has preceded us so as to prepare for us a place in the house of the Father.[62] In the Liturgy the Church should, as it were, in following him, prepare for him a dwelling in the world. The theme of watchfulness thus penetrates to the point where it takes on the character of a mission: to let the Liturgy be real, until that time when the Lord himself gives to it that final reality which meanwhile can be sought only in image.

iii. *The Judgment.* As with the return of Christ, so the judgment escapes our attempts at conceptualization. The best way to get hold of the central meaning of the doctrine is to ask, Who, according to biblical tradition, is the one who judges? At first glance, there seem to be a number of answers. To begin with, God himself is called judge.[63] But then so is Christ.[64] Finally, in Matthew 19, 28, the Twelve are told that "in the new world" they will sit on thrones and judge the twelve tribes of Israel. The same statement appears in more extended form in First Corinthians.

Do you not know that the saints will judge the world? . . . Do you not know that we are to judge angels? How much more, matters pertaining to this life![65]

In St. John, judgment is located in our present life, our present history. Even now, in our decision as between faith and nonfaith, judgment falls.[66] Naturally, this does not simply wipe out the final judgment. Rather, is that judgment brought into a new relationship with christology. Of Christ it is said:

. . . God sent the Son into the world, not to condemn the world, but that the world might be saved through him.[67]

With this we may compare:

. . . I did not come to judge the world but to save the world.[68]

And:

He who rejects me and does not receive my sayings has a judge; the word that I have spoken will be his judge on the last day.[69]

The distinction made here between Christ's own action and the effects of his word makes possible a final purification of both christology and the concept of God. Christ inflicts pure perdition on no one. In himself he is sheer salvation. Anyone who is with him has entered the space of deliverance and salvation. Perdition is not imposed by him, but comes to be wherever a person distances himself from Christ. It comes about whenever someone remains enclosed within himself. Christ's word, the bearer of the offer of salvation, then lays bare the fact that the person who is lost has himself drawn the dividing line and separated himself from salvation.

Behind the apparent diversity of ideas, patient investigation can discern a unified fundamental perspective. In death, a human being emerges into the light of full reality and truth. He takes up that place which is truly his by right. The masquerade of living with its constant retreat behind posturings and fictions, is now over. Man is what he is in truth. Judgment consists in this removal of the mask in death. The judgment is simply the manifestation of the truth. Not that this truth is something impersonal. God is truth; the truth is God; it is personal. There can be a truth which is judging, definitive, only if there is a truth with a divine character. God is judge inasmuch as he is truth itself. Yet God is the truth for us as the One who became man, becoming in that moment the measure for man. And so God is the criterion of truth for us in and through Christ. Herein lies that redemptive transformation of the idea of judgment which Christian faith brought about. The truth which judges man has itself set out to save him. It has created a new truth for man. In love, it has taken man's place and, in this vicarious action, has given man a truth of a special kind, the truth of being loved by truth.

This christological development of the idea of judgment came about, as by an inner necessity, from the primitive Christian linkage of faith in God and confession of Christ. From that development there follow quite logically further extensions of this basic New Testament notion. If judgment is transformed by christology, then the eschatological boundary is crossed not just in death but well before that, in the act of faith itself. A point we have touched on in the context of the theology of death has application in a new way in the question of the judgment. We said that the true frontier between life and death does not lie in biological dying, but in the distinction between being with the One who is life and the isolation which refuses such "being-with." We need not consider here the case of someone who through no fault of his own was unable to hear the word of Christ, and for whom such being-with may consist simply in Heidegger's "prepared readiness," the self-opening gesture of looking out in expectation. We can rightly conclude that in the final analysis man becomes his own judgment. Christ does not allot damnation. Instead, man sets limits to salvation.

Lastly, we must bear in mind that Christ is not alone. The whole meaning of his earthly life lay in his building for himself a body, in his creating for himself a "fulness." Since Christ's body truly belongs to him, encounter with Christ takes place in encounter with those who are Christ's, because they are his body. And so our destiny, our truth, if it is really constituted theologically, christologically, depends upon our relation to Christ's body and notably to its suffering members. To this extent, the "saints" are our judge. In reflecting on the nature of the Last Day (VI. a. iii.), we saw that, viewed from this angle, there is a significant interrelation between individual and general judgment. Even though the definitive truth of an individual is fixed in the moment of death, something new is contributed when the world's guilt has been suffered through to the bitter end. It is at this point that one's final place in the whole is exhaustively determined: after what one might call the solidification in their finished state of all the effects to which one has given rise. Thus the completion of the whole is not something purely external to the individual, but a reality which determines him or her in the most interior way.

It is in this context that, by way of coda, we must reflect

on the so-called "hypothesis of a final decision," as developed first by P. Glorieux and subsequently elaborated in impressive style by L. Boros. The latter formulated it in these words:

In death, the first fully personal human act becomes possible. And so death is the ontologically privileged place of emergence into consciousness, of freedom, of meeting with God, and of a decision about eternal destiny.[70]

In all probability, the dominant motive behind the development of this thesis was the sense that the fragile, and often and in many ways shadowy freedom we know during earthly life is too feeble and limited to support the weight of an everlasting and irreversible destiny. The starting point from which Glorieux approached this idea was, in point of fact, his observation that, in various crucial places, Thomas Aquinas cited a statement of John Damascene to the effect that "what the fall of the Angels meant to them, that death means to man." Aquinas, then, seems to compare human dying to that situation in which the Angels made their all-important decision.[71] Looming up in the background, therefore, is the notion that only angelic freedom would really suffice to bear responsibility for an eternal destiny. And this is where the problematic element in the thesis lies. In the last resort, it wishes to turn man into an Angel, thus secretly considering the human condition less than acceptable. One must add, too, the criticism that both empirical indications of the truth of the thesis and convincing support for it in theological tradition are lacking. Naturally, such counterargument does not in itself abolish the important question, which lay behind the original argumentation. Is it not true that, for a judgment which is to hold throughout eternity, a different freedom would be required from that which we exercise elsewhere? Admittedly, the traditional view thought overmuch in terms of one particular moment in time. The truth of a man that judgment renders definitive is that truth which has emerged as the fundamental orientation of his existence in all the pathways of his life. In terms of the sum total of decision from out of which an entire life is constructed, this final direction may be, in the end, a fumbling after readiness for God, valid no matter what wrong turnings have been taken by and by. Or again, it may be a decision to reject God, reaching down into the deepest roots of the self. But this is something that only God can determine. He knows the shadows of our freedom better than we do ourselves. But he also knows of our divine call, and unlimited possibilities. Because he knows what human weakness is, he himself became salvation as truth, yet without stripping himself of the dignity that belongs to truth.

(b) Theological Evaluation

Can the Christian hope as described above still be meaningful in the world of today? This question is all the more pressing in that for us, by contrast with our ancestors, history is not something pre-given which takes its own course in an inexorable manner. To all appearances, history has become something we can direct. We are ourselves its determining subject. History seems no longer something decreed by God or imposed by fate, but simply the result of our rational planning, through a practical reason which enjoys a manifest power over this earth. Planning has taken the place of providence, and this is all the more true in that history has now really become world history in which all partial histories have merged into the single, indivisible history of a mankind which must carry responsibility for itself. In an age when man had perforce to see the course of events as the work of higher powers, it was appropriate for him both to live in hopeful expectation of their good will and with concern to obtain it. But under present conditions this looks like a perilous and irresponsible anachronism. The shift from hope grounded on faith to a strategy of hope certified by careful theoretical calculation thus stands out as the only proper attitude.

To do justice to reality, we must make one or two distinctions here. A sphere of proper human responsibility for historical decision-making has always existed. It is simply that, in the modern period, the dimensions of that sphere have been extended, in keeping with the accelerating growth of human knowledge and power. The statement, "If anyone will not work, let him not eat,"[72] must be understood today in terms of that concept of work which is valid in a technological age. Faith does not substitute for rationality, but rather requires it. But to introduce into the necessary planning of present and future the idea that such planning might bring about the world's salvation is an abuse of rationality, and a darkening of rational counsel.

This is true in both of two senses. First, the planning of the human present and future can never be achieved by technical knowledge alone, since that knowledge specifies not goals but simply possibilities. The more central human values escape the purview of its method. Technical planning has to receive its direction by reference to values which of itself it cannot provide. Where everything is planned, humanity is sold down the river. Man does not live from bread alone: that is, as applied to our situation, man does not live from technical planning alone. In his deepest interiority, he lives by a discovery of meaning which issues from a different kind of perceiving. There is also a second limit on planning to set beside this first. The

probing of the future by human planners can never anticipate the fresh concepts and insights of a new generation.
Essentially, it cannot go beyond the experienced present of
the planners themselves. Its antennae reach the immediate present and the middle term but not the more distant
future. Human power extends so far and no further.

Taken together, these two aspects indicate the limits to
man's activity as maker. The most basic rationale of this
limit has only been touched on, however, in what we have
said so far. To grasp it, we must glance, however cavalierly,
at the historical foundations of the current strategies of
hope. The expectation of a wholly just world is by no
means a product of technological thought. It is rooted,
rather, in Judaeo-Christian spirituality. Over against the
despair that in all epochs present suffering and injustice
occasioned, other cultures defended themselves by invoking such ideas as those of the eternal return or liberation
in Nirvana. The contrasting idea of a definitive future salvation, while not exclusively restricted to the Judaeo-
Christian sphere, received its most powerful and penetrating formulation there.

The marked intra-worldly character which this idea assumed in the Old Testament led in early Christian times
to the supplementing of the transcendent hope for the
Kingdom of God by the notion of chiliasm: a thousand-
year-long reign of Christ and those who are first to rise
with him.[73] The question of the earthly realization of
the promise which this notion suggested became a burning issue for Western Christianity through the work of
Joachim of Fiore—whom we met at the outset of this
book. Joachim was convinced that God's plan for his human creatures could triumph only if it also succeeded on
earth. It seemed to follow, then, that the time of the
Church, as men have experienced it since the apostles,

cannot be the definitive form of salvation. Joachim transformed the earlier periodization of history, which reflected
the seven days of the week, into the idea of a multiplicand:
history contains three times seven days. This he did by
linking the venerable inherited schema with the doctrine
of the Trinity. In this way, it appeared to be possible to cal-
culate the third "week" of history, the time of the Holy
Spirit. The immanence of this third age created the obligation to work towards it: something Joachim tried to do
through his monastic foundations. The mingling of rational planning with suprarational goals, already observable
in the Old Testament and in Judaism, now receives systematic form. It will soon slough off the spiritual dreams
of Abbot Joachim and emerge into the political history of
Europe, where it will take the form of messianism through
planning. Such planned messianism became ever more
fascinating as the potential of planning waxed and religion
waned, though continuing, inevitably, to form human motives and hopes. Hegel's logic of history and Marx's historical scheme are the end products of these beginnings.
Those messianic goals in which Marxism's fascination
lies rest upon a faulty underlying synthesis of religion and
reason. For planning is now directed to goals which are
quite disproportionate to planning methods. And so both
the goal and the planning suffer shipwreck.

As early as the patristic Church, steps were taken to
eliminate chiliasm through an effort to preserve biblical
tradition in its proper form. The Joachimist dispute filled
the thirteenth century and, in part, the fourteenth also,
ending with a renewed rejection of this particular form of
hope for the future. The present-day theologies of liberation belong in this context. But just why did the Church
reject that chiliasm which would allow one to take up the
practical task of realizing on earth parousia-like condi-

tions? The rejection of chiliasm meant that the Church repudiated the idea of a definitive intra-historical fulfilment, an inner, intrinsic perfectibility of history. The Christian hope knows no idea of an inner fulfilment of history. On the contrary, it affirms the impossibility of an inner fulfilment of the world. This is, indeed, the common content shared by the various fragmentary pictures of the end of the world offered us by Scripture. The biblical representation of the End rejects the expectation of a definitive state of salvation within history. This position is also rationally correct, since the idea of a definitive intra-historical fulfilment fails to take into account the permanent openness of history and of human freedom, for which failure is always a possibility. In the last resort, such neo-chiliasm expresses a profound anthropological perversion. Human salvation is not to be expected from the moral dignity of man, from the deepest level of his moral personality. Rather we are to set our hopes for it on planning mechanisms, marginal to the authentically human though these may be. The values which sustain the world are turned upside down. A planned salvation would be the salvation proper to a concentration camp and so the end of humanity.

Faith in Christ's return is, therefore, in the first place, the rejection of an intra-historical perfectibility of the world. Precisely in this negative aspect, it is also the preservation of humanity against those who would dehumanize man. Of course, if this thesis—which in itself is, in any case, rationally evident—were to stand alone, then the last word would be with a posture of resigned acquiescence. And so, over and above this preliminary statement, we must add that faith in Christ's return is also the certitude that the world will, indeed, come to its perfection, not through rational planning but through that indestructible love which triumphed in the risen Christ. Faith in

Christ's return is faith that, in the end, truth will judge and love will conquer. Naturally, this victory is won only when we take a step beyond history as we know it, a step further for which history itself yearns. The historical process can only by perfected beyond itself. It is where this insight is accepted, where history is lived in the direction of its own self-transcendence, that in each and every case the process of history is thrown open to its fulfilment. Thereby, reason receives its due place, and the duty to act according to measure. Simultaneously, hope also enters into its proper realm, and is not exhausted on the laboratory counter.

The world's salvation rests on the transcending of the world in its worldly aspect. The risen Christ constitutes the living certainty that this process of the world's self-transcendence, without which the world remains absurd, does not lead into the void. The Easter Jesus is our certainty that history can be lived in a positive way, and that our finite and feeble rational activity has a meaning. In this perspective, the "antichrist" is the unconditional enclosure of history within its own logic—the supreme antithesis to the Man with the opened side, of whom the author of the Apocalypse wrote:

> Behold, he is coming with clouds,
> and every eye will see him.[74]

VII

Hell, Purgatory, Heaven

I. HELL

No quibbling helps here: the idea of eternal damnation, which had taken ever clearer shape in the Judaism of the century or two before Christ, has a firm place in the teaching of Jesus,[75] as well as in the apostolic writings.[76] Dogma takes its stand on solid ground when it speaks of the existence of Hell[77] and of the eternity of its punishments.[78]

This teaching, so contrary to our ideas about God and about man, was naturally only accepted with great difficulty. According to fragments preserved in Justinian and the Pseudo-Leontius, it was Origen who, in his ambitious attempt to systematize Christianity, the *Peri Archōn*, first proposed the idea that given the logic of God's relationship with history, there must be a universal reconciliation at the End. Origen himself regarded his outline systematics as no more than a hypothesis. It was an approach to a comprehensive vision, an approach which did not necessarily claim to reproduce the contours of reality itself. While the effect of Neo-Platonism in the *Peri Archōn* was to over-accentuate the idea that evil is in fact nothing and nothingness, God alone being real, the great Alexandrian divine later sensed much more acutely the terrible reality of evil, that evil which can inflict suffering on God himself and, more, bring him down to death. Nevertheless, Origen could not wholly let go of his hope that, in and through this divine

suffering, the reality of evil is taken prisoner and overcome, so that it loses its quality of definitiveness. In that
hope of his, a long line of fathers were to follow him: Gregory of Nyssa, Didymus of Alexandria, Diodore of Tarsus,
Theodore of Mopsuestia, Evagrius Ponticus, and, at least
on occasion, Jerome of Bethlehem also. But the main-
stream tradition of the Church has flowed along a different
path. It found itself obliged to concede that such an expectation of universal reconciliation derived from the system
rather than from the biblical witness. The dying echo of
Origen's ideas has lingered through the centuries, however,
in the many variants of the so-called doctrine of *miseri-
cordia*. These would either except Christians completely
from the possibility of damnation, or else concede to all
the lost some kind of relief from suffering—in comparison, that is, with what they really deserve.

What should we hold on to here? First, to the fact of
God's unconditional respect for the freedom of his creature. What can be given to the creature, however, is love,
and with this all its neediness can be transformed. The assent to such love need not be "created" by man: this is not
something which he achieves by his own power. And yet
the freedom to resist the creation of that assent, the freedom not to accept it as one's own, this freedom remains.
Herein lies the difference between the beautiful dream of
the Boddhisattva (c.f. above VI. 1. c.) and its realization.
The true Boddhisattva, Christ, descends into Hell and suffers it in all its emptiness; but he does not, for all that,
treat man as an immature being deprived in the final
analysis of any responsibility for his own destiny. Heaven
reposes upon freedom, and so leaves to the damned the
right to will their own damnation. The specificity of
Christianity is shown in this conviction of the greatness
of man. Human life is fully serious. It is not to be de-

natured by what Hegel called the "cunning of the Idea" into an aspect of divine planning. The irrevocable takes place, and that includes, then, irrevocable destruction. The Christian man or woman must live with such seriousness and be aware of it. It is a seriousness which takes on tangible form in the Cross of Christ.

That Cross throws light upon our theme from two directions. First, it teaches us that God himself suffered and died. Evil is not, then, something unreal for him. For the God who is love, hatred is not nothing. He overcomes evil, but not by some dialectic of universal reason which can transform all negations into affirmations. God overcomes evil not in a "speculative Good Friday," to use the language of Hegel, but on a Good Friday which was most real. He himself entered into the distinctive freedom of sinners but went beyond it in that freedom of his own love which descended willingly into the Abyss.

While the real quality of evil and its consequences become quite palpable here, the question also arises—and this is the second illuminating aspect of the mystery of the Cross for our problem—whether in this event we are not in touch with a divine response able to draw freedom precisely as freedom to itself. The answer lies hidden in Jesus' descent into Sheol, in the night of the soul which he suffered, a night which no one can observe except by entering this darkness in suffering faith. Thus, in the history of holiness which hagiology offers us, and notably in the course of recent centuries, in John of the Cross, in Carmelite piety in general, and in that of Thérèse of Lisieux in particular, "Hell" has taken on a completely new meaning and form. For the saints, "Hell" is not so much a threat to be hurled at other people but a challenge to oneself. It is a challenge to suffer in the dark night of faith, to experience communion with Christ in solidarity with his descent into the Night. One draws near to the Lord's radiance by sharing his darkness. One serves the salvation of the world by leaving one's own salvation behind for the sake of others. In such piety, nothing of the dreadful reality of Hell is denied. Hell is so real that it reaches right into the existence of the saints. Hope can take it on, only if one shares in the suffering of Hell's night by the side of the One who came to transform our night by his suffering. Here hope does not emerge from the neutral logic of a system, from rendering humanity innocuous. Instead, it derives from the surrender of all claims to innocence and to reality's perduringness, a surrender which takes place by the Cross of the Redeemer. Such hope cannot, however, be a self-willed assertion. It must place its petition into the hands of its Lord and leave it there. The doctrine of everlasting punishment preserves its real content. The idea of mercy, which has accompanied it, in one form or another, throughout its long history, must not become a theory. Rather is it the prayer of suffering, hopeful faith.

2. PURGATORY

(a) The Problem of the Historical Data

The Catholic doctrine of Purgatory received its definitive ecclesial form in the two mediaeval councils which tried to bring about reunion with the churches of the East. At the Council of Trent it was reformulated in summary fashion by way of confrontation with the movements of the Reformation. These statements already give some idea of its historical placing and ecumenically problematic quality. We have already noted (in V. 2 and 4, a.–b. above) that the New Testament left open the question of the "intermediate state" between death and the general resurrection on the Last Day. That question remained in an unfinished condition, since it could only be clarified by the gradual unfolding of Christian anthropology and its relation to christology. The doctrine of Purgatory is part of this process of clarification. In this doctrine, the Church held fast to one aspect of the idea of the intermediate state, insisting that, even if one's fundamental life-decision is finally decided and fixed in death,[79] one's definitive destiny need not necessarily be reached straight away. It may be that the basic decision of a human being is covered over by layers of secondary decisions and needs to be dug free. In the Western tradition, this intermediate state is called "Purgatory." The Eastern church has not followed the path of Western theology with its clarification of the final destiny of man. The East clung to that form of the idea of the intermediate state reached by the lifetime of John Chrysostom (who died in 407). For this reason, the doctrine of Purgatory functioned as an article dividing the churches at the attempted ecumenical reunions of Lyons in 1274 and Ferrara–Florence in 1439.[80] Naturally enough, the point around which disagreement centered was not the same as a century later with the Reformers. The Greeks rejected the idea of punishment and atonement taking place in the afterlife, yet they shared with the church of the West the practice of interceding for the dead by prayer, alms, good works, and, most notably, the offering of the Eucharist for their repose.[81] But it was in these customs, and above all in the celebration of Requiem Masses, that the Reformers saw an attack on the complete sufficiency of Christ's atoning work on the Cross.[82] Given their doctrine of justification, they were unable to concede that there might be atonement in the life to come.

Before investigating the historical roots of the problem of Purgatory, with a view to arriving at a clearer picture of the doctrinal issues involved, we must get a firmer grasp on the Catholic Church's actual teaching in the three councils I have mentioned. The texts speak of *poenae purgatoriae seu catharteriae*, "purging or purifying punishments,"[83] or, more simply, of *purgatorium*, sometimes translated as "the place of purification."[84] The term "place" is not, in fact, found in the Latin, though it is hinted at by means of the preposition "in": *in purgatorio*. All three councils approach the task of doctrinal definition by way of a *relecture* of the preceding tradition. In this process their formulations become more simple and precise. The formula adopted by Trent is the most succinct of all.

> . . . [T]he Catholic Church, instructed by the Holy Spirit, has, following the sacred writings and the ancient tradition of the Fathers, taught in sacred Councils and very recently in this ecumenical Council, that there is a purgatory, *purgatorium*, and that the souls detained therein are aided by the suffrages of the faithful and chiefly by the acceptable sacrifice of the altar.[85]

Trent adds, however, an emphatic exhortation to the bishops, urging them to do all in their power to oppose excessive subtlety, curiosity and superstition. Here the protest of the Reformation against the abuses prevalent in contemporary practice is taken up and translated into a message of reform. However, the denial of the doctrine obscured by those abuses and the religious practices associated with them is itself rejected.

The roots of the doctrine of Purgatory, like those of the idea of the intermediate state in general, lie deeply embedded in early Judaism. Second Maccabees reports that pagan amulets had been found on the Jewish fallen in the wars of the period.[86] Their deaths are interpreted as a punishment for apostasy from the Torah. According to the narrative, a prayer service was held for the fallen: "they turned to prayer, beseeching that the sin which had been committed might be wholly blotted out."[87] Moreover, money was collected to provide for a sin-offering in Jerusalem. The author praises this action as an expression of faith in the resurrection of the dead. To be sure, the text says nothing about how one ought to conceive of the purifying effect of prayer and the "intermediate state" of the sinful departed. Rather clearer in this respect is the apocryphal *Vita Adae et Evae,* a work from the first century of the Christian era, which tells of Seth's mourning for the dead Adam and of God's mercy, as proclaimed by Michael.

Rise from the body of your father and come to me and see what the Lord God is arranging concerning him. He is his creature and he has had mercy on him.

Yet this mercy incorporates penalty too:

Then Seth saw the extended hand of the Lord holding Adam, and he handed him over to Michael, saying, 'Let him be in your custody until the day of dispensing punishment at the last years, when I will turn his sorrow into joy. Then he shall sit on the throne of him who overthrew him.[88]

In the material presented by the Strack–Billerbeck collection, part of which goes back to the second century of the Christian era, there are clear signs of the idea of an intermediate Gehenna, understood as a purgatory where souls, in their atoning suffering, are prepared for definitive salvation.[89] Here, as in many other ideas about the afterlife, the Jewish religion had numerous points of contact with various currents of Greco-Roman religiosity, for which prayer for the dead had salvific potential.[90] The transition from early Judaism to early Christianity is, therefore, a gradual affair. Its phases belonged to the single continuum of tradition.

Leaving aside for the moment the controversial question as to where the New Testament contains traces of the idea of Purgatory, let us investigate instead the formation

of the Church's tradition in East and West. As early as the
second century, we can consult such representative witnesses as, in the West, Tertullian (who died soon after 220)
and in the East, Clement of Alexandria (who died rather
before 215). In the history of the doctrine of Purgatory,
Tertullian is known above all for the acts of the martyrdom of St. Perpetua, which either were composed by him
or derive from his circle. In a dream, Perpetua sees her
little brother Dinocrates who had died of cancer at an
early age. Dirty and pale, with the cancer sore from which
he died still visible, he stands in simmering heat before a
water fountain which is much too high for him to drink
from. Though terribly thirsty, he cannot slake his thirst.
Perpetua understands the message of the dream. Day and
night, she prays for her unhappy brother. Shortly, in a second vision, she is allowed to see him cleaned up, well-
dressed and with his sore healed. He can easily reach the
water now. He drinks at will and plays happily. A. Stuiber
has suggested that this text simply reproduces Late Antique conceptions about the sad lot of those who die pre-
maturely. On this view, it would have nothing to do with
the doctrine of Purgatory. Such a destiny is not the result
of guilt: the misery it brings with it cannot be interpreted
as punishment or expiation.[91] But is the right criterion
being employed here? If the fully articulated definition of
Lyons-cum-Florence-cum-Trent is to be the only possible
determination of the concept of Purgatory then one might
well come to a conclusion of the kind just described. But
in so doing, one would deprive oneself of the chance to
grasp something of the structure of the idea of Purgatory
and the historically piecemeal assembling of the elements
that compose it. It is, therefore, more just to adopt J. A.
Fischer's opinion that the essential elements of the doctrine of Purgatory crystallized out of the traditional mate-

rials offered by all three sources: Late Antique sensibility, Judaism and Christianity. The central feature of it all is the idea of a suffering on the part of the dead capable of being alleviated by prayer. The factor of guilt comes into the picture not because ethics demands it but for reasons which historians of religion study.[92] In Tertullian's Montanist essay *On the Soul* a step is taken which leads to the concept of Purgatory in its proper sense, though even here we are not dealing with an idea which is straightforwardly identical with the teaching of the mediaeval councils. Tertullian's starting point is Jesus' parabolic advice to reconcile oneself with one's opponent on the way to court, since otherwise:

. . . you will be thrown into prison. I tell you solemnly, you will not get out till you have paid the last penny.[93]

Interpreting this text in terms of human destiny in the world to come was made easier by the fact that *phylakē*, the word for "prison," was also one of the current terms for Hades.[94] For Tertullian, who had become a rigorist, the text meant that the time between death and resurrection is a time of imprisonment in which the soul has the opportunity to pay the "last penny" and so to become free for the resurrection. A new theological rationale is being offered for Hades, and this rationale "makes the interim state into a necessary purgatory for everyone."[95] Cyprian of Carthage, dying in 258, removed Tertullian's thesis from its rigorist context and gave it a new look on the basis of the tasks of a pastor in a period of persecution. In this way, Cyprian succeeded in eliminating the pagan element. He managed to work out the authentically Christian form of an insight which, though derived from the Church's Jewish roots, had earlier seemed equivalent to Greco-Roman conceptions. Cyprian's contribution set the

Western Church on its way. He asserted a definitive salvation for those who have died in faith, and notably for the martyrs. He was similarly clear about the definitiveness of Hell. His actual pastoral problem concerned the well-intentioned but weak, average Christians who did not find the strength to accept martyrdom in times of persecution. They had carried out the demands of the State religion, and thus had publicly denied Christ. Nonetheless, they wished to remain Christians and asked for reconciliation with the Church. The saying found in Matthew 5, 26 offered Cyprian an occasion for thinking through a possible continuation of penance in the afterlife. Against the protesting voices of the rigorists, this enabled him to re-admit the weak to communion with the Church. Certainly they cannot, in their present condition, enter into definitive communion with Christ. Their denial, their half-heartedness, stands in the way. But they are capable of purification. The penitential way of purification exists not only in this world but in the world to come. With this interpretation, that there is purification in the future life, the root concept of the Western doctrine of Purgatory is already formulated clearly enough.[96]

In the West, the idea of Purgatory developed in its initial stages with almost no connection with ancient philosophy. Its contacts were, rather, with the beliefs of the Christian people, marked as these were by the earlier sensibility of the classical world and of Judaism. But in turning to Clement of Alexandria, we find a very different picture. Clement's views were worked out in controversy with Valentinian Gnosis, therefore in debate with the impressive philosophical tradition of the Greek world, and notably with Platonism and Stoicism. Clement interprets our theme, and indeed Christian existence at large, in terms of the notable Greek idea of *paideia*, "education." Into this idea, he integrates the gnostic (and, prior to that,

Greco-Roman) notion of a post-mortem fire of judgment. This gives him a basis on which to carry out his exegesis of First Corinthians 3, 10–15: a text which also introduces the idea of a fire of judgment, something we shall have to look at in a moment. According to the Valentinians, the gnostic cannot be touched by that fire. It fails to reach him, since he carries the two extinguishing agents—the water of baptism and the "Wind," the Spirit, that can grant him un-failing protection. The ordinary man, however, called by the gnostics "hylicos" ("material ones"), is caught in the fire's blaze, with results at once curative and destructive. In place of this two-fold distinction, Clement speaks of the "purifying" and "educative" power of this fire.[97] He re-interprets the rather naturalistic Gnostic thinking in more human and spiritual terms. The process of man's pneu-matic purification, that catharsis which will fit him for God, begins with baptism and reaches into eternity.

Clement proved able to integrate into a most compel-ling synthesis the whole drama of Christian existence: life and death, immortality, resurrection, the Last Day. In this drama, there takes place an "ascent" whereby the soul is transformed into a *sōma*, "body," of ever greater pneu-matic perfection. This is a picture which leaves no room for the distinction between the soul and the glorified body. The two components melt into self-identity in the glori-fied subject. The idea of purification after death:

turns out to be, in this context, something of a mediating meta-physical link between the Platonic idea of the soul's immortality and the Resurrection.[98]

Just as Clement can give a place to the doctrine of the risen body by his idea of man's ascending transformation, so he can also create a significant space for the ecclesial aspect of Christian existence. The process of purification is, on all its levels, an activity of reciprocal caring. "Even beyond the threshold of death, the perfect gnostic can care for those" who stand beneath him and need him.[99] This conversion of a naturalistic into an anthropological and personalist world view gives a new twist to the question of the Last Day. The true gnostic can celebrate as the Day of the Lord that day on which he frees himself from an evil disposition and embraces the gnostic way of life. In this way, he gives fitting honor to the Lord's resurrection.[100] However, Clement does not fall into the trap of the idea of timelessness (considered above). He lights upon a profound anthropological concept of time which allows him to say that, when the one who is "ascending" reaches the highest level of pneumatic bodiliness, the *plērōma*, then at that moment he enters *sunteleia*, "perfection," and therewith the eschatological "Day of God," the eternal Today.

This would not be the place to discuss that synthesis of Christianity and Hellenism which is Clement's philosophy. His vision would certainly have something of value to offer to contemporary attempts to appropriate the biblical message in a meaningful and objective fashion—even if it is bound to a world whose concepts we cannot in many cases adopt ourselves. What is important for our present investigation is that, in a quite different context, we meet again the two basic elements of the idea of Purgatory whch we saw emerge by a gradual development in the West. In Clement as in the Western writers, the penance imposed by the Church is the concrete starting point. For him as for them, such penance is a process which can and often must continue beyond the gate of death. For him as for them, this process points up the difference between someone's valid fundamental decision, whereby he is accepted in grace, and the defective permeation of the effects of that decision throughout the being of the whole person.

We can also note that, according to these witnesses, the anchoring of a person in the Church is not something which death disrupts or destroys. Even when they have crossed over the threshold of the world beyond, human beings can still carry each other and bear each others' burdens. They can still give to each other, suffer for each other, and receive from each other. More clearly at Alexandria than in the Western tradition, this conviction rests on the Pauline–Johannine belief that the real frontier runs not between earthly life and not-life, but between being with Christ, on the one hand, and, on the other, being without him or against him.[101] The decisive step is taken in baptism: while the fundamental option of the baptismal candidate becomes definitively established with death, its full development and purification may have to await a moment beyond death, when we make our way through the judging fire of Christ's intimate presence in the companionable embrace of the family of the Church.

With suitable modifications, Clement's teaching was continued by Origen, and found acceptance wherever the theology of that great Alexandrian was considered authoritative. Finally, and scarcely changed in its central affirmations, it was put forward by Gregory of Nazianzus, whose death occurred around the year 390.[102] Alas: because the doctrine formed part of Origen's system, it shared in his downfall. Drawn into the controversy about Origen, it was dismantled along with his heritage. The crucial figure here was that of John Chrysostom, a younger contemporary of Gregory Nazianzen, dying in 407. In his homilies on First Corinthians 3, 1–17, he rejects the idea of a general restoration, *apokatastasis*, which had become linked with that of the purging fire. Chrysostom thus originated the doctrine which remains official in the Eastern churches. These churches, after the elimination of the Alexandrian attempt to synthesize Greek and Biblical thought, held to a somewhat archaic conception. The intermediate state, "Hades," applies to everyone in the period between death and resurrection. But this state contains "various levels of happiness and unhappiness," which correspond to the different levels of justification and sanctification of the faithful on earth. The saints intercede for their brethren here on earth, and we may call on them for their intercession. Through the Eucharist, through prayer and almsgiving, the living can bring "respite and refreshment" to the souls in Hades. However, the "unhappiness" to be alleviated by such actions is not taken to include a purifying or atoning suffering.[103]

(b) The Permanent Content of the Doctrine of Purgatory

In the wake of this brief historical sketch, the question remains: What is the authentic heart of the doctrine of Purgatory? What is its rationale? In listening in to the patristic discussion, we had occasion to mention First Corinthians 3, 10−15. For this text, there is a foundation, Jesus Christ, on which some build with gold, silver and precious stones, and others with wood, hay and straw. What each one has in fact built will be brought to light by the Day of the Lord.

> . . . it will be revealed with fire, and the fire will test what sort of work each one has done. If the work which any man has built on the foundation survives, he will receive a reward. If any man's work is burned up, he will suffer loss, though he himself will be saved, but only as through fire.

J. Gnilka has shown that this testing fire indicates the coming Lord himself. Echoing a passage from the prophet Isaiah,[104] it is

an image for the majesty of the self-revealed God. . . . the un-
approachability of the All-Holy.[105]

According to Gnilka, who here sets himself over against
the opinion of Jeremias,[106] this excludes any interpretation
of the text in terms of Purgatory. There is no fire, only the
Lord himself. There is no temporal duration involved,
only eschatological encounter with the Judge. There is no
purification, only the statement that such a human being
"will be saved only with exertion and difficulty."[107] But it
is by following just this exegesis that one is led to wonder
whether its manner of posing the question is correct, and
its criteria adequate. If one presupposes a naively objective
concept of Purgatory then of course the text is silent. But
if, conversely, we hold that Purgatory is understood in a
properly Christian way when it is grasped christologically,
in terms of the Lord himself as the judging fire which
transforms us and conforms us to his own glorified body,[108]
then we shall come to a very different conclusion. Does
not the real Christianizing of the early Jewish notion of a
purging fire lie precisely in the insight that the purification involved does not happen through some *thing*, but
through the transforming power of the Lord himself, whose
burning flame cuts free our closed-off heart, melting it,
and pouring it into a new mold to make it fit for the living
organism of his body? And what, in any case, can it mean
in concrete terms when Gnilka remarks that some "will
be saved only after exertion and with difficulty"? In what
does such "exertion" and "difficulty" consist? Would this
not become a merely mythical statement should it say
nothing about man himself, and, more specifically, about
the manner of his entry into salvation? Surely these terms
must refer, not to something external to man, but to the
man of little faith's heartfelt submission to the fire of

the Lord which will draw him out of himself into that purity which befits those who are God's? One really can't object that Paul is only talking here about the Last Day as
a unique event: that would be hermeneutical *naïveté*,
though exercised in the opposite sense from the type we
considered in parts V and VI of this book. Man does not
have to strip away his temporality in order thereby to become "eternal"; Christ as judge is *ho eschatos*, the Final
One, in relation to whom we undergo judgment *both* after
death *and* on the Last Day. In the perspective we are
offered here, those two judgments are indistinguishable. A
person's entry into the realm of manifest reality is an entry into his definitive destiny and thus an immersion in
eschatological fire. The transforming "moment" of this
encounter cannot be quantified by the measurements of
earthly time. It is, indeed, not eternal but a transition, and
yet trying to qualify it as of "short" or "long" duration on
the basis of temporal measurements derived from physics
would be naive and unproductive. The "temporal measure" of this encounter lies in the unsoundable depths of
existence, in a passing-over where we are burned ere we
are transformed. To measure such *Existenzzeit*, such an
"existential time," in terms of the time of this world
would be to ignore the specificity of the human spirit in
its simultaneous relationship with, and differentiation
from, the world.[109]

The essential Christian understanding of Purgatory has
now become clear. Purgatory is not, as Tertullian thought,
some kind of supra-worldly concentration camp where
man is forced to undergo punishment in a more or less arbitrary fashion. Rather is it the inwardly necessary process
of transformation in which a person becomes capable of
Christ, capable of God and thus capable of unity with the
whole communion of saints. Simply to look at people

with any degree of realism at all is to grasp the necessity of such a process. It does not replace grace by works, but allows the former to achieve its full victory precisely as grace. What actually saves is the full assent of faith. But in most of us, that basic option is buried under a great deal of wood, hay and straw. Only with difficulty can it peer out from behind the latticework of an egoism we are power-less to pull down with our own hands. Man is the recipi-ent of the divine mercy, yet this does not exonerate him from the need to be transformed. Encounter with the Lord *is* this transformation. It is the fire that burns away our dross and re-forms us to be vessels of eternal joy.[110] This insight would contradict the doctrine of grace only if pen-ance were the antithesis of grace and not its form, the gift of a gracious possibility. The identification of Purgatory with the Church's penance in Cyprian and Clement is im-portant for drawing our attention to the fact that the root of the Christian doctrine of Purgatory is the christological grace of penance. Purgatory follows by an inner necessity from the idea of penance, the idea of the constant readi-ness for reform which marks the forgiven sinner.

One vital question still remains to be cleared up. We saw that prayer for the departed, in its many forms, be-longs with the original data of the Judaeo-Christian tradi-tion. But does not this prayer presuppose that Purgatory entails some kind of external punishment which can, for example, be graciously remitted through vicarious accep-tance by others in a form of spiritual barter? And how can a third party enter into that most highly personal process of encounter with Christ, where the "I" is transformed in the flame of his closeness? Is not this an event which so concerns the individual that all replacement or substitu-tion must be ruled out? Is not the pious tradition of "help-ing the holy souls" based on treating these souls after the fashion of "having"—whereas our reflections so far have surely led to the conclusion that the heart of the matter is "being," for which there can be no substitute? Yet the being of man is not, in fact, that of a closed monad. It is related to others by love or hate, and, in these ways, has its colonies within them. My own being is present in others as guilt or as grace. We are not just ourselves; or, more correctly, we are ourselves only as being in others, with others and through others. Whether others curse us or bless us, forgive us and turn our guilt into love—this is part of our own destiny. The fact that the saints will judge means that encounter with Christ is encounter with his whole body. I come face to face with my own guilt vis-à-vis the suffering members of that body as well as with the forgiving love which the body derives from Christ its Head.

The intercession of the saints with the Judge is not . . . some purely external affair whose success is necessarily doubtful since it depends on the unpredictable benevolence of the Judge. It is above all an inner weight which, placed on the scales, can bring them to sink down.[111]

This intercession is the one truly fundamental element in their "judging." Through their exercising of such judgment they belong, as people who both pray and save, to the doctrine of Purgatory and to the Christian practice which goes with it. As Charles Péguy so beautifully put it, "J'espère en toi pour moi": "I hope in you for me."[112] It is when the "I" is at stake that the "you" is called upon in the form of hope.

This second line of reflection is actually even more important than the first which, to remind the reader, turns on the relation between Purgatory and the Church's penitential practice. Even more important because self-substituting love is a central Christian reality, and the doctrine of Purgatory states that for such love the limit of death does not exist. The possibility of helping and giving does not cease to exist on the death of the Christian. Rather does it stretch out to encompass the entire communion of saints, on both sides of death's portals. The capacity, and the duty, to love beyond the grave might even be called the true primordial datum in this whole area of tradition—as II Maccabees 12, 42−45 first makes clear.[113] Furthermore, this original "given" has never been in dispute as between East and West. It was the Reformation which called it into question, and that in the face of what were in part objectionable and deformed practices. Here, then, is where the ecumenical way ahead in this matter lies, at least as between Orthodox and Catholics. What is primary is the praxis of being able to pray, and being called upon to pray. The objective correlate of this praxis in the world to come need not, in some reunification of the churches, be determined of necessity in a strictly unitary fashion, even though the content and rationale of the Western teaching is anchored, as we have shown, in ancient tradition and central motifs of faith.

3. HEAVEN

Christian tradition uses the image of heaven, an image linked to the natural symbolic force of what is "high" or "above," in order to express that definitive completion of human existence which comes about through the perfect love towards which faith tends. Such a fulfilment is not, for the Christian, some music of the future. Rather is it sheer description of what happens in the encounter with Christ, itself already present in its fundamental elements. To raise the question of "heaven" is thus not to float free from earth in a balloon of enthusiastic fantasy. It is to come to know more deeply that hidden presence by whose gift we truly live, even though we ourselves continually permit it to be camouflaged, and to withdraw from us, displaced by the many objects that occupy the foreground of our lives.

Heaven, therefore, must first and foremost be determined christologically. It is not an extra-historical place into which one goes. Heaven's existence depends upon the fact that Jesus Christ, as God, is man, and makes space for human existence in the existence of God himself.[114] One is in heaven when, and to the degree, that one is in Christ. It is by being with Christ that we find the true location of our existence as human beings in God. Heaven is thus primarily a personal reality, and one that remains forever shaped by its historical origin in the paschal mystery of death and resurrection. From this christological center, all the other elements which belong to the tradition's concept of heaven may be inferred. And, in pride of place, from this christological foundation there follows a theological affirmation: the glorified Christ stands in a continuous posture of self-giving to his Father. Indeed, he *is* that self-giving. The paschal sacrifice abides in him as an enduring presence. For this reason, heaven, as our becoming one with Christ, takes on the nature of adoration. All cult prefigures it, and in it comes to completion. Christ is the temple of the final age;[115] he is heaven, the new Jerusalem; he is the cultic space for God. The ascending movement of humanity in its union with Christ is answered by the descending movement of God's love in its self-gift to us. And so worship, in its heavenly, perfected form, entails an immediacy between God and man which knows of no setting asunder. This is what theological tradition calls the vision of God. Thomists and Scotists dispute whether this fundamental act is better called the vision of God or the love of God: it all depends on one's anthropological starting point.

But in the last analysis, the point of it all is the same: God totally permeates the whole man with his plenitude and his utter openness. God is "all in all," and thus the human person enters upon his boundless fulfilment.

The christological statements made here also have their ecclesiological aspect. If heaven depends on being in Christ, then it must involve a co-being with all those who, together, constitute the body of Christ. Heaven is a stranger to isolation. It is the open society of the communion of saints, and in this way the fulfilment of all human communion. This is not by way of competition with the perfect disclosure of God's Face, but, on the contrary, is its very consequence. It is because the Church knows this that there is such a thing as the Christian cult of the saints. That cult does not presuppose some mythical omniscience on the part of the saints, but simply the unruptured self-communion of the whole body of Christ—and the closeness of a love which knows no limit and is sure of attaining God in the neighbor, and the neighbor in God.

But from this an anthropological element does indeed emerge. The integration of the "I" into the body of Christ, its *disponibilité* at the service of the Lord and of others, is not the self's dissolution but a purification which is, at one and the same time, the actualization of its highest potential. This is why heaven is individual for each and every one. Everyone sees God in his own proper way. Everyone receives the love offered by the totality in the manner suggested by his own irreplaceable uniqueness.

To him who conquers, I will give some of the hidden manna, and I will give him a white stone, with a new name written on the stone, which no one knows except him who receives it.[116]

In this light, one can understand why the New Testament, and the whole of tradition with it, calls heaven not only sheer grace through the gift of love but also "reward." It is "reward" in that it is a response to *this* life-way, *this* biography, this particular person with his actions and experiences. The Scholastics took these insights further and gave them systematic form. Drawing, in part, on extremely venerable traditions, they spoke of the special 'crowns' of martyrs, virgins and doctors. Today, we are rather more circumspect where such assertions are concerned. It is sufficient to know that God gives each and every person his fulfilment in a way peculiar to this or that individual, and that in this way each and all receive to the uttermost. Perhaps such reflections should encourage us, not so much to consider this way or that privileged in the Church, but rather to recognize the task of enlarging the vessel of our own life. But once again, this enlargement is not meant to ensure that in the world to come we have the largest barn possible in which to store our wealth, but rather to be able to distribute all the more to our fellows. In the communion of the body of Christ, possession can only consist in giving, the riches of self-fulfilment in the passing on of gifts.

The cosmological dimension of the christological truth we are considering has occupied our thoughts earlier and in some detail. The "exaltation" of Christ, the entry of his humanity into the life of the triune God through the resurrection, does not imply his departure from this world but a new mode of presence to the world. In the imagistic language of the ancient credal symbols, the mode of existence proper to the risen Lord is that of "sitting at the right hand of the Father." It is sharing in God's sovereign power over history, a power which is effective even where it is concealed. Thus the exalted Christ is not stripped of his worldly being but, by coming to transcend the world, is related to it afresh. "Heaven" means participation in this new mode of Christ's existence and thus the fulfilment of what baptism began in us. This is why heaven escapes spatial determination. It lies neither inside nor outside the space of our world, even though it must not be detached from the cosmos as some mere "state." Heaven means, much more, that power over the world which characterizes the new "space" of the body of Christ, the communion of saints. Heaven is not, then, "above" in a spatial but in an essential way. This enables us to pronounce upon the legitimacy, as well as the limitations, of the traditional images. They retain their truth so long as they evoke transcendence over, and freedom from, the world's constraints, and the power of love which overcomes the world. They become false if they either remove heaven altogether from relation with this world, or if they attempt to integrate it totally into the world, as some kind of upper story. Scripture, accordingly, never tolerates the monarchical supremacy of a single image. By utilizing many images, it keeps open a perspective on the Indescribable. In particular, by announcing a new heaven and a new earth, the Bible makes it clear that the whole of creation is destined to become the vessel of God's Glory. All of created reality is to be drawn into blessedness. The world—God's creature—is what the Scholastics would call an "accidental" element in the final joy of the redeemed.

Heaven is in itself eschatological reality. It is the advent of the finally and wholly Other. Its own definitiveness stems from the definitiveness of God's irrevocable and indivisible love. Its openness vis-à-vis the total eschaton derives from the open history of Christ's body, and therewith of all creation which is still under construction. Heaven will only be complete when all the members of the Lord's body are gathered in. Such completion on the part of the body of Christ includes, as we have seen, the "resurrection of the flesh." It is called the "Parousia" inasmuch as then the presence of Christ, so far only inaugurated among us, will reach its fulness and encompass all those who are to be saved and the whole cosmos with them. And so heaven comes in two historical stages. The Lord's exaltation gives rise to the new unity of God with man, and hence to heaven. The perfecting of the Lord's body in the *plērōma* of the "whole Christ" brings heaven to its true cosmic completion. Let us say it once more before we end: the individual's salvation is whole and entire only when the salvation of the cosmos and all the elect has come to full fruition. For the redeemed are not simply adjacent to each other in heaven. Rather, in their being together as the one Christ, they *are* heaven. In that moment, the whole creation will become song. It will be a single act in which, forgetful of self, the individual will break through the limits of being into the whole, and the whole take up its dwlling in the individual. It will be joy in which all questioning is resolved and satisfied.

Appendices

Between Death and Resurrection: Some Supplementary Reflections

1. A Clarification from the Congregation for the Doctrine of the Faith on the Question of Eschatology

On 17 May 1979, the Holy See's Congregation for the Doctrine of the Faith made public, with the approval of the Pope, a "Letter on Certain Questions in Eschatology" addressed to all bishops and episcopal Conferences. This document proceeds from a conviction which had become ever more crystal clear in recent meetings of the Synod of Bishops. It thus linked together, in quite conscious fashion, the papal teaching office with that of the episcopal body and thereby addressed a word to the bishops' Conferences for their careful consideration. The Synods had become increasingly aware that the Church of today must meet a twofold obligation. On the one hand, she must stand fast in complete fidelity to the fundamental truths of the faith. On the other hand, in the spiritual upheaval of our age, she also finds herself most urgently committed to the task of interpretation, to the end that the selfsame faith may be communicable now as before. Interpretation and fidelity may stand towards each other in a certain relationship of tension; but precisely in this relation do they belong inseparably to each other. Only the person who makes the truth accessible once again, who actually mediates it, remains true to it; but only the one who remains true to it interprets it correctly. An interpretation that is unfaithful ceases to be a genuine interpretation and becomes a falsification. This is why insistence on fidelity does not mean the renunciation of interpretation, nor does it constitute a plea for "the sterile repetition of ancient formulae." On the contrary: it involves a decisive call to objective interpretation. If, at the end of my interpretative activity, I no longer occupy a reverent posture towards the interpreted word, if I can no longer in all honesty speak *with* the text, then I have betrayed my interpreter's role. "They should let the Word stand": this well-known observation of Martin Luther's could well be taken as the marching orders for any and every interpretative gambit that desires to be true to its own calling.

The fidelity about which the document mentioned above speaks is to be exercised in relation to the "fundamental truths of faith." What does that mean? The Letter to the Romans would answer this question by pointing to our baptismal confession: in a splendid formulation that Letter describes it as a copy and continuation of the unfolding of the divine decrees, from creation to the final fulfilment in the resurrection from the dead. This reference to baptismal confession is not only appropriate and meaningful in that it can call Bible and Fathers to witness in its defense.[1] It *is* those things because, in addition, it highlights the inseparable togetherness of faith and life—of faith, prayer and worship. "The truths of faith" are not, then, an ideological package which the Christian finds somebody saddling him with. One becomes a Christian by baptism, which is a voluntary acceptance of one's induction into the common form of faith in the Triune God. Membership in the Church is achieved in the concrete order through the common prayer of the confession of faith which is at one and the same time the presence of the baptismal mystery and access to the present Lord. If I cease to be able to give real assent to the Creed, or to any part of it, the content of baptism, my belonging to that community of faith and confession which is the Church, cannot remain unimpaired. The confession of faith, which on such an understanding is brought back into the very center of the picture, is, for its part, not a collection of propositions so much as a structure. As the Roman document itself indicates, it is a structure whose inner coherence, the unity of what is believed, comes to expression as the coherence and unity of a single whole. One cannot obliterate a part without losing the totality.[2]

On the basis of these presuppositions, the Roman statement addresses itself to the article of the Creed which concerns hope for the life everlasting, and has this to say:

If Christians have no reliable hold on the content of the words 'life everlasting', then the promises of the Gospel evaporate, as does the meaning of creation and redemption, while even earthly life is robbed of its hope (cf. Hebrews 11,1).

The Congregation for the Doctrine of the Faith regards this as a threat which has actually materialized:

Who can fail to see that here a subtle and penetrating doubt cuts ever deeper into hearts?

It draws attention to the fact that the disputed questions of theology now being debated so publicly are such that by virtue both of their subject matter and their gravity they cannot leave the majority of believers unaffected.

For in point of fact, the existence of the soul and the meaning of life after death are under discussion, and people ask themselves what happens between the death of the Christian and the general resurrection. All of this causes confusion for believers since they find their accustomed manner of speaking and concepts that are dear to them no longer recognisable.

At this point, a second characteristic feature of the Roman document manifests itself: since it places a premium on the communicability of thought in language, it necessarily places a premium also on the synchronic and diachronic continuity of language, as indeed on the near alliance of the language of prayer (which in the Church is essentially diachronic and thus "catholic") and the language of theology. Because the "fundamental truths of faith" belong to all believers, and are, as a matter of fact, the concrete content of the Church's unity, the fundamental language of faith cannot be regarded as something for experts to work out. And for the same reason, that language which is the bearer of unity cannot be manipulated at will. Theology as an academic discipline needs technical language; as interpretation, it tries to translate its shared materials in ever new ways. But in both of these respects theology is beholden to the basic language of faith, a language which can only be developed in peaceful continuity with the common life of the praying Church, and which cannot endure sudden ruptures. The Roman document identifies the two complementary, not contradictory, tasks which arise at this point, and does so with some emphasis. On the one hand theology must research, discuss, experiment; on the other hand, theology cannot thus create for itself its own object, being ever thrown back as it is onto the "essence of faith," the faith of the Church. To penetrate and develop this essence, rather than to change or replace it, is theology's task, and, in truth, with such a task to perform theology has work enough to do.[3]

On the basis of these methodological commitments, the Roman text develops its own substantive affirmations whose essential content may be summarized under two headings:

1. The resurrection of the dead that we confess in the

Creed concerns the *whole* man. It is "for the elect nothing other than the extension of Christ's resurrection to all."

2. As for the intermediate state "between" death and resurrection, "the Church" affirms "the continuity and independent existence of the spiritual element in man after death," an element which is "endowed with consciousness and will," so that the "human I" continues in being. In order to refer to this element, the Church employs the term "soul." The Roman document is aware that this word "soul" appears in the Bible with varying significations. Yet it insists that "there is no solid reason for rejecting this term. Much more is it considered as a verbal instrument which is simply unavoidable for the retaining of the Church's faith." The word "soul," as a vehicle for a fundamental aspect of the Christian hope, is here reckoned to be part of that fundamental language of faith whose anchor is the faith of the Church. That language is indispensable for communion in the reality in which faith believes, and therefore is not merely something that the theologian can take up or leave alone at his discretion.

The Church's teaching office has hereby entered into a theological debate which it sees as touching the limits of theology: the dismantling of the concept of the soul, which in the course of the last half century has become more and more apparent, is not just a matter for scholars to discuss. Here the linguistic substrate of faith, faith's fundamental language, is *en jeu*. That boundary-point has been reached where, over and above the question of interpretation, the loss threatens the *interpretandum*, the objective content itself. But what objective content *is* that? In the space of a short essay we cannot hope to survey all the multiple aspects of the panorama which this question opens up. But we can hope to get an idea of current trends in their main outline.

2. *The Background of the Modern Controversy*

As I have already mentioned, the New Testament does not provide any clearly delimited concept of "soul." From the vantage-point of the Lord's resurrection, it contemplates our own rising again in which our destiny will be one with his. And yet the New Testament is also aware, and this time in full continuity with the faith of the Judaism of its day, that in between the first Easter and our own resurrection human beings do not sink into nothingness. The description of this intermediate state, which hitherto was carried out with the help of such terms as "Paradise," "Abraham's bosom," "lying under the altar," "dwelling in the 'place of refreshment'," is now strikingly integrated into a christological context: the person who dies is with the Lord; whoever is with the Lord does not die. Two points are clear:

a. Human beings live on "with the Lord" even before the resurrection.

b. This living on is not yet identical with the Resurrection which comes only "at the end of days" and will be the full breaking in of God's Lordship over the world.

At first, people did not bother themselves too much about the anthropological tools at the service of such assertions. Only as a result of a very slow process was the Christian concept of man as a body–soul unity formulated on the basis of these basic data of faith. Describing how the "soul" is the bearer of the intermediate state was an even more protracted business. One can say that the formation of this concept first reached a degree of completeness in Thomas Aquinas, and so in the high mediaeval period. However, the word "soul" had already become a key word for Christian believing and praying in the patristic age. In that age, it gave expression to the certainty that the human I would endure undestroyed, in continuity, beyond death. Thus a picture of what it is to be human grew up for which the "immortality of the soul" and the "resurrection from the dead" were not opposites, but rather complementary affirmations for the single, albeit phased, hope of which Christians were certain. The first breach of this certainty came with Luther, who cast doubt on the usefulness of the idea of the soul, on precisely the same grounds which have brought about the crisis of that idea in the Catholic Church of our own century. Until this point, what we can observe is the growth of a language for hope in the community of faith, a community which, in its diachronic unity, had protected the identity of what was believed as, little by little, terms developed, and a holistic vision of the reality at the foundation of faith was formed. Development and identity could not be contraries, since the common "subject," the Church, held both together. But for Luther the Church had ceased to be the protector of identity. On the contrary, she was the arrogant corrupter of the pure Word. Tradition is no longer the perpetual liveliness of the Origin, but its adversary. The correct understanding of the beginnings must now be sought not in the Church's living understanding, but in the historical understanding of the Bible. Development is henceforth a nugatory category, since it lacks a vehicle. With this, a fixation on biblical terminology becomes unavoidable, and the rejection of the concept of the soul likewise. For the Bible did not have to have an overview which it could express as a synthesis of the individual contributory elements in that idea. This separation of Origin and tradition is linked in Luther to an inner opposition to the Hellenic or philosophical strand in Christianity. Historic Christianity rests on a fusion of the biblical inheritance with Greek thought[4]: this synthesis must be disentangled, and a non-Hellenic Christianity sought.

As in other areas so here too Luther's radicalism turns out to be, in the history of thought, an anticipation of what would only later come to full actuality. As to Lutheran Orthodoxy, at first it did no more than perpetuate the Church's faith in its traditional form, though under changed tokens, and with certain definite modifications. Not until the great crisis of tradition in the Enlightenment, and the gradually attained victory of historicism in the nineteenth century did the changed relationship to tradition produce an effect on the broad scale. Now at last the historian would place himself outside the living subject of tradition, reading history backwards, not forwards, seeking to distill its original meaning in its pure form. In Catholic theology, a crisis was prepared from the time of the reception of historical-critical interpretation of the Bible, officially recognized as legitimate with Pius XII's encyclical on Scripture study.[5] The crisis became manifest after the Second Vatican Council: under the impact of the claims of the wholly new, the earlier continuum of tradition was relegated to the abandoned space of the "preconciliar." The impression arose that Christianity in all its aspects was to be sketched out anew. The long prepared questions, in the realm of eschatology as elsewhere, took on the force of elementary powers that would toss the fabric of tradition almost carelessly to one side. It speaks volumes for the speed with which all this happened that within a year of the Council the Dutch Catechism had already put the doctrine of the immortality of the soul behind it, substituting in its place a remarkably obscure anthropology of resurrection-by-stages.[6] Indeed, the Missal of Paul VI dared to speak of the soul only here and there, and that in timorous fashion, otherwise avoiding all mention of it where possible. As for the German rite of burial, it has, so far as I can see, obliterated it altogether.

That such a deeply rooted and central feature of Christian faith and prayer could disappear so quickly must surely arouse astonishment. This process is not to be ascribed primarily to changed insights about man. Rather is it, as with Luther, first and foremost the expression of a basic change in relationship to tradition. To this degree it is symptomatic of a quite general crisis of Catholicism itself, for the latter is essentially characterized by a definite relation to tradition. Precisely this relation to tradition, proper to Catholicism, has now become unintelligible. One must say more: it has become unintelligible because it stands in opposition to the understanding of history found in a technological world with its counter-historical rationality. Looking from this angle, we can see that the power of the new vision of things to carry all before it, and the remarkable lostness of what is Catholic in the modern world, is itself correspondingly intelligible.

Let us try to grasp what is going on from yet another perspective. Modifying an image used by Kolakowski, we could say that the intercourse of the historical-critical method with its object may be compared with a kind of necrophilia.[7] The individual data are arrested in their finitude and fixed fast in their pastness. As already suggested, the student tries to establish in its purest possible form the finite specificity of each item from the past. In relation to the Christian faith, this means the attempt to isolate the most primitive from the welter of later constellations, so as to get at, ultimately, the message of Jesus in all its "purity." Once the Jesus of the "Sayings-Source" has been located, everything of later provenance can be explained away as a human garnish, its ingredients analyzed and combined. The true key-master of so archeologically conceived a Gospel can only be the historian. People forget that there might be in history a continuous Subject, in whom development is faithful to an Origin whose plenary authority the Subject carries within her own life.

For such an attitude, the anthropological synthesis that Christian tradition has put together from out of the individual elements of biblical faith must be both meaningless and suspect. Tradition's concept of the soul is not, in fact, to be found in so many words, or in its unity, in the New Testament writings. For the direction that theological thought has taken since the Council, two further motives were decisive. First, we must mention here a more virulent reappearance of the anti-Hellenic syndrome that had become virtually a basic category of description for historians of dogma in the practice of their craft since its inception.[8] The content of this syndrome, its significance, and its limitations had never really been thoroughly worked out. This negative attitude towards whatever was Greek was aided and abetted by two no less basic features of the contemporary scene. One is scepticism about ontology, about talk of being, for ontology seems to go against the grain of present day function- and act-centered thinking, and indeed to be unacceptable to it. In theology, people liked to set over against ontological thought, now denounced as static, the historical and dynamic approach of Scripture. Thus the ontological was counterposed to the dialogical and the personal. The other feature which assisted anti-Hellenism was the fear, reaching almost panic proportions, of any accusation of dualism. To see man as a being compounded of body and soul, to believe in a continued existence for the soul between the death of the body and its resurrection, seemed like a betrayal of the biblical and modern recognition of the unity of man, the unity of the creation. It would be a kind of fall from out of the biblical thought-world of creation into a Greek dualism which split the world into spirit and matter.

3. Content and Problematic of the New Attempts at a Solution

But what hope, then, remains for the human being after death, if the distinction of body and soul is thus denied? Luther had at least got to grips with the issue by representing man between death and resurrection as "asleep." But the question arises, Who is it that is asleep? The concept of sleep can hardly be employed to describe the gradually disintegrating body. But if there is something distinct from the body which goes on living, why should it not be called the soul? If, on the other hand, the term "sleep" is meant to express the temporary suspension of the existence of a human being, then that human being in his self-identity simply exists no longer. The reawakening of resurrection would be for him a new creation. The man who rises at the resurrection may be like the man who died but he cannot be the same as he—since it necessarily follows that with death the man who was has reached his definitive end. But in this case one has failed to maintain the very teaching on resurrection which one set out to save. And anyway we know now that by "sleep" the Bible is in no sense ascribing to the dead a condition of unconsciousness, much less that of a break-up of existence. This expression was simply an economical portmanteau term for being dead—a term which Christians filled with their own content, namely, the idea of (conscious) life with the Lord.[9]

In the face of this disorientation of thought, Catholic theologians in the last fifty years and especially since the Second Vatican Council have sought another way out. In continuity with the ideas of Troeltsch and Barth they stress the complete incommensurability of time and eternity. The person who dies steps outside time. He enters

upon the "end of the world," which is not the final day of
the cosmic calendar but is, rather, something alien to the
diurnal round of this world's time. With such thoughts as
these Barth tried to throw light on the imminent expectation of a coming end to the world on the part of Jesus and
the early Christians. The end of time, as time's boundary,
is not only very close but reaches into time's very midst.
This starting-point for reflection is then utilized to explain resurrection: when a person, by his dying, enters
into non-time, into the end of the world, he also enters, by
the same token, into Christ's return and the resurrection
of the dead. There is, therefore, no "intermediate state."
We have no need of the soul in order to preserve the identity of the human being. "Being with the Lord" and resurrection from the dead are the same thing. A solution of
striking simplicity has been found: resurrection happens
in death.

But here a question suggests itself. According to this
idea, a human being is simply indivisible. Without the
body he just does not exist: that belief is what makes
people seek out this way of thinking. Now no one can
doubt that after death man's *body* remains in the world of
space and time. It does not "rise," but is laid in the tomb.
That abolition of time which reigns beyond death does
not, then, hold good for the body. But in that case, for what
does it hold good, granted that nothing in man is separable
from the body? Or is there in fact something which, amid
the spatio-temporal disintegration of the body, is distinguishable from the body and makes its sortie from a temporal order which now for the first time takes the body
wholly into its own possession? And if there is such a
something, then why not call it the soul? Indeed, with
what right can one call it the body, when it obviously has
nothing to do with man's historical body and its materi-

ality? And how can there really be no dualism if one pos-
tulates a post-mortem second body (which one surely
must, on this hypothesis), whose origin and mode of existence remain obscure?

A second set of questions also require an answer. How
can history be, at one point (other than God!) already at its
end, when in reality it is still unfolding? The fundamental
idea—in itself perfectly correct—of the "incommensurability" between the time of this world and the time of the
world to come must surely have been misunderstood and
over-simplified. (One should speak of "eternity" only in
relation to God himself.) What future can history and the
cosmos expect? Will they ever come to their fulfilled
wholeness, or will an everlasting duality separate time
from an eternity that time can never reach? The answers
given to these questions are not entirely harmonious, nor
do they claim completeness.[10] But the inner logic of the
whole scheme points towards a declaration that a temporal end of history and a fulfilment of the cosmos are superfluous. If the resurrection has already happened, and
the individual is already encompassed by the achieved end
of the world, then this is really the only logical solution.

Once one begins to weigh the profit and loss entailed by
this entire mental operation, the whole enterprise must
appear dubious. Basically, the rejection of the soul under-
mines the resurrection, because a "resurrection" which
concerns neither matter nor the concrete historical world
is no resurrection at all. If a single word has to be fitted out
with so many hermeneutical adjuncts that in the end it is
being used in a way that goes counter to its direct meaning, then something has gone wrong with the relation between language and thought. Here we see a concrete case
of how language is not indefinitely manipulable. I do not
mean in the least to deny that these new ideas, whose

overall orientation I have tried to describe here in con-
densed form, have brought to light some important particular insights. In many respects, it was thoroughly useful and well-warranted to try a one-off experiment, and see
whether the common content of theological thought *could*
be set out in a new terminology, without recourse to the
idea of the soul. But whoever looks at the results in an un-
biased manner must surely say that in the event, what was
being tried proved to be impossible. One cannot just go
back two thousand years and retreat into the language of
the Bible. G. Lohfink, speaking as an exegete, has put this
point well and with unmistakable clarity: biblicism is
not a genuine possibility.[11] In any case, the "new way"
goes beyond the Bible both in language and thought. Indeed, it forms its own terminology in a more innovative
fashion than did Tradition. There is no through road here
to the "pure Word" of Scripture, nor to a more satisfactory
conceptual logic. Instead, what has happened is that proclamation has lost its language. To be sure, one can bring
the believer to the conclusion that there is no immortality
of the soul. But no preaching idiom will ever make him
understand that his dead friend is, *by that very fact*, risen
from the dead. Such a use of the term "resurrection" is a
typical exercise of *lingua docta*, the language of academics
with a historical theory on the brain. It is not a possible
expression of the common, and commonly understood,
faith. Even apart from the fact that the tortuous hermeneutical considerations that are necessary as background for the understanding of this formula could never
be incorporated into actual proclamation, the academic
theologian has here taken up residence in a ghetto whose
language and thought are only available to other theologians, and where linguistic and intellectual communication with the wider community has been shut down. This

is why reference to the word "soul," that indispensable verbal dwelling-place of the common content of doctrine, is indeed obligatory, as the Congregation for the Doctrine of the Faith has reminded us. This is why, too, that Congregation was right to take under its protection the ideas both of the resurrection of the whole man and of the immortality of the soul as being realities that belong inseparably with each other.[12]

4. Basic Outline of a New Consensus

In the context of present-day philosophical discussion, the fear engendered by the idea of the soul and the connected anxiety lest one receive a verdict of "Guilty of dualism!" have long been pointless. J. Seifert has made a shrewd analysis of the equivocations found in the term "dualism," distinguishing no less than eight dissimilar positions which have been crammed into the shell of that word and so brought under a common suspicion which, in the light of their mutual contradictoriness, is hardly appropriate.[13] Among the most important developments of the philosophical discussion of the issue we may note that the outstanding neurophysiologist J. Eccles (a Nobel prize-winner) and the philosopher K. Popper (normally regarded as a positivist) are united in their rejection of a neurophysiological monism and materialism. The one using a natural-scientific approach, the other a rigorously logical approach, they have found themselves obliged to abandon such a conception of man, and to elaborate in its place a "pregnant dualistic position"—where the word "dualism" is used in a completely value-free sense for the relative independence of consciousness and its corporeal instrument.[14] They have co-published a study, *The Self and its Brain*, whose title is sufficiently expressive of its content. The self possesses the brain as its physiological substrate, and uses it as its instrument. Eccles, quite correctly given his method, leaves open thereby the question of the immortality of the soul. He writes:

The coming to be, as the disappearance, of our existence are two sides of the same mystery—as the final level of the soul-body problem will recognise. What becomes of our consciousness after the death of the brain? Its wondrous instrument disintegrates, and ceases to respond to its cognitive outreach. Will the self be renewed in other forms of appearance? This question lies beyond what science can know, and a scientist should guard against the hasty interjection of a definitive 'no'.[15]

Certainly, a theologian who comes today to the defense of the existence and immortality of the soul, in the sense which Christian tradition gives to it, can expect to find opponents on many sides. But he does not affirm something which, from a philosophical or natural-scientific standpoint, is meaningless and indefensible. On the contrary: he takes up his stand against intellectual hubris and that historical forgetfulness whose waters seem set to spread far and wide. He makes a bid in support of a kind of thinking which is at once more exact and more comprehensive, and he may be sure that he does not stand alone. The theory of resurrection in death, by contrast, demolishes bridges that would lead to the intellectual commonwealth of philosophical thought, as well as to the history of Christian thought. The real methodological background to this whole proceeding is the change in the manner of conceiving the relationship of faith and reason, as well as a change in relation to tradition, to the inner unity of the history of faith.

Earlier in these reflections we had already seen that a rupture in the continuity of tradition is the basic problem that underlies the revolutionizing of particular theological themes. History is no longer a presence, mediated in trustworthy guise by the continuum which is tradition. Rather must what is past be continually refound through reconstruction by the historical method. But now a second aspect of the crisis becomes apparent, namely, uncertainty about how to tackle the relation between faith and reason. Just as the historical method wishes to distill the pure quintessence of the past and solidify it in its aboriginal form, so also ought what is theological to be purged of every philosophical additive. The mistrust of historical reason for philosophical reason plays a decisive role here. It is rarely noticed that in both questions we are dealing with modes of rationality and that, consequently, historical reconstruction can hardly visualize faith in its pure state with an entirely innocent eye. Obviously, we cannot treat this question, *expresso modo*, in this appendix. Yet two remarks may well be in place in connection with the question whether the linkage of resurrection faith to belief in the immortality of the soul may not rest upon an unacceptable importation of philosophy into faith.

1. Historically, it must be affirmed quite unambiguously that the concept of soul found in Christian tradition is in no sense a simple borrowing from philosophical thought. In the form in which Christian tradition has understood it, it exists nowhere outwith that tradition. Christian tradition has seized upon preexisting insights, elements of thought and language of diverse kinds, has purified and transformed these in the light of faith, and fused them into a new unity. This new unity derived from the logic of faith, and renders that logic capable of expression. Christian novelty has found its most vigorous expression in this context in the formula of the soul as "form of the body." Thomas Aquinas took this formulation from Aristotle, yet gave it, in terms of his own thought, a fundamentally new significance. Thus, the Council of Vienne was able to find in it the valid expression of Christian anthropology, and,

during the controversies of that time, to take it under its wings as the linguistic form of faith itself.[16] On the basis of belief in creation, and of the Christian hope which corresponds to that faith, a position has been reached which transcends both monism and dualism. It should be counted among those fundamental, elemental, insights into the nature of man that ought never to be lost. For a Christian (and especially a thinking man) should not regard monism as less dangerous and fatal than dualism. In terms of this anthropological formula of Thomas', I can agree with a remark of G. Greshake's, rightly understood: "For me, the concept of a body-free soul is, as an idea, a non-starter."[17] It is thoroughly obvious from this starting-point (of Thomas') that man throughout his life "interiorizes" matter. Consequently, even in death he does not relinquish this connection. Only so can his relation to resurrection be meaningful.[18] But by the same token, one does not need to disavow the concept of soul, nor to substitute in its place a new body. It is not that some kind of body holds the soul fast, but that the soul itself, in its continuing existence, retains within itself the matter of its life, and therefore tends impatiently towards the risen Christ, towards the new unity of spirit and matter which in him has been opened for it.[19] It follows from the logic of language here that it is uniquely fitting to speak of the living on of the *soul*. The Christian concept of the soul necessarily includes those elements of which Greshake has reminded us. That they should indeed constantly be called to mind afresh may heartily be conceded.

2. To such a degree is it justified to call the mind the continuing integration of matter-become-body in the soul that emphasis may be so placed as to give the impression that this is the really essential condition of the life everlasting. But that is false. Matter is, rather, death's condi-

tion for life. But what, then, does our expectation of the life everlasting rest upon for human beings at large? What factor can warrant it? The debate over dualism and monism has managed to push the heart of the matter out of our field of vision. We could put it like this: What gives rise to man's longing for survival? Not the isolated I, but the experience of love. Love wills eternity for the beloved and therefore for itself. The Christian response to our problem is, therefore: Immortality does not inhere in a human being but rests on a relation, on a *relationship*, with what is eternal, what makes eternity meaningful. This abidingness, which gives life and can fulfil it, is truth. It is also love. Man can therefore live forever, because he is able to have a relationship with that which gives the eternal. "The soul" is our term for that in us which offers a foothold for this relation. Soul is nothing other than man's capacity for relatedness with truth, with love eternal. And in this way, we can get right the real order of priorities: the truth and love that we call "God" give man eternity, and because in the spirit and soul of man matter is integrated, matter attains in him to the fulfilled completeness of the resurrection. In this connection, an example may illustrate the relation of faith to the philosophy that preceded it. Plato had recognized that immortality can only come from that which *is* immortal, from the truth. He saw that for human beings hope for eternal life is based on a relation to the truth. But in the last resort, the truth is an abstraction. When, in the event, someone entered the world who could say of himself "I am the Truth" (John 14, 6), the significance of Plato's assertion was fundamentally altered. The formula according to which truth grants immortality could be received as right and proper in all its amplitude, but it was now fused with another formulation:

I am the resurrection and the life; he who believes in me, though he die, yet shall he live. (John 11, 25)

A formula had become a form of life: in relationship with Christ truth can be loved, and so "being with the Lord" is life, "whether we wake or sleep" (cf. I Thessalonians 5, 10; Romans 14, 8f.).

Since this is how things are, belief in immortality and resurrection is finally identical with belief in God himself. It can only be grounded in him, even though, when so grounded, it is perfectly logical. Because God is first concrete for us in Christ, so is our own hope first concrete through faith in Christ. This does not render rationality superfluous, but brings unity to its own fumbling efforts and steadies them. Such relation to Christ does not, however, arise from the reconstructive activity of historical reason, but through the plenary authority of the communitarian history of faith, that is, in the Church. And once again, that in turn does not render historical rationality superfluous, but furnishes its knowledge with a center that can integrate it into a unity. It is now fundamental for the future of theology that it should return to a positive attitude towards the living unity of Christian history. Only thus will it treat of the Living One. Only so can development and identity subsist together, and only where development within identity is possible is there life. That simply makes it clear yet again that the language of faith which has grown up in the community of faith is a living reality, which cannot be silenced at will. Only the person who is blessed with the common speech can lead a common life.[20]

APPENDIX II

Afterword to the English Edition

This book first appeared in 1977. Since that date, the discussion it aroused has focussed almost entirely on the problem of the body–soul relationship, and the question of the soul's immortality. In my handling of these themes, I took up a position which was sharply opposed to the post–conciliar consensus of a seeming majority of Catholic theologians. For, in the work of the latter, the theory of a resurrection *in* death, and a consequent rejection of the concept of the soul, had made considerable inroads. Then in 1979, to my surprise, the Roman Congregation for the Doctrine of the Faith published an explanatory document on this very issue. That document regarded the idea of the soul as indispensable for the discourse and thinking that belong with faith. The appearance of this text gave me the opportunity to clarify my own position once again, and also to offer, in brief compass, a judgment of my own on what were at that time the more recent publications concerning this topic. The resultant essay has been presented here in the form of an Appendix, as a further explication of the subject to round off the material found in this book.

This afterword will take, in the first place, the shape of a short report on the subsequent debate about immortality and resurrection. This will be followed by some indications of further difficulties attaching to the eschatology theme. It was while writing this book that I came to realize that these particular knotty points exist. They could usefully receive closer attention in theological discussion.

1. Short Report on the Further Progress of the Controversy About Resurrection and Immortality

In the last few years, the production of eschatological literature has further expanded. Accounts of the subject as a whole have been presented by H. Küng,[1] H. Vorgrimler,[2] F. J. Nocke,[3] J. Auer[4] and M. Kehl.[5] In the great triptych of theological aesthetics, dramatics and logic in which Hans Urs von Balthasar has transcribed anew the vision of faith in a conversation with the wisdom of the world, the final volume of his *Theodramatik* is devoted to the "Final Act."[6] This is certainly no manual of eschatology; and yet, with its profound analysis of the essence of Christian hope, of the pain of God, of judgment and the consummation, it makes a foundational contribution to a deepening of the eschatology theme. Concern for these aspects of eschatology could well release the subject from a narrowly anthropological concept of its own task, while avoiding the excessively inventorial approach of the classical heuristic schemes. The special contribution of Kehl lies in his analysis of the formulation of mankind's corporate hope, from Kant to Benjamin. At the same time, where the questions of classical theology are concerned, he persists in sharing that fashionable (better: *superficial*) consensus which prevents him from taking seriously the question of the soul. Hans Küng's position is, in this respect, categorical: yet at least it has the merit of highlighting one consequence of the doctrine of resurrection *in* death—a consequence both unavoidable and, in practice, generally ignored. This is the impossibility, on these ground rules, of praying for the dead. When Küng proposes to allow at any rate a modest place for such intercessory prayer for the departed, the internal contradictoriness of this position is apparent.[7] Vorgrimler and Nocke are more careful here, but their accounts do not yield any insights that can take us substantially further.

A significant step forward in the discussion *can* be made, however, thanks to a number of recent monographs. In the context of an encyclopaedia article, the Vienna dogmatician R. Schulte offered a first attempt at a better balanced and philosophically more carefully worked out view of the problem of the body–soul relationship.[8] Similarly, the Christmastide meeting of German dogmatic theologians, from 2 to 5 January 1985, dealt usefully with the topic of the soul as a "problematic concept in Christian eschatology."[9] At this meeting philosophers, exegetes, and both fundamental and dogmatic theologians made their voices heard. What had hampered the earlier discussion was not least a lack of philosophical seriousness. The simplemindedness with which the concepts of time and eternity were handled showed an absence of awareness of that quite fundamental reflection which the Fathers and the Middle Ages had dedicated to this question. Hypotheses can only be questionable when they rest on such insecure foundations as the assumption that dying means an exit from time to non-time, or that the nontemporal is straightforwardly identifiable with eternity. In this discussion, there was a notable paucity of reflection on what makes human existence human, how in that existence the new element of the intellectual and the psychic have their own roles to play in unison with the physical and the biological. The papers read at the conference I have mentioned led to greater thoughtfulness about these issues: and more progress is still needed in this direction.

In this context I would like to refer to two English-

language investigations which could well provide fresh
stimulus for philosophical thought. J. C. Eccles, whose
views were touched on in Appendix I, has in the meantime
clarified further, in collaboration with D. N. Robinson, the
concept of man found in his view of the brain–mind relationship. (Evidently, this last is not in any simple way to
be identified with the body–soul relation.)[10] Here once
again, the question of the interplay between the biological
realm and the phenomenon of spirit, and of the reciprocal
immanence and distinction of these, is reflected on in its
multiple aspects. Not for the first time, it becomes im-
pressively clear how far a purely scientific analysis of
the phenomenon of man can take us, and where such a
method comes up against limits it can never cross. Eccles
cannot, indeed does not wish to, develop a genuine meta-
physic of the human, and therefore must naturally ex-
clude a theory of immortality. What he can show, however, is that there are no compelling grounds for accepting
a reductive materialism. Rather are there more pressing
reasons for accepting the immateriality and survival of
mind, and especially of the personal soul after the death of
the body.[11]

A rewarding, if compressed, attempt to work out a new
philosophical conception here on the basis of acquain-
tance with the contemporary human sciences is that of
Albert Shalom.[12] To try to sum up in a few lines the subtle
analyses of this study would be hubristic. Nevertheless, I
would like at least to indicate how the author seeks to
press forward to a new vision of subjectivity and personhood by way of a deepened reflection on the nature of
time. The interrelationship of "internalization" and "deployment" is for him the key that will unlock the remarkable twofold nature of man. For, on the one hand, that nature is harnessed to the outer flux of the biological world,

and, on the other, it transcends that world in the permanence of a self-identical abiding interiority. For Shalom, this mutually ordering relationship of outer and inner, of biological centrifugality and spiritual centripetality, should replace the "body–soul" formula which, it must be confessed, he considers only in that static and dualistic form which Descartes had given it. I support Shalom in his rejection of Cartesian dualism, for the fact is that in Cartesian thought the inner unity of creation, bonded together in the being of man, is lost to view. Furthermore, I am convinced that Shalom's fundamental anthropological formula of deployment and internalization can broaden and deepen the classical anthropology in a substantial way. His book contributes important new elements to the philosophical (and theological) discussion with the human sciences. To be sure, I am not of the opinion that this model can substitute for a rightly understood notion of body and soul, as that is found with increasing maturity in Christian history (and nowhere else!) on the basis of its biblical foundations. That body–soul idea remains unavoidable. But it can be carried over into such categories of temporality and there find its further extension, its better protection against misconceptions, and a purer grasp of its own personalist significance.[13]

This brings me to another aspect of the discussion of the same theme. The quest for a correct understanding of soul, immortality and resurrection was, throughout this entire debate, rendered more difficult, not to say blocked off altogether, by a wholly schematic comprehension of the relation between Hellenic and biblical thought. The joy of Greek culture in the body was overlooked, as was the insistent orientation of that culture towards the *polis*, with its common life of "justice." Hellenic thinking was identified with a body–soul dualism, set over against a Hebraic

stress on this-worldliness, itself affirmed in a fashion
equally lacking in a sense of perspective. In this regard, the
doctoral work of H. Sonnemanns on Hellenic and Christian anthropology and eschatology is illuminating, and
could draw back forgotten truths from the theological sub-
conscious.[14] What I was able only to hint at in merest outline in my own eschatological study receives here a fuller
exposition, and I may perhaps be allowed to draw readers'
attention to Sonnemann's account as filling out the historical aspect of this dimension of my own presentation.

Important clarifications issued more recently from a
source where I had not expected them. The Evangelical
theologian Fritz Heidler has surveyed anew the "biblical
teaching on the immortality of the soul" from the viewpoint of Lutheran theology. In his important book, he
boldly sets his face against the Evangelical progenitors of
the theory of total death, and of resurrection *in* death,
against, that is, such figures as Karl Barth, Helmut Thielicke and Eberhard Jüngel, on whose work Catholic theologians too have come to depend in considerable measure.[15] Heidler shows in incisive fashion that the total
datum of biblical theology can find appropriate expression
only with the recognition of the immortality of the soul.
To my astonishment, he also holds that this recognition
corresponds to the real intention of Luther's theology. I
would commend Heidler's book both for the amplitude
and depth it brings to the biblical question, and also for its
ecumenical value in relation to Evangelical theology.

Of late, the hitherto most determined opponent of the
concept of the soul, G. Greshake, has also come to modify
his position, and to bring it somewhat closer to my own,
in a book coauthored with the Vienna exegete J. Kremer.[16]
Greshake now expressly recognizes the just value of the
concept of the soul, yet persists in his thesis about resur-

rection in death. In a—by and large—very positive review, his Freiburg colleague J. H. Verweyen remarks on this point: "Unless transformed through accompaniment by saving clauses, the formula 'resurrection in death' can only elicit considerable misunderstanding. It so easily steers away our attention from the decisive twin poles of the beginning and consummation of our share in Christ's resurrection, by suggesting, though not fully intending, the fulfilment of the individual in the temporal moment of death."[17] One can only agree. As this debate proceeds, it becomes ever clearer that the true function of the idea of the soul's immortality is to preserve a real hold on that of the resurrection of the flesh. The thesis of resurrection in death dematerializes the resurrection. It entails that real matter has no part in the event of the consummation. This theory reduces Christian hope to the level of the individual. If individual men and women *qua* individuals can, through death, enter upon the End, then history as such remains outside salvation and cannot receive its own fulfilment. The battle-lines are drawn up, in fact, in precisely the reverse of the order that one might expect. Denial of the soul and affirmation of resurrection in death mean a spiritualistic theory of immortality, which regards as impossible true resurrection and the salvation of the world as a whole. The doctrine of immortality that tells us that our "I" is, as it were, confirmed in God through Christ's resurrection and thereby tends expectantly towards the future resurrection—this alone can safeguard the realism of the Bible.

Finally, I would like to refer to the publication in Leipzig in 1986 of a dissertation, originally produced at Erfurt, in which G. Nachtwei has undertaken an analysis of my eschatology in the context of my entire theological work.[18] This book appears to me to be the most comprehensive and objective overall evaluation that has yet appeared of the discussion opened by my *Eschatologie* in the German-speaking countries. One of the vital services of this study was to allow the range of questions involved their full depth and breadth. For I had not attempted to repristinate a "Hellenic" or Neo-Scholastic theory of the body and the soul. Rather was my concern to give these concepts their rightful place in a "dialogical" anthropology conceived in the context of Scripture and the Fathers. It is because Nachtwei reestablishes this positive framework that in his study polemical narrowness dissolves, and contrary propositions lose their hardness. His following through the line of argumentation to its pastoral consequences is valuable as well. He calls attention to the fact that the most "up-to-date" eschatological theses were in many cases turned straight into preaching and catechesis, without any intervening interval to allow a suitable pause for reflection. Indeed, offering an account of how theological theses are to be converted into preaching has become one of the tasks of a dogmatic treatise. To my mind, such damage to the language of proclamation is a sign of the fact that we are on the wrong track: preaching should not be for theology a sort of final, derivative *précis* of the latter's scientific discourse. The contrary of this position is much closer to the truth. The kerygma is theology's point of departure, and its goal. If, *en route,* theological reflection attacks the kerygma, it is not the kerygma that suffers shipwreck, but theology.

And this brings me to a further point which concerns me very much. Before the appearance of Nachtwei's major work, the discussion of my eschatology had limited itself, as I have said, almost exclusively to the body–soul problem.[19] To my dismay, the impression arose that I reduced the whole of eschatology to this single question. Noth-

ing could be further from my intention. I must confess
that, through my own experience of the crisis into which
preaching had entered, the dispute about the soul was
something weighty and central for me. Speaking as a theologian, I consider this to be, in the last analysis, not a debate about philosophy but about the capacity of faith to
become proclamation, and about the resurrection. As already suggested, it is paradoxically the case that resurrec-
tional realism depends on the "soul": a realism about faith
in God's power from whose compass materality is not excluded. Hereby hangs too the Christian belief in the salvation of the world and of history, and, lastly, the possibility
of praying, in any meaningful sense of that word, for our
dead. As a theologian, I do not regard philosophy as being,
ultimately, a study which we pursue for philosophy's sake.
And yet how the very case at hand demonstrates that the
integrity of faith depends on rigor of philosophical thinking, such that careful philosophizing is an irreplaceable
part of genuine theological work! Or to put it in other
words: on such theological grounds as these, the philosophical and anthropological question became for me a vital one, even though I treated it as a theologian and tried to
incorporate it within the wider totality of a theological
eschatology.

In this context, I would like to underline an insight into
method to which I addressed myself at the end of Appendix I. During the course of the last century, Cardinal Newman and Vladimir Solovyev referred with some emphasis
to the category of development as the key concept for a
kind of theological thinking that would be appropriate to
Catholic dogma. This insight has not however borne fruit
in modern theology, because the problem of the interrelationship of exegesis, Church and dogma has remained un-
solved. To the student of historical texts, treated accord-

ing to the criterion of scientific method, the enduring subjecthood of the Church in the midst of temporal change is not exactly a favorite topic. And yet this subject (the Church) also lives in an exchange of deployment and internalization. Where attention is exclusively directed to the succession of phenomena (of texts), the binding power of internalization is forgotten. There remains only a mere succession of contradictory stages in faith and ecclesial life. As between Scripture, the Fathers, the Scholastics and the modern age, no inner living context suggests itself: one stands before a sequence of but partly reconcilable texts. In view of this discontinuity in the language of faith, contemporary theology has no other option save to fall back on the most ancient of its texts. If one takes up this attitude, one can certainly not speak of "resurrection in death" (for that is wholly unbiblical); but equally, one is also disallowed from substituting the formula "immortality of the soul." Fundamentally, there remains only the effort to attach to whatever one takes to be primitive and Jesus-like a semi-illuminating philosophy one has concocted for oneself. It is surely plain that no faith capable of sustaining human living lies this way. And so the case of the theme of resurrection-and-immortality turns out to be simply an example of something that is needful for theology in general. Everything depends on the capacity of theology to leave off its fixation with deployment, and find its way back to that ecclesial identity which holds all together. In this way, theology will be able to grasp faith in the living dynamic of its development. For that self-identity does not in any way rigidify, but rather renders ever deeper that which it embraces.

2. Further Fundamental Matters from My Book

Next to the question of the anthropological basis of Christian eschatology, the writing of my book brought me into contact with other fundamental matters which were no less important for me. My theological formation over the last forty years was profoundly marked by the dominance of an exegesis which, so far as the heart of the matter was concerned, was indebted to Albert Schweitzer's concept of the radically imminent eschatological character of the preaching of Jesus—and this notwithstanding the various novel methodological subtleties that had been introduced. It is my impression that this basic position is still today the governing one despite the varied shifts in exegesis and theology that have taken place. The really exciting question is supposed to be not whether in this or that detail in his ideas about time Jesus was mistaken, but whether the original message is, in its core proclamation, tenable at all, so that it is only by interpretation that it can be made usable in our lives. But this raises two quite fundamental issues for modern theology. The first concerns the problem as to how we can arrive at a correct understanding of Scripture. Do we have to stick with the *opinio communis* of the exegetes, or is that just one element, albeit an important one, in our commerce with Scripture? If there is no further court of appeal beyond the present generation of exegetes, then the last two or three generations, including our own, could only proceed on the assumption that Jesus' message is intrinsically incapable of being appropriated by us, so that it is actually we ourselves who must first bring it into a meaningful form. On the other hand, there can be no dodging the issue by retreating into a position for which historical rationality and its expression in exegesis are regarded as unimportant for faith. Such a flight from reason would contradict fundamentally the very nature of Christian faith. This is why I was concerned to work out an exact position vis-à-vis the foundations of contemporary exegesis, and, at the same time, to ask just where the latter opens itself out into the hermeneutic of faith. Engagement with the problematic of imminent expectation and so with the wider problem of the proper interpretation of Scripture at large was and is at the heart of my book. For me, as its opening chapter indicates, the eschatology question is identical with the question of the essence of Christianity itself. Sections 2 and 3 of the book grapple directly with this issue, but, in point of fact, the entire work is written from this vantage point, which I resume more particularly in section 6. It would please me very much if this issue, which is really and truly so central, might be taken up again and discussed in a way that would extend and deepen what I had to say. The matter of immortality and resurrection is no more than an aspect of this wider whole.

Furthermore, the ecumenical question also exercised me in working out my ideas on eschatology. First and foremost, the theology of death (section 4 of my study) was motivated by the desire for a realistic anthropology. Each and every human being is a suffering being. The moment of death is not our first experience of finitude. Finitude presses daily on body and on soul. We must prepare ourselves for encounter with that limit which, whether we are more aware of it or less, is the recurrence of suffering. This is a primordial human question. I tried to ask it in as concrete a way as I could, not using my own wisdom but seeking to understand that of the Bible, and to make it mine, ours. In the course of so doing I discovered that the factor of interconfessional division also enters in here: the question of what human "works" are worth, and where their own limit should be placed. It struck me that the debate over justification (by works or through faith), which in its classic form is of hardly more than historical interest, becomes at this point a matter of concrete human concern, and one, moreover, that is placed within reach of its resolution. In this sense I meant that particular section of my book to be something of a tacit conversation with the Reformed churches. In like manner, I also tried to give the question of Purgatory a new twist, on the basis of Scripture and Fathers, and to put it in its ecumenical context. It would give me pleasure if this part of my study were also discussed and proved able to stimulate wider reflection.

Finally, I had in mind two last dimensions of the eschatology question which are especially important today. One concerns the relation of the concrete, cosmic expectations that belong to faith with our current world-picture. Hardly anybody seems to recognize today how vital it is to guard against a false physicalism in the interests of defending the frontiers of authentic religious expression. There is a great danger of so withdrawing faith from material reality that one will end up in a new Docetism, beginning with christology and ending with eschatology. As far as the form of Christ's self-presentation is concerned, only his word will be of consequence and not his flesh. (To defend the virginal birth of Jesus and his bodily resurrection seems quite indecent to some commentators, so far has this Docetism penetrated in many quarters.) Naturally, in this case, our bodies have no more to do with resurrection, and the world can go on forever just as it chooses, for— after all—one rises again in the act of dying. There is no room left in the divine promise for history or materiality. One of my principal concerns was to find the right intermediary course between physicalism on the one hand and Docetism on the other. The other unavoidable problem was that generated by present-day political theology, which comes close to dissolving the Eschaton into Utopia. I have explained in the introduction to my book why I think it is wrong to change eschatology into a treatise on political theology, or into a generalized theology of hope. I have also tried to respond to the basic questions which those theologies throw up, and to do so by way of adherence to the concrete form of Christian hope. In this context, I may refer the interested reader to my new book *Kirche, Ökumene und Politik* where I have dealt with this constellation of themes in a more thorough manner.[20]

My *Eschatologie* was written for German readers. It is an unfortunate consequence of this that I had in my sights only a tiny fraction of the English language literature. I should have liked to use this Afterword to make good this deficiency at least by a little. Alas, my present office does not allow me to read with that serenity and patience which would be prerequisites for this. I can only ask my readers in English speaking countries to show forbearance. At the same time, I would like to thank most sincerely all those who have made the English translation possible, especially Father Aidan Nichols, O.P., who has awaited my nearly always highly tardy answers to his letters with great patience. I hope that this little book will be a help to both theologians and believers at large in the English-speaking world, as they seek after a living faith which will be, in the midst of all the questions of the present hour, a power that makes for hope.

JOSEPH CARDINAL RATZINGER
Rome,
Feast of St. Teresa of Avila, 1987

Notes

A NOTE ON THE CURRENT VOLUME

1. See S. Sykes, *The Identity of Christianity. Theologians and the Essence of Christianity from Schleiermacher to Barth* (London 1984).

2. J. Ratzinger, *Volk und Haus Gottes in Augustins Lehre von der Kirche* (Munich 1954).

3. J. Ratzinger, *Die Geschichtstheologie des heiligen Bonaventura* (Munich 1959).

4. See especially J. Ratzinger, "Heilsgeschichte, Metaphysik und Eschatologie," in *Theologische Prinzipienlehre. Bausteine zur Fundamentaltheologie* (Munich 1982), pp. 180–199, as well as the present work.

INTRODUCTION

1. H. U. von Balthasar, "Eschatologie," in J. Feiner, J. Trütsch, F. Böckle, *Fragen der Theologie heute* (Einsiedeln 1957), p. 404.

2. J. Weiss, *Die Predigt Jesu vom Reiche Gottes* (Göttingen 1892); A. Schweizer, *Skizze des Lebens Jesu* (Tübingen 1901); ibid. *Von Reimarus zu Wrede. Eine Geschichte der Leben-Jesu-Forschung* (Tübingen 1906).

3. M. Werner, *Die Entstehung des christlichen Dogmas* (Bern-Tübingen 1941).

4. D. Wiederkehr, *Perspektiven der Eschatologie* (Einsiedeln 1974).

5. *Didache* X.6.

6. Cf. K. G. Kuhn, "maranatha," TWNT IV, pp. 470–475.

7. F. J. Dölger, *Sol Salutis*, 2nd ed. (Münster 1925); E. Peterson, "Die geschichtliche Bedeutung der jüdischen Gebetsrichtung," in *Frühkirche, Judentum und Gnosis* (Freiburg 1959), pp. 1–14; "Das Kreuz und das Gebet nach Osten," ibid. pp. 15–35.

8. Zechariah 12, 10; Apocalypse 1, 7.

9. FGJ p. 35.

10. See H. J. Jaschke, *Der Heilige Geist im Bekenntnis der Kirche. Eine Studie zur Pneumatologie des Irenaeus von Lyon im Ausgang vom altchristlichen Glaubensbekenntnis* (Münster 1976).

11. Apocalypse 20, 2–7.

12. See U. Hommes, J. Ratzinger, *Das Heil des Menschen. Innerweltlich-christlich* (Munich 1975), pp. 33ff.

PART ONE. THE ESCHATOLOGICAL PROBLEM

1. J. Jeremias, *Neutestamentliche Theologie* I (Gütersloh 1971), p. 105.

2. R. Schnackenburg, *Gottes Herrschaft und Reich* (Freiburg 1959), pp. 23–47.

3. Ibid. p. 37.

4. Cited ibid. p. 38.

5. F. Hahn, *Christologische Hoheitstitel*, 3rd ed. (Göttingen 1966), pp. 133–279, especially pp. 193–218; see also J. Ratzinger, *Einführung in das Christentum* (Munich 1968), pp. 164ff.

6. Cf. J. Jeremias, *Neutestamentliche Theologie* I (op. cit.), pp. 110–115.

7. Mark 1, 15.

8. Matthew 12, 38–42; Luke 11, 29ff.; Matthew 16, 2.

9. J. Schmid, *Das Evangelium nach Markus*, 2nd ed. (Regensburg 1950), p. 28.

10. K. L. Schmidt, "basileia," TWNT I, p. 591.

11. Cf. Matthew 20, 1–16; Luke 18, 9–14; 17, 7–10; 15, 11–32; 15, 1–10; 7, 36–50; Mark 4, 26–29.

12. Cf. Matthew 10, 16; 19, 17; 7, 21–33; 25, 31–40.

13. Matthew 7, 11 and parallels.

14. Mark 10, 18.

15. J. Jeremias, *Neutestamentliche Theologie* I (op. cit.), p. 104.

16. F. Mussner, *Praesentia Salutis. Gesammelte Studien zu Fragen und Themen des Neuen Testamentes* (Düsseldorf 1967) p. 95.

17. Cf. K. L. Schmidt, "basileia" (art. cit.), p. 591.

18. Luke 11, 20.

19. Matthew 24, 48; Luke 12, 45; cf. Matthew 25, 5.

20. II Peter 3, 4.

21. H. Conzelmann, *Die Mitte der Zeit. Studien zur Theologie des Lukas*, 4th ed. (Tübingen 1962), p. 183.

22. On the question of dating, see W. G. Kümmel, *Einleitung in das Neue Testament*, 17th ed. (Heidelberg 1973), pp. 89ff. and 119ff. A general attack on the now customary dating is launched by J. A. T. Robinson in *Redating the New Testament* (London 1975).

23. E. Grässer, *Das Problem der Parusiaverzögerung in den synoptischen Evangelien und in der Apostelgeschichte* (Berlin 1957), pp. 217ff.

24. Daniel 12, 11 (and cf. 11, 32; 9, 27).

25. Hosea 9, 7; Jeremiah 46, 10; Deuteronomy 32, 35.

26. Luke 21, 24 (cf. Zechariah 12, 3; Psalm 79, 1; Isaiah 63, 18; Daniel 9, 26; I Maccabees 3, 45–51; Daniel 12, 7; Tobit 14, 5).

27. Matthew 24, 29.

28. Cf. Internationale Theologenkommission, *Die Einheit des Glaubens und der theologische Pluralismus* (Einsiedeln 1973), especially pp. 17–29, 36–42.

29. K. Barth, *Der Römerbrief*, 2nd ed. (Munich 1922), p. 298.

30. Cf. F. M. Braun, *Neues Licht auf die Kirche* (Einsiedeln 1946), p. 116.

31. K. Barth, *Der Römerbrief* (op. cit.), p. 240.

32. Ibid. p. 234.

33. Ibid. p. 243; cf. F. M. Braun, *Neues Licht auf die Kirche* (op. cit.), p. 114.

34. See H. Küng, *Rechtfertigung. Die Lehre Karl Barths und eine katholische Besinnung* (Einsiedeln 1957), p. 26.

35. This point is evidenced in G. Hasenhüttl, *Der Glaubensvollzug. Eine Begegnung mit Rudolf Bultmann aus katholischem Glaubensverständnis* (Essen 1963), especially pp. 165–177.

36. O. Cullmann, *Christus und die Zeit. Die urchristliche Zeit- und Geschichtsauffassung*, 2nd ed. (Zurich 1948), pp. 43ff.

37. Ibid. p. 47.

38. Ibid. p. 55.

39. Ibid. p. 71.

40. Ibid. p. 72.

41. O. Cullmann, *Heil als Geschichte* (Tübingen 1965), p. 313.

42. C. H. Dodd, *The Parables of the Kingdom* (London 1935), p. 198.

43. Ibid. p. 207.

44. Ibid. p. 202.

45. Ibid. p. 203.

46. Ibid. p. 210; Isaiah 64, 4; I Corinthians 2, 9.

47. J. Moltmann, *Theologie der Hoffnung* (Munich 1964), p. 12.

48. Ibid. pp. 13ff.

49. Cf. G. Greshake, G. Lohfink, *Naherwartung—Auferstehung—Unsterblichkeit*, 2nd ed. (Freiburg 1976), pp. 30–34.

50. See G. E. Kafka, U. Matz, *Zur Kritik der Politischen Theologie* (Paderborn 1973), especially pp. 18ff.

51. See e.g., S. Silva, *Glaube und Politik: Herausforderung Latinamerikas. Von der christlich inspirierten Partei zur Theologie der Befreiung* (Frankfurt 1973), pp. 192–228.

52. Luke 6, 35; Matthew 5, 9.

53. Philippians 2, 5–11.

54. Isaiah 45, 23.

55. Job 15, 8.

PART TWO. DEATH AND IMMORTALITY

1. J. Pieper, *Tod und Unsterblichkeit* (Munich 1968), p. 192.
2. P. Althaus, *Die letzten Dinge. Lehrbuch der Eschatologie*, 6th ed. (Gütersloh 1956); E. Jüngel, *Tod* (Stuttgart, Berlin 1971).
3. On this, see the special issue of *Concilium* 11, 5 (1975), and notably J.-M. Pohier's contribution at pp. 352–362.
4. See, for example, H. von Glasenapp, *Die fünf grossen Religionen* I (Düsseldorf 1952), p. 29; C. Regamey, in F. König, *Christus und die Religionen der Erde* (Freiburg 1951), I. pp. 73ff.; for the Greek world, P. Hoffmann, *Die Toten in Christus. Eine religionsgeschichtliche und exegetische Untersuchung zur paulinischen Eschatologie* (Münster 1966), pp. 26ff.
5. J. Pieper, *Über die platonischen Mythen* (Munich 1965); U. Duchrow, *Christenheit und Weltverantwortung. Traditionsgeschichtliche und systematische Struktur der Zweireichelehre* (Stuttgart 1970), pp. 61–80.
6. As shown by F. Mussner, *Die Auferstehung Jesu* (Munich 1969).
7. Cf. I Samuel 28, 3–25. Detailed material may be consulted in P. Hoffmann, *Die Toten in Christus* (op. cit.), pp. 61–73, and especially pp. 67ff.
8. Qoheleth 2, 16ff.
9. Job 19, 22–25.
10. Psalm 16, 9b–10, 11b–c.
11. H. J. Kraus, *Psalmen* I (Neukirchen 1960), p. 127.
12. Especially verses 23–28.
13. H. J. Kraus, *Psalmen* I (op. cit.), p. 511.
14. Psalm 73, vv. 4ff.
15. Ibid. v. 9.
16. Ibid. v. 22.
17. Ibid. vv. 24, 26.
18. A. von Harnack, *Das Wesen des Christentums* (Leipzig 1900; 1950), p. 28.
19. H. J. Kraus, *Psalmen* I (op. cit.), p. 520.
20. Wisdom 3, 1ff.; 16, 13; cf. also 2, 3.
21. Apocalypse 20, 13ff.
22. I Corinthians 15, 26.
23. Philippians 2, 6–11.
24. O. Cullmann, *Unsterblichkeit der Seele oder Auferstehung der Toten?* (Stuttgart 1962), p. 19.
25. P. Althaus, "Retraktionen zur Eschatologie," in *Theologische Literatur Zeitung* 75 (1950), p. 256.
26. Ibid. pp. 257–260.
27. G. Greshake, *Auferstehung der Toten* (Essen 1969), p. 387.

28. *A New Catechism. Catholic Faith for Adults* (New York 1982), p. 474.

29. Ibid. p. 473.

30. G. Greshake, *Auferstehung der Toten* (op. cit.), p. 387.

31. G. Greshake, G. Lohfink, *Naherwartung—Auferstehung—Unsterblichkeit* (op. cit.), p. 77.

32. Ibid. p. 80.

33. Mark 12, 18–27.

34. Exodus 3, 6.

35. I Corinthians 15, 17.

36. Ibid. 15, 16.

37. John 11, 25a.

38. Ibid. 11, 25b.

39. Ibid. 6, 39ff.; 6, 44 and 54; 11, 24; 12, 48.

40. Luke 16, 19–31.

41. M. Luther, *Werke. Kritische Gesamtausgabe* (Weimar 1883ff.) *Tischreden* 5, 219; cf. P. Althaus, "Retraktionen zur Eschatologie" (art. cit.), p. 255.

42. I.e. P. Hoffmann, *Die Toten in Christus* (Münster 1966).

43. Cf. Mark 12.

44. R. Meyer, "kolpos," TWNT III, pp. 824–826; cf. B. Trémel, "Der Mensch zwischen Tod und Auferstehung nach dem Neuen Testament," *Anima* 11 (1956), pp. 313–331.

45. Luke 23, 43.

46. Luke 16, 19–29.

47. Apocalypse 6, 9.

48. Josephus, *The Jewish War* II.8.11, tr. W. Whiston, in *The Whole Genuine Works of Flavius Josephus* (London 1839), III, p. 376; cf. also *The Jewish Antiquities* XVIII.1, 5.

49. K. Schubert, *Die Gemeinde vom Toten Meer* (Munich, Basel 1958), p. 96.

50. Ibid. p. 98.

51. P. Hoffmann, *Die Toten in Christus* (op. cit.), pp. 41ff.

52. Ibid. pp. 163ff.

53. Acts of the Apostles 7, 59.

54. J. Jeremias, "paradeisos," TWNT V, p. 769.

55. John 1, 18.

56. Ibid. 13, 23.

57. Represented by I Thessalonians 4, 13 - 5, 11, and I Corinthians 15, 12–58.

58. P. Hoffman, *Die Toten in Christus* (op. cit.), pp. 186–206.

59. Ibid. p. 237.

60. Ibid. p. 238.

61. P. Hoffmann, *Die Toten in Christus* (op. cit.), pp. 253–258.

62. R. Bultmann, *Der zweite Brief an die Korinther* (Göttingen 1976), pp. 132–146.

63. Ibid. p. 144.

64. II Corinthians 4, 16.

65. Ibid. 5, 9; cf. Philippians 1, 24ff.

66. J. Gnilka, *Der Philipperbrief* (Freiburg 1968), p. 92.

67. John 11, 25.

68. For Clement, see now K. Schmöle, *Läuterung nach dem Tode und pneumatische Auferstehung bei Klemens von Alexandrien* (Münster 1974).

69. For these creeds, see DS 2; 5; 10–64; for the Creed of Nicaea–Constantinople, see DS 150; for the (Pseudo-) Athanasian Creed, DS 76.

70. E.g. Psalm 136, 25; Jeremiah 25, 31; Psalm 65, 3.

71. DS 72.

72. Ibid. 540.

73. Ibid. 325.

74. Ibid. 684.

75. Ibid. 801.

76. Ibid. 1000.

77. Ibid. 856–858.

78. See PL CLXXXIII.375; 705; CLXXXII.993; 579.

79. Apocalypse 6, 9ff.

80. DS 1002.

81. M. Luther, *Werke* (op. cit.), *Tischreden* 5, p. 219.

82. U. Duchrow, *Christenheit und Weltverantwortung* (Stuttgart 1970), p. 71: Greek in origin is precisely what Orphism is not!

83. *Republic* 589 a 7ff.

84. U. Duchrow, *Christenheit und Weltverantwortung* (op. cit.), p. 61.

85. G. Dumézil, *L'Idéologie tripartite des Indo-Européens* (Brussels 1958), and other works by this author.

86. U. Duchrow, *Christenheit und Weltverantwortung* (op. cit.), p. 79.

87. *Phaedo* 114d.

88. Cf. also the great vision in *Phaedrus* 245c–250c.

89. *De anima* B. 2, 412a 19ff.

90. *De generatione animalium* B. 3, 736b 28; 3, 737a 10; 6, 744b 22.

91. P. Hoffmann, *Die Toten in Christus* (op. cit.), p. 42.

92. F. Guntermann, *Die Eschatologie des hlg. Paulus* (Münster 1932), p. 38; cf. P. Hoffmann, *Die Toten in Christus* (op. cit.), p. 211.

93. *Libri X in Canticum canticorum* 2, 5, = PG XIII, 126B–127A. Here cited in the translation by R. P. Lawson, *Origen. The*

Song of Songs. Commentary and Homilies (London 1957, = *Ancient Christian Writers* 26), pp. 134–135.

94. P. Hoffmann, *Die Toten in Christus* (op. cit.), p. 125.

95. A. Pegis, "Some Reflections on Summa contra Gentiles II. 56", in *An Etienne Gilson Tribute* (Milwaukee 1959), p. 177.

96. T. Schneider, *Die Einheit des Menschen. Die anthropologische Formel 'anima forma corporis' im sogenannten Korrektorienstreit und bei Petrus Johannis Olivi* (Münster 1972), pp. 23, 27.

97. DS 902.

98. P. Althaus, "Retraktionen zur Eschatologie" (art. cit.), p. 256.

99. Matthew 5, 8.

100. John 17, 3.

101. Cf. Gregory of Nyssa, *De beatitudinis, Oratio* 6, PG XLIV.

102. H. Meyer, *Thomas von Aquin*, 2nd ed. (Paderborn 1961), p. 269; cf. T. Schneider, *Die Einheit des Menschens* (op. cit.), p. 29.

103. Ibid.

104. A. Pegis, *At the Origins of the Thomistic Notion of Man* (New York 1963), p. 58, cited in T. Schneider, *Die Einheit des Menschen* (op. cit.), p. 50.

105. J. Pieper, *Tod und Unsterblichkeit* (op. cit.), p. 96.

106. Genesis 3, 3.

107. John 9.

108. Philippians 2, 5–11.

109. Matthew 10, 30 and parallels.

110. H. Schlier, *Das Ende der Zeit* (Freiburg 1971), pp. 71ff.

PART THREE. THE FUTURE LIFE

1. A. Vögtle, *Das Neue Testament und die Zukunft des Kosmos* (Düsseldorf 1970), pp. 232ff.

2. G. Greshake, *Auferstehung der Toten* (Essen 1969), pp. 386ff.

3. Ibid. p. 393.

4. Ibid. p. 410.

5. I Corinthians 15, 35.

6. As shown by F. Mussner, *Die Auferstehung Jesu* (Munich 1969), pp. 101–120.

7. I Corinthians 15, 50.

8. John 6, 55.

9. Ibid. 6, 63.

10. Cf. especially I Corinthians 15, 20–28, and the entire book of the Apocalypse.

11. G. Kretschmar, "Auferstehung des Fleisches. Zur Früh-

geschichte einer theologischen Lehrformel," in *Leben angesich-ten des Todes* (Tübingen 1968, = Thielecke *Festchrift*), pp. 106ff.

12. Ibid. p. 114.

13. I Corinthians 15, 50.

14. G. Kretschmar, "Auferstehung des Fleisches" (art. cit.), p. 123.

15. Logion 23.

16. G. Kretschmar, "Auferstehung des Fleisches" (art. cit.), p. 127.

17. *De resurrectione* 8, cf. G. Kretschmar, "Auferstehung des Fleisches" (art. cit.), p. 134.

18. *Adversus Haereses* V. 31, 1.

19. G. Kretschmar, "Auferstehung des Fleisches" (art. cit.), p. 129.

20. Cited ibid.

21. Ibid. p. 133.

22. T. H. C. Van Eijk, *La Résurrection des morts chez les Pères Apostoliques* (Paris 1974), pp. 170–178: a discussion of the im-plausible constructions offered by W. Bieder, "Auferstehung des Fleisches oder des Leibes?," *Theologische Zeitschrift* 1 (1945), pp. 105–120.

23. *Excerpta in Psalmum* 1, = PG XII, 1093A–1096B.

24. See the catalogue of problems in T. Schneider, *Die Einheit des Menschen* (Münster 1973), pp. 59–63: the book's whole ac-count of the debate is worth consulting.

25. *In Leviticum homiliae* VII, 1–2. Here translated into En-glish from the text offered in M. Borret, S.J. (ed.), *Origène. Homé-lies sur le Lévitique* I (Paris 1981, = *Sources Chrétiennes* 286), pp. 298–323.

26. Cf. C. Regamey, in F. König, *Religionswissenschaftliches Wörterbuch* (Vienna 1956), pp. 445ff.

27. G. Greshake, *Auferstehung der Toten* (op. cit.), p. 406.

28. K. Rahner, *Zur Theologie des Todes* (Freiburg 1958), p. 22.

29. I Corinthians 15, 28.

30. G. Greshake, *Auferstehung der Toten* (op. cit.), p. 386.

31. Ibid.

32. Cf. Adorno's postulate of "the resurrection of the flesh" as a condition of true justice in Th. W. Adorno, *Negative Dialektik* (Frankfurt 1966), pp. 205, 393.

33. Mark 13, 37.

34. J. Daniélou, "Christologie et eschatologie," in A. Grill-meier, H. Bacht (eds.), *Das Konzil von Chalkedon* III (Würzburg 1954), pp. 280–286.

35. Mark 13, 6; 21–23.

36. Ibid. 13, 7ff.

37. Ibid. 13, 8.
38. Ibid. 13, 9–13.
39. Ibid. 13, 14.
40. Daniel 9, 27; 11, 31; 12, 11.
41. Mark 13, 10.
42. Ibid. 13, 14–27.
43. II Thessalonians 2, 8; cf. 2, 3.
44. Apocalypse 13, 1–18.
45. *XL Homiliarum in Evangelia, Libri Duo,* I.1, = PL 76, 1077f.
46. I Thessalonians 5, 3.
47. Luke 17, 26–30; cf. Matthew 24, 37–39.
48. Mark 13, 10; 13, 30; cf. ibid. 9, 1.
49. W. Beinert, *Die Kirche—Gottes Heil in der Welt. Die Lehre von der Kirche nach den Schriften des Rupert von Deutz, Honorius Augustodunensis und Gerhoh von Reichersberg* (Münster 1973), p. 347.
50. Romans 11, 25–32.
51. E. Käsemann, *An die Römer* (Tübingen 1973), pp. 299–304.
52. II Thessalonians 3, 10ff.
53. See E. Peterson, *Eis Theos. Epigraphische, formgeschichtliche und religionsgeschichtliche Untersuchungen* (Göttingen 1926); "Die Einholung des Kyrios," *Zeitschrift für systematische Theologie* 7 (1929–30), pp. 682ff.; E. Grässer, *Das Problem der Parusieverzögerung in den synoptischen Evangelien und in der Apostelgeschichte* (Berlin 1957), pp. 121ff.
54. A. Grillmeier, *Mit ihm und in ihm. Christologische Forschungen und Perspektiven* (Freiburg 1975), p. 406.
55. Matthew 25, 1ff.
56. T. Maertens, *Heidnisch-jüdische Wurzeln der christlichen Feste* (Mainz 1965), pp. 41–44.
57. Galatians 4, 3; 9; Colossians 2, 8; 20; on the present situation of Christians; on their eschatological destiny. Matthew 24, 29–31; II Peter 3, 10, *et al.*
58. T. Maertens, *Heidnisch-jüdische Wurzeln der Christlichen Feste* (op. cit.), p. 42.
59. Galatians 4, 3; Colossians 2, 8.
60. Cf. especially John 14, 15–31.
61. R. Guardini, *Der Herr* (Würzburg 1937), pp. 542–548; cf. the commentaries of Bultmann and Schnackenburg on the Fourth Gospel.
62. John 14, 2f.
63. II Thessalonians 1, 5; I. Corinthians 5, 13; Romans 2, 3ff.; 3, 6; 14, 10; cf. also Matthew 10, 28 and parallels; Matthew 6, 4; 6; 15; 18.

64. Matthew 25, 31–46; 7, 22f.; 13, 36–43; Luke 13, 25–27; I Thessalonians 4, 6; I Corinthians 4, 4f.; 11, 32; II Corinthians 5, 10.

65. I Corinthians 6, 2ff.; cf. Daniel 7, 22; Wisdom 3, 8; Apocalypse 3, 21.

66. John 3, 17f.; 9, 39; 12, 47f.

67. Ibid. 3, 17.

68. Ibid. 12, 47.

69. Ibid. 12, 48.

70. L. Boros, *Mysterium Mortis. Der Mensch in der letzten Entscheidung,* 9th ed. (Olten, Freiburg 1971), p. 9.

71. Ibid. p. 181.

72. II Thessalonians 3, 10.

73. Cf. Apocalypse 20; among the Fathers, preeminently Justin, *Dialogus cum Trypho* 80, 1; Irenaeus, *Adversus Haereses* V. 31ff.

74. Apocalypse 1, 7.

75. Matthew 25, 41; 5, 29 and parallels; 13, 42, 50; 22, 13; 18, 8 and parallels; 5, 22; 18, 9; 8, 12; 24, 51; 25, 30; Luke 13, 28. See for materials J. Gnilka, "Hölle. Die Aussagen der Schrift," LThK V pp. 445–446.

76. II Thessalonians 1, 9; 2, 10; I Thessalonians 5, 3; Romans 9, 22; Philippians 3, 19; I Corinthians 1, 18; II Corinthians 2, 15; 4, 3; I Timothy 6, 9; Apocalypse 14, 10; 19, 20; 20, 10–15; 21, 8.

77. DS 72; 76; 801; 858; 1351.

78. Ibid. 411.

79. DS 1000; see V. 3.

80. Notably in the Bull of Union for the Greeks of 6. 7. 1439.

81. J. N. Karmiris, "Abriss der dogmatischen Lehre der orthodoxen katholischen Kirche," in P. Bratsiotis, *Die orthodoxe Kirche in griechischer Sicht,* 2nd ed. (Stuttgart 1970), pp. 15–120, and especially pp. 112–120.

82. *Confessio Augustana* XXIV, in *Die Bekenntnisschriften der evangelisch-lutherischen Kirche,* 6th ed. (Göttingen 1967).

83. DS 856; cf. 1304.

84. Ibid. 1580; 1820.

85. Ibid.

86. II Maccabees 12, 32–46.

87. Ibid. 12, 42.

88. *Vita Adae et Evae* 46–47; J. H. Charlesworth (ed.), *The Old Testament Pseudepigrapha* II (London 1985), pp. 288; 290.

89. H. L. Strack, P. Billerbeck, *Kommentar zum Neuen Testament aus Talmud und Midrasch* (Munich 1922–1926), IV.2, pp. 1044–1047; 1050–1056; 1101ff.

90. K. Schmöle, *Läuterung nach dem Tode und pneumatische Auferstehung bei Klemens von Alexandrien* (op. cit.), p. 136.

91. A. Stuiber, *Refrigerium interim. Die Vorstellungen des Zwischenzustandes und die frühchristliche Grabeskunst* (Bonn 1957), pp. 61ff.

92. J. A. Fischer, *Studien zum Todesgedanken in der alten Kirche* I (Munich 1954), pp. 259ff.

93. Matthew 5, 26 and parallels.

94. E. Stauffer, *Die Theologie des Neuen Testaments*, 4th ed. (Stuttgart 1948), pp. 196; 296, note 697. Cf. also G. Bertram, *phulakē*, TWNT IX, pp. 237–240; W. Bauer, *Griechisch-deutsches Wörterbuch*, 5th ed. (Berlin 1958), col. 1716: i.e., *phulakē, sub loc.*

95. J. A. Fischer, *Studien zum Todesgedanken in der alten Kirche* I (op. cit.), p. 258.

96. Cyprian, *Letters* 55, 20; CSEL III.2, p. 638. See J. A. Fischer, *Studien zum Todesgedanken in der alten Kirche* I (op. cit.), pp. 267ff.

97. K. Schmöle, *Läuterung nach dem Tode und pneumatische Auferstehung bei Klemens von Alexandrien* (op. cit.), pp. 60ff.

98. Ibid. p. 135.

99. Ibid. p. 138.

100. Ibid. p. 140.

101. Philippians 1, 21; John 3, 16–21.

102. J. Gnilka, *Ist I Kor 3, 10–15 ein Schriftzeugnis für das Fegfeuer? Eine exegetische-historische Untersuchung* (Düsseldorf 1955), pp. 27ff.

103. J. N. Karmiris, "Abriss der dogmatischen Lehre der orthodoxen katholischen Kirche" (art. cit.), pp. 113–117.

104. Isaiah 66, 15ff.

105. J. Gnilka, *Ist I Kor 3, 10–15 ein Schriftzeugnis für das Fegfeuer?* (op. cit.), p. 126.

106. J. Jeremias, "geenna," TWNT I, p. 656.

107. J. Gnilka, "Fegfeuer II. Lehre der Schrift," LThK IV, p. 51.

108. Romans 8, 29; Philippians 3, 21.

109. H. U. von Balthasar, "Eschatologie," in J. Feiner, J. Trütsch, F. Böckle, *Fragen der Theologie heute* (Einsiedeln 1971), p. 411.

110. H. U. von Balthasar, "Eschatologie im Umriss," in *Pneuma und Institution. Skizzen zur Theologie* IV (Einsiedeln 1974), p. 443.

111. Ibid. p. 441.

112. Cited in P. Engelhardt, "Hoffnung II. Überlieferung," LThK V, p. 422.

113. Perhaps this is already clear, indeed, in Sirach 7, 33.

114. K. Rahner, "Auferstehung des Fleisches," in *Schriften zur Theologie* II (Einsiedeln 1955), p. 221.

115. John 2, 19.

116. Apocalypse 2, 17b.

APPENDIX I

1. Cf. Romans 6, 17: baptism as a being given over to the "standard of the teaching," whereby a credal confession or catechism-type synthesis of the most important credal contents is brought into play. Cf. E. Käsemann, *An die Römer* (Tübingen 1973), pp. 171ff; H. Schlier, *Der Römerbrief* (Freiburg 1977), pp. 208ff.; J. Ratzinger, "Kirche und wissenschaftliche Theologie," in W. Sandfuchs (ed.), *Die Kirche* (Würzburg 1978), pp. 83–95, especially pp. 91ff.

2. Cf. on this H. de Lubac, *Credo* (Einsiedeln 1975), pp. 29–56.

3. The Roman text says expressly on this point, 'Naturally, this is not a matter of reducing or even hindering theological research, research which is in itself of great service to the faith of the Church. . . ." In the final section of the clarification, this is reaffirmed: "The difficulties bound up with these questions lay heavy responsibilities on the theologians whose task, for its part, is assuredly irreplaceable. Just so, they have a claim to our encouragement and to that space for free manoeuvre which their methods legitimately require."

4. This has been shown—if somewhat unilaterally—by, in particular, W. Kamlah, in his *Christentum und Geschichtlichkeit. Die Entstehung des Christentums* (Stuttgart 1951).

5. *Divino afflante*, 30. 9. 1943; extracts appear in D.S. 3825–3831.

6. In its German dress, *Glaubensverkündigung für Erwachsene* (Freiburg 1969), pp. 524–529, and notably p. 525: "They are present, to be awakened." P. 627 speaks of an existence continued in the act of being awakened." The clarification issued by the cardinalatial commission of 15. 10. 1968 which adopted a critical position on several points in this catechism, had nothing to say on this. How far the displacement of the idea of the soul has gone may be seen from the avoidance of any clear statement of the soul's immortality in the catechism licensed for the dioceses of Aachen and Essen, a catechism which, for its fidelity to the tradition, was simply deluged by cascades of angry comment: see *Botschaft des Glaubens* (Donauwörth–Essen 1978), p. 368, section 547. The far-reaching capitulation of the liturgical reformers in the face of the new terminology made a deep mark here.

7. L. Kolakowski, *Die Gegenwärtigkeit des Mythos* (Munich 1973), pp. 95ff. This author used the image for man's technical-rational intercourse with nature.

8. Cf. on this theme the essay, so rich in both materials and perspectives, of A. Grillmeier, "Hellenisierung-Judaisierung als Deuteprinzipien der Geschichte des kirchlichen Dogmas," in idem,

Mit ihm und in ihm. Christologische Forschungen und Perspekti-
ven (Freiburg 1975), pp. 423–488.

9. Cf. the fundamental account of this area in P. Hoffmann, *Die Toten in Christus*, 3rd ed. (Münster 1978).

10. Thus, more clearly than hitherto, G. Greshake and G. Lohfink in the third edition of the *quaestio disputata: Naherwartung—Auferstehung—Unsterblichkeit. Untersuchungen der christlichen Eschatologie* (Freiburg 1978), especially pp. 151–155 (Lohfink); 178ff. (Greshake). W. Pannenberg has given convincing expression to the impossibility of doing without the idea of a real end to history as the locus for the resurrection of the dead in his *Die Auferstehung Jesu und die Zukunft des Menschen* (= Eichstätter Hochschulreden 10; Munich 1978), pp. 14–18.

11. E.g. op. cit. p. 145.

12. For this reason, the introduction of this model in radical fashion would also render Christ's resurrection problematic. For when it is said that every Christian experiences anew what happened to Christ in his own awakening to the risen life, the removal of the dimensions of bodiliness and history from the Lord's resurrection is at any rate close at hand.

13. J. Seifert, *Das Lieb-Seele-Problem in der gegenwärtigen philosophischen Diskussion* (Darmstadt 1979), pp. 126–130. Further philosophical literature on the subject is indicated in this study.

14. J. C. Eccles, "Hirn und Bewusstsein," in *Mannheimer Forum* 77/78, pp. 9–65, and here at p. 15. See also idem, *The Human Mystery* (Berlin 1979); C. R. Popper and J. C. Eccles, *The Self and its Brain. An Argument for Interactionism* (Berlin 1977).

15. J. C. Eccles, "Hirn und Bewusstsein," p. 65.

16. Cf. T. Schneider, *Die Einheit des Menschen. Die anthropologische Formel 'anima forma corporis' im sogenannten Korrektorienstreit und bei Petrus Johannes Olivi* (Münster 1972).

17. G. Greshake, op. cit. p. 179. Greshake here speaks of a "difference of substance" between us in whose light he "would like to retain" his own position, p. 180. We must try once again to narrow down the difference which separates us. Personally, I have always taken from the *anima-forma-corporis* formula the idea of the abiding relatedness of the soul to the body. The soul renders itself temporal in the body, and thus integrates bodiliness within its own reality. That the soul is already, in the moment of death "come to its fulfilment," ibid., I regard as incompatible with the openness of history, for which the resurrection has not yet taken place, as II Timothy 2, 18 emphasizes.

18. G. Greshake, op. cit. pp. 170ff.

19. Ibid. pp. 172ff., with reference to an important study by L. Scheffczyk, *Auferstehung* (Einsiedeln 1976), pp. 290ff.

20. The same methodological problem lies at the root of the dispute about the theme of priesthood. The method of archeological reconstruction, working on the linguistic resources of the New Testament, will naturally be brought to deny that the Church has a priesthood, and to see in the *de facto* existence of that priesthood only a restoration of what belongs to the Old Testament, or to paganism. It is not realized that, by way of living development, through a synthesis of the diverse New Testament elements concerned, something new, namely the Christian priesthood, grew into being. The same holds good of the concept of sacrament: cf. J. Ratzinger, *Zum Begriff des Sakraments* (= Eichstätter Hochschulreden 15, Munich 1979). Yes, indeed: the foundations of possibility for a truly Catholic theology depend upon this point.

APPENDIX II

1. H. Küng, *Ewiges Leben?* (Munich 1982).
2. H. Vorgrimler, *Hoffnung auf Vollendung. Aufriss der Eschatologie* (Freiburg 1980).
3. F. J. Nocke, *Eschatologie* (Düsseldorf 1982).
4. J. Auer, *'Siehe, ich mache alles neu.' Der Glaube an die Vollendung der Welt* (Regensburg 1984). Auer, following here the philosopher H. E. Hengstenberg, wishes to distinguish between the concrete phenomenon "body" and "bodiliness" as a metaphysical principle in the constitution of man. The distinction between "body" (physical) and "bodiliness" (metaphysical) seems to me to be justified. But it does not solve the problem of the personal bearer of "bodiliness" and therefore it does not solve the problem of the resurrection either. The fact that a metaphysical "bodiliness" belongs to man after death as before it points to a constant of his metaphysical constitution, but not to the event that we term "resurrection." Nevertheless, careful reflection on this aspect of the question might help to loosen up fixed positions and contribute to an anthropologically more profound view of immortality and resurrection.
5. M. Kehl, *Eschatologie* (Würzburg 1986).
6. H. U. von Balthasar, *Theodramatik IV. Das Endspiel* (Einsiedeln 1983).
7. H. Küng, op. cit. p. 180: "We should neither be praying for definite 'poor souls' in 'Purgatory'—the kind of prayer of little faith that is supposed to go on for a lifetime, nor praying with a scarcely intelligible kind of prayer carried out 'with' or directed 'to' the dead. What should be proposed is prayer for the dying, and for the dead, rather, a revential, loving thinking about them, to-

gether with a commending of them to the grace of God—in the living hope that the dead are definitively with God: *Requiescant in pace!* May they rest in peace!"

8. R. Schulte, "Leib und Seele," in F. Böckle, F. X. Kaufmann, K. Rahner, and B. Welte, (eds.), *Christlicher Glaube in moderner Gesellschaft* 5 (Freiburg 1980), pp. 5–61.

9. W. Breuning, (ed.), *Seele, Problembegriff christlicher Eschatologie* (Freiburg 1986). A predominantly philosophical collection, G. Pöltner and H. Vetter, *Das Leib-Seele-Problem* (Vienna 1986), moves in the same direction. In this context, I would also like to draw attention to the fact that the philosophical section of the *Görresgesellschaft* devoted its 1985 labors to the theme "Leib und Seele. Ein altes und ein neues Problem der Philosophie." The person charged with collating the various reports of this occasion, the Giessen philosopher Hans Michael Baumbartner, summed up the drift of the papers and discussions by remarking, "The upshot of the discussion was a generally shared conviction that neither an elimination of what was meant by the soul nor a reduction of that meaning (whether real or merely linguistic) would be justifiable—and that not only from a philosophical point of view but also from those of the theory of science and indeed of natural science itself." *Jahres- und Tagungsbericht der Görresgesellschaft* (Cologne 1986), p. 118.

10. J. C. Eccles and D. N. Robinson, *The Wonder of Being Human. Our Brain and Our Mind* (New York and London 1984).

11. Ibid. p. 172.

12. A. Shalom, *The Body–Mind Conceptual Framework and the Problem of Personal Identity* (Atlantic Highlands, New Jersey, 1985).

13. A possible helpful contribution here is that of D. Connell, "Substance and the Interiority of Being," in *Neue Zeitschrift für systematische Theologie und Religionsphilosophie* 25 (1983), pp. 68–85. In a critical encounter with various notions espoused by Bergson, the author shows that interiority demands substantiality.

14. H. Sonnemanns, *Seele-Unsterblichkeit-Auferstehung. Zur griechischen und christlichen Anthropologie und Eschatologie* (Freiburg 1984). W. Jaeger's *The Theology of the Early Greek Philosophers* (Oxford 1947) remains fundamental for following the journey of Greek thought from the beginnings up to Plato.

15. F. Heidler, *Die biblische Lehre von der Unsterblichkeit der Seele: Sterben, Tod, ewiges Leben im Aspekt lutherischer Anthropologie* (Göttingen 1983). A position on our question worth looking at is that of the Evangelical systematic theologian J. Bauer in his *Einsicht und Glaube* (Göttingen 1978), pp. 7–49. Bauer presents a "plea for Plato," but then proceeds to separate out the

ideas of resurrection and immortality as essentially different. A careful examination of this position would be valuable, but cannot be carried out here.

16. G. Greshake and J. Kremer, *Resurrectio mortuorum. Zum theologischen Verständnis der leiblichen Auferstehung* (Darmstadt 1986).

17. H. J. Verweyen, review of the above in *Theologische Revue* 83 (1987), pp. 313–316.

18. G. Nachtwei, *Dialogische Unsterblichkeit. Eine Untersuchung zu Joseph Ratzingers Eschatologie und Theologie* (Leipzig 1986).

19. H. Vorgrimler introduces my book to his readers with the remark that "This book is not like the other books in the series [i.e. the *Kleine katholische Dogmatik*] in that it is not concerned to give the complete coverage proper to a dogmatic treatise. The author tries to offer a positive evaluation of Platonism, and engages in debate with political theology and with the hypotheses of G. Greshake and G. Lohfink," op. cit. pp. 10ff. I can only regard this statement as a misdirecting of the reader. I was *much* concerned with the objective comprehensiveness proper to a treatise, and tried to achieve it in a way that was both concise and contemporary.

20. J. Ratzinger, *Kirche, Ökumene und Politik* (Einsiedeln, 1987).

Select Bibliography

GENERAL WORKS

Alberione, J., *The Last Things* (Boston 1964).

Badham, P., *Christian Beliefs about Life after Death* (London 1976).

von Balthasar, H. U., "Eschatology," in J. Feiner *et al.* (eds.), *Theology Today: Renewal in Dogma* I (Milwaukee 1965), pp. 222–244.

Galot, J., *The Mystery of Christian Hope* (New York 1977).

Garrigou-Lagrange, R., *Life Everlasting* (St. Louis and London 1952).

Gleason, R. W., *The World to Come* (New York 1958).

Guardini, R., *The Last Things* (New York 1954).

Hick, J., *Death and Eternal Life* (San Francisco 1980).

Küng, H., *Eternal Life?* (London 1984).

Macquarrie, J., *Christian Hope* (London 1978).

Schillebeeckx, E., "The Interpretation of Eschatology," in Schillebeeckx, E., and B. Willems (eds.), *The Problem of Eschatology* (New York 1969, = *Concilium* 41), pp. 42–56.

Schmaus, M., *Dogma 6: Justification and the Last Things* (London 1977).

Schnackenburg, R., *God's Rule and Kingdom* (New York 1963).

Simpson, M., *The Theology of Death and Eternal Life* (Dublin and Cork 1971).

van der Walle, A., *From Darkness to the Dawn* (London 1984).

Williams, M. E., "Eschatology (Theological Treatment)," *New Catholic Encyclopedia* 5, pp. 533–538.

Winklhofer, A., *The Coming of his Kingdom* (New York 1963).

PART ONE

II. The Exegetical Data

1. A Word on Method

Brown, R. E., *The Critical Meaning of the Bible* (London 1981).

———. *Biblical Exegesis and Church Doctrine* (London 1985).

Childs, B. S., *The New Testament as Canon. An Introduction* (Philadelphia 1984).

Frei, H., *The Eclipse of Biblical Narrative* (Yale 1974).

Gadamer, H. G., *Truth and Method* (New York 1975).

Maier, G., *The End of the Historical–Critical Method* (St. Louis, Missouri 1977).

Marlé, R., *Introduction to Hermeneutics* (London 1967).

Mascall, E. L., "History and the Gospels," in *Theology and the Gospel of Christ* (London 1977), pp. 65–120.

Stuhlmacher, P., *Historical Criticism and Theological Interpretation of Scripture* (Philadelphia 1977).

2. *The Meaning of Jesus' Proclamation of the Kingdom of God*

Hahn, F., *The Titles of Jesus in Christology. Their History in Earliest Christianity* (London 1969).

Jeremias, J., *New Testament Theology I. The Proclamation of Jesus* (London 1972).

Ladd, G. E., *Jesus and the Kingdom. The Eschatology of Biblical Realism* (New York 1964).

Lundström, G., *The Kingdom of God in the Teaching of Jesus* (Edinburgh and London 1963).

Perrin, N., *The Kingdom of God in the Teaching of Jesus* (London 1963).

Schmidt, K., "basileia," TDNT I, pp. 579–593.

Schnackenburg, R., *God's Rule and Kingdom* (London and New York 1963).

3. *The Expectation of an Imminent End*

Beasley-Murray, G. R., *Jesus and the Future. An Examination of the Criticism of Eschatological Discourse in Mark 13 with Special Reference to the Little Apocalypse Theory* (London 1954).

Conzelmann, H., *The Theology of St Luke* (London 1961).

Corell, A., *Consummatum Est: Eschatology and Church in the Gospel of St John* (New York 1958).

Davies, W. D., and D. Daube (eds.), *The Background of the New Testament and its Eschatology. In Honour of Charles Harold Dodd* (Cambridge 1956).

Knight, G. A. F., "Eschatology in the Old Testament," *Scottish Journal of Theology* 4 (1951), pp. 355–362.

Martin, F., "Eschatology (In the Bible)," NCE 5, pp. 524–533.

Marsh, J., *The Fulness of Time* (London 1952).

Wilder, A. N., *Eschatology and Ethics in the Teaching of Jesus* (New York 1950).

III. Word and Reality in Contemporary Appreciation

1. The Panorama of Solutions

von Balthasar, H. U., *The Theology of Karl Barth* (New York 1972).

Barth, K., *The Epistle to the Romans* (London 1968).

Bultmann, R., *History and Eschatology. The Presence of Eternity* (New York 1962).

———. *Theology of the New Testament* (New York 1951–1955).

Cullmann, O., *Christ and Time. The Primitive Christian Conception of Time and History* (London 1952).

———. *Salvation in History* (London 1967).

Dodd, C. H., *History and the Gospel* (London 1952).

———. *The Parables of the Kingdom* (London 1961).

Kee, A. (ed.), *A Reader in Political Theology* (Philadelphia 1974).

———. *The Scope of Political Theology* (London 1978).

Küng, H., *Justification. The Doctrine of Karl Barth and a Catholic Reflection* (New York 1964).

Meeks, M. D., *Origins of the Theology of Hope* (Philadelphia 1974).

Metz, J. B., *Theology of the World* (New York 1969).

Moltmann, J., *The Crucified God. The Cross of Christ as the Foundation and Criticism of Christian Theology* (London 1976).

———. "Exegesis and the Eschatology of History," in *Hope and Planning* (London 1971), pp. 56–98.

———. "Theology as Eschatology" in Herzog, F. (ed.), *The Future of Hope. Theology as Eschatology* (New York 1970), pp. 1–50.

———. *The Theology of Hope* (New York 1967).

2. Preliminary Conclusions

von Balthasar, H. U., *A Theology of History* (London 1963).

Daniélou, J., *The Lord of History. Reflections on the Inner Meaning of History* (London 1958).

PART TWO

IV. The Theology of Death

Aries, P., *The Hour of Our Death* (New York 1981).

———. *Western Attitudes toward Death* (Baltimore 1975).

Boros, L., "Death: a Theological Reflection," in Taylor, M. (ed.), *The Mystery of Suffering and Death* (New York 1973), pp. 139–155.

———. *The Moment of Truth. Mysterium Mortis* (London 1965).

Charles, R. H., *A Critical History of the Doctrine of a Future Life in Israel, in Judaism and in Christianity*, 2nd ed. (London 1913).

Ernst, C., "The Theology of Death," *Clergy Review* 44 (1959), pp. 588–602.

Gatch, M., *Death: Meaning and Morality in Christian Thought and Contemporary Culture* (New York 1969).

Helling, M., *What Are They Saying About Death and Christian Hope?* (New York 1978).

Hick, J., *Death and Eternal Life* (San Francisco 1980).

Pelikan, J., *The Shape of Death. Life, Death and Immortality in the Early Fathers* (Nashville 1961).

Rahner, K., *On the Theology of Death*, 2nd ed. (London 1965).

Rohde, E., *Psyche: the Cult of Souls and Belief in Immortality among the Greeks* (London 1925).

Rush, A. C., *Death and Burial in Christian Antiquity* (Washington, D.C. 1941).

Wright, J. H., "Death (Theology of)," NCE 4, pp. 686–695.

V. The Immortality of the Soul and the Resurrection of the Dead

1. The State of the Question

Cullmann, O., *Immortality of the Soul or Resurrection of the Dead? The Witness of the New Testament* (London 1955).

2. The Biblical Data

Bultmann, R., *The Gospel of John. A Commentary* (Oxford 1971).
———. *Theology of the New Testament* (New York 1951–1955).

Gnilka, J., *The Epistle to the Philippians* (New York 1971).

Jeremias, J., "paradeisos," TDNT V, pp. 765–773.

Meyer, R., "kolpos," TDNT III, pp. 824–826.

Reicke, B., "Body and Soul in the New Testament," *Studia Theologica* 19 (1965), pp. 200–212.

Schubert, K., *The Dead Sea Community. Its Origins and Teachings* (London 1959).

Stendahl, K. (ed.), *Immortality and Resurrection* (London 1965).

3. The Documents of the Church's Magisterium

Barnard, L. W., "Justin Martyr's Eschatology," *Vigiliae Christianae* 19 (1965), pp. 86–98.

McWilliam Dewart, J. E., *Death and Resurrection* (Wilmington, Delaware 1986, = Message of the Fathers of the Church 22).

Douie, D. L., "John XXII and the Beatific Vision," *Dominican Studies* 3 (1950), pp. 154–174.

Florovsky, G., "Eschatology in the Patristic Age," *Studia Patristica* 2 (1957), pp. 235–250.

Forshaw, B., "Benedictus Deus," NCE 2, pp. 304–305.

Kirk, K. E., *The Vision of God* (London 1931).

Lampe, G. W. H., "Early Patristic Eschatology," *Scottish Journal of Theology. Occasional Papers* 2 (1953), pp. 17–35.

Lienhard, J. T., "The exegesis of I Corinthians 15, 24–28 from Marcellus of Ancyra to Theodoret of Cyrus," *Vigiliae Christianae* 37 (1983), pp. 340–357.

Mollat, G., "Benedict XII," NCE 2, pp. 275–276.

Prestige, L., "Hades in the Greek Fathers," *Journal of Theological Studies* 24 (1923), pp. 476–485.

Wolfson, H. A., "The Immortality of the Soul and Resurrection in the Philosophy of the Church Fathers," *Harvard Divinity School* 22 (1956–1957), pp. 5–40.

4. Theological Unfolding

González-Ruiz, J.-M., "Should We De-mythologise the 'Separated Soul'?" in Schillebeeckx, E., and B. Willems (eds.), *The Problem of Eschatology* (New York 1969, = *Concilium* 41), pp. 82–96.

Pegis, A., *At the Origins of the Thomistic Notion of Man* (New York 1963).

———. "Some Reflections on *Summa Contra Gentiles* II. 56," in *An Etienne Gilson Tribute* (Milwaukee 1959), pp. 169–188.

Pieper, J., *Death and Immortality* (London 1969).

PART THREE

VI. The Resurrection of the Dead and the Return of Christ

1. What Does "The Resurrection of the Dead" Mean?

Cornelis, H., *et al.*, *The Resurrection of the Body* (Notre Dame, Indiana 1964).

Darragh, J. T., *The Resurrection of the Flesh* (London 1921).

Durrwell, F. X., *The Resurrection* (London 1960).

McElwain, H. H., "Resurrection of the Dead," NCE 12, pp. 419–427.

Rahner, K., "The Hermeneutics of Eschatological Assertions," *Theological Investigations* IV (London 1966), pp. 323–346.

———. "The Resurrection of the Body," *Theological Investigations* II (London 1963), pp. 203–216.

Sider, R. J., "The Pauline Conception of the Resurrection Body in I Corinthians XV," *New Testament Studies* 21 (1974–1975), pp. 428–439.

Stanley, D. M., *Christ's Resurrection in Pauline Soteriology* (Rome 1961).

Williams, R., *Resurrection* (London 1982).

2. The Return of Christ and the Final Judgment

Ceroke, C. P., and S. J. Duffy, "Parousia," NCE 10, pp. 1032–1039.

Glasson, T. F., *His Appearing and His Kingdom. The Christian Hope in the Light of History* (London 1953).

——. *The Second Advent. The Origin of the New Testament Doctrine*, 3rd ed. (London 1963).

Moore, A. L., *The Parousia in the New Testament* (Leiden 1966, = Supplements to *Novum Testamentum* XIII).

Nolan, B. M., "Some Observations on the Parousia and New Testament Eschatology," *Irish Theological Quarterly* XXXVI.4 (1969), pp. 283–314.

Robinson, J. A. T., *Jesus and his Coming* (London 1957).

VII. Hell, Purgatory, Heaven

Arendzen, J. P., *Purgatory and Heaven* (New York 1960).

Buis, H., *The Doctrine of Eternal Punishment* (Philadelphia 1957).

Dalton, M. J., *The Theology of Salvation and Damnation* (Dublin and Cork 1977).

Daniélou, J., *Origen* (New York 1955).

Fortman, E., *Everlasting Life after Death* (New York 1976).

von Hügel, F., "What Do We Mean By Heaven? And What Do We Mean By Hell?," *Essays and Addresses on the Philosophy of Religion* (London 1921–1949), pp. 195–226.

Jeremias, J., "geenna," TDNT I, pp. 657–658.

Le Goff, J., *The Birth of Purgatory* (London 1984).

Ombres, R., "Latins and Greeks in Debate over Purgatory, 1230–1439," *Journal of Ecclesiastical History* 35 (1984), pp. 1–14.

——. *The Theology of Purgatory* (Dublin and Cork 1978).

Paternoster, M., *Thou Art There Also. God, Death and Hell* (London 1967).

Perham, M., *The Communion of Saints. An Examination of the Place of the Christian Dead in the Belief, Worship and Calendars of the Church* (London 1980).

Pontifex, M., "The Doctrine of Hell," *Downside Review* 71 (1953), pp. 135–152.

Rahner, K., "Purgatory," *Theological Investigations* XIX (London 1984), pp. 181–193.

Rowell, G., *Hell and the Victorians* (Oxford 1974).

Rowlands, C., *The Open Heaven. A Study of Apocalyptic in Judaism and Early Christianity* (London 1982).

Simon, U. E., *Heaven in the Christian Tradition* (New York 1958).

Sykes, S. W., "Life after Death: the Christian Doctrine of Heaven," in McKinney, R. W. A. (ed.), *Creation, Christ and Culture* (Edinburgh 1976), pp. 250–271.

.Thompson, W., "The Doctrine of Hell," *The Ecumenist* 10 (1972), pp. 33–37.

Thurston, H., *The Memory of Our Dead* (London 1915).

Walker, D. P., *The Decline of Hell* (London 1964).

Ware, K. T., "One Body in Christ: Death and the Communion of Saints," *Sobornost* 3, 2 (1981), pp. 179–196.

Index of Names

Andorno, T. W., 282
Althaus, P., 73, 104–105, 150–151, 278, 281
Aristotle, 24, 77, 144, 148, 149, 178
Auer, J., 262, 288
Augustine, 182–184

Bachofen, J. J., 76
Bacht, H., 282
Balthasar, H. U. von, 1, 262, 275, 285, 288
Barth, K., 3, 47–48, 56, 251–252, 266, 277
Bauer, J., 289
Bauer, W., 285
Baumbartner, H. M., 289
Beinert, W., 283
Bernard of Clairvaux, 137
Bertram, G., 285
Bieder, W., 282
Billerbeck, P., 221, 284
Billot, L., 181
Bloch, E., 193
Boros, L., 208, 283
Bratsiotis, P., 284
Braun, F. M., 277
Breuning, W., 289
Bultman, R., 36–37, 48–50, 51, 54, 56, 57, 58, 118–119, 126–127, 280, 283

Clement of Alexandria, 133, 222, 224–227, 231
Clement of Rome, 172
Connell, D., 289
Conzelmann, H., 37, 276

Cullmann, O., 51–55, 57, 104, 277, 278
Cyprian, 223–224, 231, 285

Daniélou, J., 195–197
Descartes, R., 265
Didymus of Alexandria, 216
Diodore of Tarsus, 216
Dodd, C. H., 55–56, 57, 277
Dölger, F. J., 6, 275
Duchrow, U., 280
Dumézil, G., 280
Durandus of Saint-Pourçain, 181

Eccles, J., 255–256, 264, 286, 289
Einstein, A., 23
Empedocles, 141
Engelhardt, P., 285
Epicurus, 102
Evagrius Ponticus, 216
Feuling, D., 181
Fischer, J. A., 222, 285
Flavius Josephus, 122–123, 279

Gerhoh of Reichersberg, 200
Glasenapp, H. von, 278
Glorieux, P., 208
Gnilka, J., 228, 280, 283, 285
Grässer, E., 276, 283
Gregory Nazianzen, 227
Gregory of Nyssa, 151–152, 216, 281
Greshake, J., 108, 179, 188, 191, 258, 266, 277, 278, 279, 282, 286, 290

Grillmeier, A., 282, 283, 286
Guardini, R., 283
Guntermann, F., 280

Hahn, F., 276
Harnack, A. von, 89, 278
Hasenhüttl, G., 277
Hegel, G. W. F., 212, 217
Heidegger, M., 201
Heidler, F., 266, 289
Hengstenberg, H. E., 288
Hettinger, F., 181
Hippolytus, 172
Hoffmann, P., 120, 125–126, 278, 279, 280, 281, 286
Homer, 77, 141
Hommes, U., 276

Irenaeus, 175, 283

Jaeger, W., 289
Jaschke, H. J., 275
Jeremias, J., 228, 276, 279, 285
Jerome, 216
Joachim of Fiore, 13, 211–212
Jochanan, Rabbi, 28
John Chrysostom, 219, 227
John Damascene, 208
John of the Cross, 217
Jüngel, E., 73, 266, 278
Justin, 174–175, 283
Justinian, 215

Käsemann, E., 283, 286
Kafka, G. E., 277
Kamlah, W., 286
Karmiris, J. N., 283, 285
Kehl, M., 262, 263, 288
Kolakowski, L., 249, 286
König, F., 278, 282
Kraus, H. J., 87–89, 278
Kremer, J., 266, 290
Kretschmar, G., 172, 176, 281, 282
Kuhn, K. G., 275
Kümmel, W. G., 276

Küng, H., 262–263, 277, 287, 288

Laforêt, N. J., 181
Lohfink, G., 110, 182, 254, 277, 286
Louis the Bavarian, 137
Lubac, H. de, 286
Luther, M., 104, 105, 119–120, 125, 139, 242, 247–249, 279

Maertens, G., 283
Marcuse, H., 193
Marx, K., 212
Matz, U., 277
Meyer, H., 281
Meyer, R., 279
Michael Palaeologos, 136
Michel, A., 181
Moltmann, J., 57–58
Mussner, F., 276, 278, 281

Nachtwei, G., 267–268, 290
Newman, J. H., 269
Nocke, F. J., 262, 263, 288

Ockham, William of, 137
Origen, 33, 34, 133, 145–146, 176–177, 179, 185–187, 215, 227

Pegis, A., 149, 281
Péguy, C., 232
Peter, patriarch of Antioch, 135
Peterson, E., 6–7, 275, 283
Pieper, J., 70, 278, 281
Plato, 24, 73, 77–79, 112, 141–143, 148, 259
Plotinus, 144–145, 278
Pohier, J., 278
Pöltner, G., 289
Pomponazzi, P., 140
Popes: Benedict XII, 136, 138;

Gregory the Great, 198–
199; John XXII, 138; Leo IX,
135; Paul VI, 248; Pius XII,
248
Popper, K., 255, 287
Pseudo-Leontius, 215
Pythagoras, 23, 141

Rahner, K., 191, 282, 285
Ratzinger, J., 275, 286, 288,
290
Regamey, C., 278, 282
Robinson, D. N., 264, 289
Robinson, J. A. T., 276

Sandfuchs, W., 286
Scheffczyk, L., 287
Schell, H., 181
Schlatter, A., 104
Schleiermacher, F., 70
Schlier, H., 160, 281, 286
Schmid, J., 276
Schmidt, K. L., 276
Schmöle, K., 280, 284
Schnackenburg, R., 276, 283
Schneider, T., 281, 282, 287
Schubert, K., 122, 279
Schulte, R., 263, 289
Schweitzer, A., 1, 35, 47, 275
Seifert, J., 255, 286
Shalom, A., 264, 265, 289
Silva, S., 277
Socrates, 73, 79, 102

Solovyev, V., 269
Sonnemann, H., 266, 289
Strange, C., 104
Stauffer, E., 285
Strack, H. L., 221, 284
Stuiber, A., 285
Sykes, S., 275

Tatian, 41
Teilhard de Chardin, 154, 191
Tertullian, 172, 222, 223, 230
Theodore of Mopsuestia, 216
Thérèse of Lisieux, 65, 188,
217
Thielicke, H., 266
Thomas Aquinas, 24, 148–
149, 153, 155, 159, 178,
179–181, 191, 208, 246,
257–258
Trémel, B., 279
Troeltsch, E., 47, 251

Valentinus, 173–176
Van Eijk, T. H. C., 282
Verweyen, J. H., 267, 290
Vetter, H., 289
Vögtle, A., 166–168
Vorgrimler, H., 262, 288, 290

Weiss, J., 1, 19, 35, 47, 275
Werner, M., 2, 275
Wiederkehr, D., 275

Index of Subjects

Abraham, 119, 122, 139, 186
Aevum, 110 ff., 182
Antichrist, 196, 200, 214
Anthropology, 64 ff., 142, 146 ff.
Apocalyptic, Jewish, 194
Aristoteleanism, 148 ff., 180
Ascension (of Christ), 139
Assumption (of Mary), 107

Baptism, 115
Being, 77 ff., 94
Beyond, 12 ff., 100
Bodiliness, Body, 107–109, 147–149, 158, 168 ff., 176 ff.
Bodiliness, of Christ, 115, 158, 190, 207, 235
Buddhism, 187 ff.

Chiliasm, 13, 176, 211 ff.
Christology, 12, 25, 32, 34 ff., 56, 62 ff., 97 ff.
Communion, 89 ff., 93 ff., 117, 159
Communion of saints, 8 ff., 159, 186, 232 ff.
Community, 13, 76 ff., 81 ff.
Cosmos, 6 ff., 62, 191–194, 202, 237–238
Cross, 7, 64, 97 ff., 102–103, 218
Cultus, imperial, 201–202; of the dead, 76, 84

Death, 4, 9 ff., 11 ff., 62, 69–103, 107; in contemporary society, 69 ff.; in cultural history, 75 ff., 80 ff., 83 ff.

Decline, consciousness of, 3
De-eschatologizing, 2
De-mythologizing, 114
Docetism, 273
Doctrine, development of, 269 ff.
Dualism, 255 ff., 265

Early Jewish theology, 120
Emancipation, 61 ff., 156
End of world, 6 ff., 11, 19, 35, 37 ff.
Enlightenment, Greek, 77; Israelite, 85; Modern, 1
Eschatology, consequent, 1, 35; existential, 35 ff., 47; temporal, 9, 29, 35, 37 ff., 47; realized, 55 ff.
Eternity (cf. Aevum), 107 ff., 157 ff., 181 ff.
Ethics, 29 ff., 101 ff.; political, 59
Eucharist, 6 ff., 56
Exegesis, 1, 19 ff.
Existentialism, 3

Faith, confession of (Creed), 11, 114
"Final decision," hypothesis of, 207 ff.
Fortune, 14
Franciscan Order, 13
Future, 3, 8 ff., 13, 52 ff., 57, 209 ff.

Gnosis, 146, 172 ff., 224
God, 24 ff., 82 ff., 89, 118, 154 ff., 206, 260

Grace, 30 ff.
Greek thought, 73 ff., 140 ff.,
    150 ff., 224, 247, 265 ff.

Heaven, 4, 24 ff., 189 ff., 233 ff.
Hell, 4, 150, 215 ff.
Hermeneutics, 106, 115 ff., 177
Hinduism, 187
Historical Jesus, 19
Historical-critical method,
    19 ff., 249 ff., 271 ff.
History, 4, 109 ff., 166, 184 ff.,
    209 ff.; theology of, 13, 195
Hope, 1 ff., 4 ff., 8, 15, 57 ff.,
    118, 209 ff.; Old Testament,
    26 ff., 65 ff.; prophetic, 27

Idealism, 33, 73
Images, 129 ff., 201 ff., 237 ff.
Imminent expectation, 19 ff.,
    32, 34, 35–45, 53, 56, 110
Immortality, 83, 91, 143 ff.; of
    soul, 4, 73 ff., 79 ff., 93 ff.,
    104–161, 256
Individualization of Christian-
    ity, 5, 11 ff.
Intermediate state, 106, 118,
    119 ff., 123 ff., 168 ff., 218,
    245, 252

Joy, 32, 64, 185 ff.
Judgment, 3, 10 ff., 190, 201 ff.,
    232; Last Judgment, 194 ff.
Justice, 76 ff., 90 ff., 93, 100,
    265
Justification, 99, 272 ff.

Kingdom of God, 2, 19 ff., 24 ff.
Knowledge, historical, 19 ff.;
    scientific, 21 ff.

Last Day, 119, 191, 194 ff.
Liberal theology, 1 ff., 47, 48
Liberation, 9, 35, 62, 212
Life, 72, 80 ff., 86 ff., 90 ff.,
    93 ff., 99 ff., 101 ff.

Love, 94 ff.

Martyrdom, 90 ff., 93 ff., 101,
    111 ff., 122, 132, 224
Marxism, 3, 12, 50, 193, 212
Matter, 108 ff., 158, 166 ff.,
    169, 172, 179, 181 ff., 258
Messiah, 27 ff., 61, 124
Messianism, 3, 59, 61
Metaphysics, 51 ff., 69 ff., 97
Moses, 113, 250
Mystery cult, 141, 145

Natural science, 22 ff., 48 ff.
Nature, law of, 78 ff.

Old Testament, 43

Paradise, 121, 124, 129 ff.
Parousia, 5, 8, 38 ff., 109 ff.,
    194 ff.
Past, 9 ff., 53 ff.
Penance, 29 ff., 231
Person, 11 ff., 65, 108, 151,
    180 ff.; of Jesus, 29 ff., 33, 35
Pharisees, 113
Platonism, 73, 77 ff., 104,
    112 ff., 143, 224
Pneumatology, 11, 34 ff.
Politics, 79
Political ethics, 59 ff.
Politicized eschatology, 3,
    27 ff.
Positivism, 72
Praxis, 152; of hope, 4, 100; of
    world transformation, 14,
    57 ff.
Prayer, 5 ff., 222, 231, 262 ff.
Present, 9, 13, 29, 34, 44 ff.,
    183, 209 ff.
Purgatory, 4, 189, 218 ff., 273

Reality, 21, 46 ff., 77 ff., 91
Redemption, 31, 65
Relation, 154 ff., 187
Religion, 3, 143

Resurrection, 72 ff., 82, 87, 90,
    112 ff.; of Jesus, 6, 44, 111,
    113 ff.; of the body, 106, 169,
    175, 177–181, 191–193,
    244 ff., 267; of the dead,
    104 ff., 165 ff., 251 ff.; of the
    flesh, 133, 172 ff.
Return of Christ, 194 ff., 201 ff.
Rome, 201

Sacrament, 55–56
Sadducees, 112
Saint, 9, 186, 207, 232, 235
Salvation, 13 ff., 61 ff., of soul,
    5, 13 ff.; presence of, 9, 13,
    29, 33 ff., 45
Saving history, 51 ff.
Science, 22 ff., 48 ff.
Secularization, 3
Sheol, 81 ff., 87 ff., 120, 146,
    149, 156
Sickness, 69 ff., 81, 86 ff.
Signs (of End), 194 ff.
Sin, 84
Sleep of death, 125, 131, 251
Soul, 106, 140 ff., 146–150,
    155, 160, 177 ff., 245, 246 ff.,
257 ff., 256 ff.
Spirit, 191 ff.
Spiritualization, 13 ff., 176
Stoics, 101, 123, 144, 224
Substitution, 232
Suffering, 90 ff., 93 ff., 101 ff.,
    188, 215, 220; substitution-
    ary, 85 ff., 215 ff., 227

Temple, Jerusalem, 6
Theology, black, 58; of hope,
    3, 44, 57–60, 262, 273; of
    liberation, 3 ff., 57 ff., 213; of
    revolution, 58–60; political,
    58–60, 79, 273
Time, 51 ff., 106 ff., 181 ff.
Truth, 19 ff., 78 ff., 98 ff.,
    101 ff., 241 ff., 259

Utopia, 13, 273

Vision of God, 133 ff., 151

Work, 210
World, transformation of,
    13 ff., 58 ff., 253

Index of References

OLD TESTAMENT

Genesis
  3, 3: 156

Deuteronomy
  32, 35: 277

I Samuel
  28, 3–25: 278

Tobit
  14, 5: 277

Job, 88, 91
  15, 8: 64, 277
  19, 22–25: 85, 278
  19, 26: 172

I Maccabees
  3, 45–51: 277

II Maccabees, 90
  12, 32–46: 220
  12, 42–45: 233

Psalms
  16 (especially verses 19 ff.): 87 ff.
  65, 3: 280
  73 (especially verses 23–28): 88 ff.
  73, 4 f.: 278
  73, 9: 278
  73, 22: 278
  73, 24–26: 278
  73, 25: 278
  79, 1: 277
  90 (89), 4: 36
  95, 7: 28
  136, 24: 280

Ecclesiastes, 88
  2, 16 f.: 278

Wisdom
  2, 3: 278
  3, 1 ff.: 278
  3, 8: 284
  16, 13: 278

Sirach
  7, 33: 285

Isaiah, 27, 86 ff.
  45, 23: 63 ff.
  53: 91
  53, 9–12: 87
  63, 18: 277
  66, 15 f.: 228, 285

Jeremiah
  25, 31: 280
  46, 10: 277

Ezechiel
  28, 2: 196

Daniel
  7, 22: 284
  9, 26: 277
  9, 27: 276, 283
  11, 31: 283
  11, 32: 276
  11, 36: 283
  12, 2: 90
  12, 7: 277
  12, 11: 276, 283

Hosea
  9, 7: 277

Zechariah
  12, 3: 277
  12, 10: 275

NEW TESTAMENT

Matthew
  5, 8: 151, 281
  5, 9: 277
  5, 22: 284
  5, 26 and parallels: 223, 224
  5, 29 and parallels: 284
  5, 45: 277
  6, 4; 6; 15; 18: 283
  7, 11 and parallels: 33, 276
  7, 21–23: 276
  7, 22 f.: 284
  8, 12: 284
  10, 16: 276
  10, 28 and parallels: 283
  10, 30 and paral-

lels: 158, 281
12, 38–42: 276
13, 36–43: 284
13, 42; 50: 284
16, 2–4: 276
18, 8 and paral-
  lels: 284
18, 9: 284
19, 7: 276
19, 28 and paral-
  lels: 205
20, 1–16: 276
22, 13: 284
24, 15–22: 38
24, 22: 38
24, 23 f.: 38
24, 26–28: 38
24, 29: 277
24, 29–31: 39,
  283
24, 37–39: 283
24, 48: 276
24, 51: 284
25, 1 ff.: 283
25, 5: 276
25, 30: 284
25, 31–40: 276
25, 31–46: 284
25, 41: 284

Mark
1, 15: 276
4, 26–29: 276
9, 1: 283
10, 18: 33
12: 115, 279
12, 18–27:
  113–114
13 and parallels:
  38
13: 196 ff.
13, 6: 196, 282
13, 7 f.: 196, 282
13, 8: 196, 283
13, 9–13: 196,
  283

13, 10: 196, 199,
  283
13, 14: 196, 283
13, 14–20: 38
13, 14–27: 196,
  283
13, 20: 38
13, 21–23: 38,
  196, 282
13, 24–27: 38 ff.
13, 30: 199, 283
13, 37: 196, 283

Luke
6, 35: 277
7, 36–50: 276
11, 20: 276
11, 29 f.: 276
12, 45: 276
13, 25–27: 284
13, 28: 284
15, 1–10: 276
15, 11–32: 276
16, 19–29: 279
16, 19–31: 124,
  279
17, 7–10: 276
17, 20 f.: 32 ff.
17, 26–30: 199,
  283
18, 9–14: 276
21, 20–23: 38
21, 24: 277
21, 25–28: 39 ff.
23, 43: 124, 279

John 36 ff., 42, 151
1, 18: 279
2, 19: 285
3, 16–21: 285
3, 17 f.: 284
6: 116 ff., 281
6, 39 ff.: 279
6, 44; 54: 279
6, 55 f.: 281
6, 63: 192, 281

9: 281
9, 39: 284
11: 116 ff.
11, 24: 279
11, 25: 129, 279,
  280
12, 47 f.: 205, 284
12, 48: 205, 279,
  284
13, 23: 279
14, 2 f.: 283
14, 15–31: 283

Acts of the
  Apostles
7, 59: 279

Romans
2, 3 ff.: 283
3, 6: 283
6, 1–14: 114 ff.
6, 17: 286
8, 29: 285
9, 22: 284
11, 25–32: 283
14, 10: 283

I Corinthians
1, 18: 284
3, 1–17: 227
3, 10–15: 225,
  228
4, 4 f.: 284
5, 13: 283
6, 2 f.: 284
11, 32: 284
15: 92 ff., 115 ff.,
  171
15, 12–58: 279
15, 16; 17: 116,
  279
15, 20–28: 281
15, 24: 137
15, 26: 278
15, 28: 282
15, 35–53: 169 ff.

15, 50: 173, 192
15, 50ff.: 173ff.

II Corinthians
2, 15: 284
4: 127
4, 3: 284
4, 16: 280
5, 1: 170
5, 1–10: 127ff.
5, 6–10: 128
5, 8: 128
5, 9: 280
5, 10: 284

Galatians
4, 3: 283
4, 9: 283

Ephesians
2, 6: 170

Philippians
1, 21: 128, 285
1, 21–26: 128
1, 23: 126, 128ff.
1, 24f.: 128ff.
2, 5(6)–11: 63ff.,
    278, 281
2, 6: 63
3, 19: 284
3, 21: 285

Colossians
2, 8: 283
2, 20: 283

3, 1ff.: 173
3, 1–3: 170

I Thessalonians
4, 6: 283
4, 13–15, 11:
    279
4, 16: 126
5, 3: 199, 284
5, 10: 126

II Thessalonians
1, 5: 283
1, 9: 284
2, 3: 196
2, 3–10: 196
3, 10: 284
3, 10ff.: 283

I Timothy
6, 9: 284

II Timothy
2, 18: 116, 287

II Peter
3, 4: 36, 276
3, 10: 283

I John
2, 18–22: 197

II John
7: 197

Apocalypse 281
1, 7: 214, 275,
    284
2, 17b: 285
3, 21: 284
6, 9: 279
6, 9ff.: 137, 280
13, 1–18: 283
14, 10: 284
19, 20: 284
20: 284
20, 2–7: 276
20, 10–15: 284
20, 13ff.: 278
21, 8: 284

JEWISH WRITINGS

Ethiopian Enoch
22: 120, 147

4 Esdras: 121

The Life of Adam
and Eve
46–47: 284

VALENTINIAN
GNOSIS

Gospel of Philip,
Cogion: 173
23

Letter to Rheginus:
193